Ethnolinguistics and Cultural Concepts

'Ethnolinguistics' is the study of how language relates to culture and ethnicity. This book offers an original approach to ethnolinguistics, discussing how abstract concepts such as truth, love, hate and war are expressed across cultures and ethnicities. James W. Underhill seeks to situate these key cultural concepts within four languages (English, French, Czech and German). Not only do these concepts differ from language to language, but they go on changing over time. The book explores issues such as how far meaning is politically and culturally influenced, how far language shapes the thought of ethnic groups, and how far their thought shapes language, and the role of individuals in the consolidation of cultural concepts. It offers a clear and thought-provoking account of how concepts are understood, and will be welcomed by those working in the fields of sociolinguistics, linguistic anthropology, discourse analysis, semantics and pragmatics.

JAMES W. UNDERHILL is a senior lecturer in the Department of English at the Université Stendhal, Grenoble, France.

Ethnolinguistics and Cultural Concepts

Truth, Love, Hate and War

James W. Underhill

CAMBRIDGE
UNIVERSITY PRESS

CAMBRIDGE UNIVERSITY PRESS
Cambridge, New York, Melbourne, Madrid, Cape Town,
Singapore, São Paulo, Delhi, Mexico City

Cambridge University Press
The Edinburgh Building, Cambridge CB2 8RU, UK

Published in the United States of America by Cambridge University Press, New York

www.cambridge.org
Information on this title: www.cambridge.org/9781107010642

First published 2012

Printed in the United Kingdom at the University Press, Cambridge

A catalogue record for this publication is available from the British Library

Library of Congress Cataloguing in Publication data
Underhill, James W. (James William)
   Ethnolinguistics and cultural concepts : truth, love, hate and war /
   James W. Underhill.
      p.   cm.
   Includes bibliographical references and index.
   ISBN 978-1-107-01064-2 (hardback)
   1. Anthropological linguistics.   I. Title.
   P35.U495 2012
   306.44′089–dc23
   2012000289

ISBN 978-1-107-01064-2 Hardback

for Henri Meschonnic (1930–2009), poet, translator,
linguist and thinker

Contents

Preface

Truth, love, hate and war – war, hate, love and truth: these are the themes of this book on language and worldviews. In the following pages, we will penetrate into the complex veins and arteries which feed gut emotions, loving and hating, and seek to discern the ways in which the ultimate expression of anger, war, becomes manifest in language, and the strategies politicians and journalists use in order to make an apology for war. War will be inspired by the desire to protect people and values, or so the rhetorical strategies used would have us believe. Hate will be inspired by love. Hate of our enemies and of forms of evil will fuel a passion for war, a passion which will define us and define our enemies.

This was the state of affairs which Shakespeare's Romeo despaired over when he saw how much the noble sentiments of love and faithfulness became perverted into hating and fighting: the spoiling for a brawl which other characters in *Romeo and Juliet*, Tybalt and Mercutio, accepted as a natural state of affairs. Seeing his friend Benvolio fail in his diplomatic peace-keeping role, and get drawn into the fight, he cried out:

> O me! What fray was here?
> Yet tell me not, for I have heard it all.
> Here's much to do with hate, but more with love.
> Why then, O brawling love, O loving hate,
> O anything of nothing first create;
> O heavy lightness, serious vanity,
> Misshapen chaos of well-seeming forms.
> > Act 1: sc.1: Shakespeare, (1987/90)
> > *Volume III: Tragedies*: 1057

Conflicting, paradoxical feelings – brawling love and loving hate – will churn up emotions and set the agenda for war in 2003, a war of military invasion but also a war of culture and ideology, a war which will entail a reorganisation of the means by which the very concept of 'war' is used in English. War has not only transformed the Middle East, it has transformed the ways we think about civil society. And that transformation has engendered (and partly been engendered by) the way war is presented, understood and promoted as a strategy of imposing political will.

Can we escape war, and redefine hate and love? Attempting to do so will involve striving to understand the way the three concepts are entangled. This will take us deep into the English speaker's worldview, into the conceptual and emotional centre of his or her manner of perceiving the world and what goes on there. This entails penetrating deeply into the intimate spheres of the imagination. And in seeking entry into those zones of conscious and semi-conscious reflection, we will be weighing up what truth and love mean in and of themselves. They will not simply be seen as aspects of lies and lying, and hate and hating, though truth does, inevitably, posit as its antithesis, untruth, bad faith. And love – as we all know – often leads to spite and aggression.

Writers such as Shakespeare and philosophers such as Augustine, Aquinas and Buber have unveiled, defined and discussed the complexities of loving and hating, and sought to circumscribe the very limits and the essence of truth. Their work is unfinished. Philosophers and writers will continue to enlighten and inspire us in seizing upon those emotions which take us by the guts. In dissecting and defining them, they will instruct us as to our own natures, and the role those emotions play (or should play) in this world. But though the poetics of thought, the study of the way language shapes our conceptual and emotional relationship to the world, is ultimately philosophical in nature, this is not – strictly speaking – a philosophical book.

This is a book about language. Or rather, this is a book about languages. Ethnolinguistics is the study of the way worldviews construct the complex and flexible frameworks within which we think and feel. To say 'within which' is already misleading: we are not 'confined' to or by language. We live 'in' language and we love 'in' language, just as we hate 'in' language. We tell the truth or choose to lie, once more 'in' language. But we are not the playthings of language. Language is our adventure: we contribute to shaping it, we follow its logic, but we open up new vistas within language. Studying thinking-in-language involves investigating the geography of our understanding. Like land developers we can transform our linguistically painted landscape. Ultimately language is not a prison. But nor is it a mere tool, a means: it is an ongoing act of creation. Consequently, at one level we are as much the producers as the products of language.

Worldviews emerge within our own language, visions of the world, conceptual worlds, which oppose and contradict one another: incompatible ideologies which seek to exclude one another. But there is a worldview which is implicit in the deeper frameworks of the language system we speak. At this level, French and German shape the imagination, the understanding and the desires of the French and the Germans. Their sensitivity to the world, all of the conceptual connections which French and German people take for granted, appear to us curious, at times almost incomprehensible. Learning to navigate within their waters, we come to realize that we are entering another world-view. And at this stage we realize that the world is always grasped and represented 'in' language. We realize that our English language imposes its own constraints upon us, just as the richness and depth of expression in English, both past and present, has opened up for us a wonderful means of expression: one which allows us to enter the worlds of philosophers such as John Locke and the worlds of writers such as Shakespeare. Languages cultivate the mind, just as the mind cultivates language, constantly reinvigorating its potential for expression.

Recognising that languages are complex systems of conceptual and emotional patterning is part of the ethnolinguistic project. Recognising that languages pattern understanding differently, and that they thereby present slightly different worlds to us, is the crux of the ethnolinguistic approach. We will be investigating English, French, German and Czech. Why not Russian? Why not Arabic? Indeed, why not? Though comparative linguistics often takes on board multiple languages and draws up dauntingly impressive tables of details concerning linguistic diversity, it is my firm belief that language study which relies on second- and third-hand sources is of little use in opening up worlds – other worlds – to us.

I share with Humboldt and with Whorf a fascination with non-Indo-European languages, but remain sceptical about what can be understood until one comes to grips with actually communicating in a foreign tongue. Moving beyond the Indo-European mindset might well take us beyond the limits of 'Western' conceptions of society, history, time and space. But unlike many researchers working at the level of grammar and relying upon second-hand accounts, I believe it is all too easy to fall into schematic and simplistic conceptions about the understanding of people of cultures other than our own. Believing that we can understand other cultures and languages, and believing that we can understand them 'in' English, is very often the tacit belief that is shared by those people who speak about languages they do not speak to people who understand them no better than themselves.

Comparative linguists often believe they can leave speech behind, leave content behind, leave meaning behind, in focusing on the supposedly 'deeper' levels of language, grammatical form and construction. This appears to me an absurd misunderstanding of the very nature of philology (*filia-logos*), the love of language. If we leave meaning behind, we leave people behind. And language is about people, it is about us.

I have therefore chosen to study only languages which I speak and which I can discuss at the level of discourse analysis. Discussing speech and discourse strategies transforms ethnolinguistics into a 'cross-lingual discourse analysis'. Corpus study will become essential when we engage foreign languages at this level. For this reason two of the four studies (love and war) will focus upon strategically defined corpora.

Truth, love, hate and war: are these private or public concepts? Do love and truth belong to the realm of intimacy, or do they belong to the world of politics? Is hating an inner seething of twisted emotions deep within us, or is it the very bond which binds us to our enemies, private and political, and thereby defines us and gives our lives meaning? War may, at first sight, appear purely political, but as our case study will show, a vast array of metaphorical 'wars' figure in the imagination – and the truly intimidating thing about propaganda is that it will reach deep into our imagination and seize upon those imaginary wars in order to manipulate us and to realign our feelings in relation to real wars. Real wars, meanwhile, will gradually be deprived of their 'reality', as they are masked by perverted positive representations of problem solving and liberation.

Language is both personal and political. The ethnolinguist must face up to this. For that reason, the arduous task we are setting off on is that of moving into politically charged foreign territory. This book does not offer readers an easy entry into exotic thought-worlds: it invites readers to ponder upon fragments. Starting with truth, love, hate and war, we will try to reach out within the thought-worlds of other language systems in order to gain a greater understanding of the way living, breathing individuals struggle with words and refashion their own worlds, the way they debate questions and dispute answers, the way they define and redefine the way they think and feel about each other.

Acknowledgements

I wish to thank the editors of the groundbreaking internet forum for metaphor research based in Germany, metaphoric.de, for allowing me to publish here some of the findings of a study on war propaganda which were first published by them online at a time when grappling with metaphoric manipulation was of urgent importance. The speed with which they acted made sure my work made some impact. In this book, those findings have been put in perspective in the context of the present American administration's attempt to escape the rhetoric they got themselves caught up in during the first decade of the twenty-first century. For helpful reactions and comments on my research, I must thank Christine Raguet, Luise von Flotow and the late Michel Viel. For stylistic help with the English text, I would like to express my warmest thanks to Shaeda Isani, Dawn Rivière and John Reid. The presentation of the Czech language was greatly improved by Tamara Ibehová, and the German would not have escaped slips and errors without the invaluable help of Steffi Arzt, Marko Pajević and Cornelia Chladek. I should, however, be held responsible for any errors in analysis or translation. Thanks also to the editorial staff of Cambridge University Press for their help, support and astute insights.

1   Hope, Obama and the neoconservative worldview

On 2 November 2009, the www.nowpublic.com website published an article whose title made manifest the journalist's scepticism concerning US policy in the Middle East. That title read, 'Is Obama Delivering Hope and Change? What happened to Yes We Can?' Obama had been elected principally because he had convinced voters of his unshakable faith in the American people and his belief in their capacity to find a way out of the cynicism engendered by the Bush administration. Obama urged Americans to forge a new optimism which would inspire them to achieve collectively great things at a time when many were suffering from the global crisis of capitalism, rising unemployment and homelessness. Part of his package was an implicit promise that America would shake off its international reputation – tarnished by neoconservative foreign policy – and rise once more as a symbol of freedom. As the defenders of justice and democracy, they would lead the world onwards into a twenty-first century which had opened with the catastrophe of 9/11. In place of overbearing foreign policy, Obama promised respect and diplomacy, in place of lies and deception, he promised truth and transparency. In place of the carnivorous pursuit of capital accumulation that was pillaging other countries (while impoverishing whole sectors of society at home), Obama promised the world he would consider the greater good of the planet while seeking to protect the interests of his nation.

Obama's second book, *The Audacity of Hope* (2006), can hardly be considered 'audacious' (since hope is fundamental to the American worldview and since the USA sincerely believes in itself as 'The Land of Hope and Glory'): nevertheless, that book did affirm clearly, calmly and with conviction, the ideas that one man believed would help regenerate the world of politics and domestic policy. The language of Obama was the language of hope, and that hope seemed to emanate from an entirely different moral dimension from the one the Bush administration had created for Americans. Obama's vision of the world seemed radically different: inspired, healthy, authentic.

The worldview of neoconservatives had taken hold of the Bush administration, and that worldview had taken hold of the American people. Fear and cynicism were eating away at the core of American society. And while one of Bush's more

1

successful rhetorical ploys had been to contrast the 'decadent' Old World which had lost its 'moral compass', with his own crusading, by the end of his second term in office, few people believed the USA was leading anyone anywhere other than deeper into trouble. It was a hard lesson for the American people to learn: that they had been duped by their leaders. And it was harder still to be forced to admit that those who had been portrayed as posturing fools, cowards, traitors and Machiavellian manipulators seeking to advance their own agendas (charges made concerning France, Germany and Russia) had in fact been well-advized to refuse to engage in the war in Iraq alongside American troops.

The disappointment and despondency of the American people expressed itself in language: not only in the positions taken up, but in the very words of American English. Existing words seemed impotent to express the outrage, disgust and contempt for the administration that had impoverished the nation through waging a war that had served only to enrich a minute fraction of the country's business community. And when words appear impotent, creativity takes hold of language and generates new forms of expression: neologisms are coined to describe new realities. It became commonplace to speak of being 'iraqued' as in the following example:

We were *Iraqued* – that is, we were attacked not for anything we'd done but for someone's inflated fears of what we might do; shot, gassed ... (www.starhawk.org, 8 December 2003)

At other times, the entire Bush administration was characterized as a capitalist plot, a war machine whose sole purpose was to generate fear in order to smoke-screen the ravenous pursuit of the wealth and power of one class of American society. Certain Americans spoke of the 'Bush Crime Sindicket' (see www. youtube.com, The Bush Crime Syndicate (part 2/2), 26 February, 2012). Others spoke of 'Iraquet', the manipulation of the media and the misuse of federal funds in an economic war of benefit to a small minority of Americans (see the song, 'Iraquet', written by Rowlands and Robertson, copyright 2002, www.geocities.ws/daverowlands77/hopeandfade/lyrics/Iraquet.htm, 26 February, 2012). Politicians were compared to gangsters: they were deemed something akin to the 'robber barons' of nineteenth-century industrial Britain or the new oligarchs of post-Soviet Russia.

The average American was suffering. True, it would be somewhat perverse to focus upon the American malaise at the expense of empathising with the real victims of the Bush administration. The bombing of civilians, the destruction of whole neighbourhoods, the disruption of production, distribution, hospitals and schools in both Iraq and Afghanistan certainly produced countless real victims. Surely, such victims deserve more sympathy than American citizens in general and the soldiers who naively signed up to do their duty and to serve blindly Uncle Sam. Nevertheless, it should not be forgotten that life for American citizens in general became harder, became darker, became embittered under the

Bush administration. The Americans' faith in the political class had been seriously shaken by the end of Bush's two terms in office. And if we are to understand something of the way in which Obama will try to navigate his nation and negotiate with the world, we must understand to what extent he and the whole American people were unable to escape the transformation of the American worldview which took place in the years following Bush's election.

But change in worldviews comes hard. Obama too was to some degree the accomplice of the reigning ideology of the first decade of the twenty-first century. To claim that Obama is a neoconservative would be absurd. Obama struggled against the Bush administration, denounced the war in Iraq and tirelessly critiqued foreign and domestic strategy throughout both Bush's terms in office. Nevertheless, two facts must be borne in mind. To oppose an argument, we must, inevitably, to a certain extent, embrace and condone the terms upon which that argument is based. That is to say, we do not escape the concepts imposed upon us by our opponents. To this extent, opposition presupposes a certain degree of 'conceptual complicity'. Secondly, the neoconservatives had transformed the American worldview to such a degree that it would be naive to imagine that Obama could have won the election without engaging in the fundamental arguments of the neoconservatives and without accepting their concepts.

Like most worldview-transforming movements, the neoconservatives harnessed tradition and radically transfigured it. The form that emerged would allow them to use tradition as a means of propelling their own interests within the framework of future policy. Hope was fundamental. The New World was a utopia-project, a religious crusade. The story is well known. Once on the American continent, the 'settlers moved steadily west and southwest, successive administrations described the annexation of territory in terms of "manifest destiny" – the conviction that such expansion was preordained, part of God's plan to extend what Andrew Jackson called "the area of freedom" across the continent'. The words could be those of any US citizen, the lines from a school book on history, or the lines from a speech from a politician from any of the American parties. In fact, they come from Obama's *The Audacity of Hope* (281). True, the inverted commas are his too. Obama offers a careful critique of both the history of American foreign policy and the Cold War era which generated antagonism and fear. He claims that 'American foreign policy has always been a jumble of warring impulses' (280), and he lucidly admits that many countries recognize the history of the colonisation of America 'for what it was – an exercise in raw power' (281).

What is remarkable, however, considering the astuteness of Obama, and given his evident desire to be honest with himself and with the American people, is that he fails utterly to escape the fundamental concepts which were to equip the neoconservatives with their moral agenda for war. Obama accepts the concept of 'manifest destiny'. The God-given right of the settlers to take up residence is not denounced. That same moral crusading was transposed onto the Old World during the First and Second World Wars, and, in turn, to the Middle East when the Bush administration set about transforming the whole world in the image of the New World. While it is true that Obama criticized neoconservative foreign policy, he did not question the legitimacy of their expansionist policy. What he found fault with was the technical and tactical means by which the neoconservatives proposed to set about the task of remodelling the world. Obama briefly quoted John Quincy Adams, who claimed that America should not venture abroad 'in search of monsters to destroy' (quoted in Obama 2006: 280). But he quickly forgot Quincy's advice that Providence has charged America with the task of making a new world, not reforming the old (*ibid.*).

That Obama opposed the Bush administration and attacked its policies is irrefutable, but he did not question the underlying forces driving their policies. He did not stand outside their 'world', but walked right in and took his stance within the coordinates of their political and economic agenda. We think in language, and Obama, even when he opposed the Bush administration, was thinking within the language of the neoconservatives.

The concepts of the settlers were to shape the discourse of the neoconservatives during the nineties and most of all after 9/11. Saddam Hussein was represented as an 'outlaw': a figment of the frontier imagination – and the USA became a sheriff. European leaders were invited to fulfil their civic duty in joining the posse. Obama did not denounce such rhetoric, nor did he critique the notion of 'rogue states'. Indeed, though the tone is not his habitual mode of expression, Obama did not disapprove of what he called 'our desire to slap down rogue states' (290). Obama did criticize – and loudly too – the 'bad execution' of the war in Iraq (302). He considered it 'a failure of conception', a project plagued by 'a series of ad hoc decisions, with dubious results' (*ibid.*). Besides, as he put it: 'What I sensed, though, was that the threat Saddam posed was not imminent, the Administration's rationales for war were flimsy and ideologically driven' (294).

Nevertheless, Obama engaged the arguments of the neoconservatives on their own terms. He took his stance without denouncing the debate. As a result, he wholeheartedly embraced the concept of 'security'. In analysing Woodrow Wilson's initial reticence at the beginning of the First World War, Obama could have been writing his own autobiography. Though tempted to avoid involvement in conflicts in Europe, Wilson finally understood after German U-boat attacks on American vessels, that neutrality was untenable. Obama concluded: 'America had emerged as the world's dominant power – but a power whose prosperity Wilson now understood to be linked to peace and prosperity in faraway lands' (282).

Obama went on to explain: 'It was in an effort to address this new reality that Wilson sought to reinterpret the idea of America's manifest destiny. Making "the world safe for democracy" didn't just involve winning a war, he argued: it was in America's interest to encourage the self-determination of all people, and provide the world a legal framework that could help avoid future conflicts' (282–3). Given the complexity of America's foreign relations (which Obama seems to understand full well), what is frightening here is his manifest faith in the vocation of the American people. The American people not only can, they *must* change the world. Obama's conviction is unshakable on this point. For this reason, Obama takes to heart the words of Theodore Roosevelt:

The United States of America has not the option as to whether it will or will not play a great part in the world … It *must* play a great part. All that it can decide is whether it will play that part well or badly. (Roosevelt, quoted by Obama 2006: 282)

The neoconservatives openly declared their adherence to this concept of America's vocation. For them, America was a world-transforming project. What they added to traditional American beliefs were three elements:

1. The unscrupulous pursuit of economic gain. The argument behind this was logical enough: a strong economy made for a strong nation. Inevitably, however, such a policy, in practice, constantly confused private or corporate interests with national interests.
2. A culture of fear.
3. The conviction that since the end of the Cold War, history had come to an end, and that no nation, no culture, no ideology and no economic model could oppose the will of the world (which had been revealed to the American people, and which had already been realized in their constitution).

The crucial question for our own times is to what degree Obama's administration can escape the neoconservative worldview. The task will take more than skill and integrity: it will require an entire critique of the underlying principles which construct that worldview. It will require coming to understand the way in which the neoconservatives have succeeded in harnessing tradition and framing the debates driving American foreign policy.

Hope will not suffice. On the contrary, hope may well prove to be Obama's failing, his hubris. It may well bring about his downfall. A belief that America can change the world for the better and that Obama's administration can clear up after the Bush administration may well transform 'Yes We Can!' into 'How the Hell Could We Have Hoped to?' Although Obama cannot be fairly condemned for the failure of the wars in Iraq and Afghanistan to come to an acceptable closure, Bush's wars have now, in a very real sense, become 'Obama's wars'. In September 2010, Bob Woodward published his book entitled *Obama's Wars*, questioning the legitimacy of sending 30,000 more troops to Afghanistan under the command of a president who seems not to endorse the war in principle. And April 2011 saw the publication of book with a similar title, James Gannon's *Obama's War: Avoiding Quagmire in Afghanistan.* The role is not enviable: Obama has stepped into the world created by the neoconservatives and is expected to find a solution, a way out.

As expected, the President's popularity took a serious blow during the November elections to the Senate in 2010, and on 3 November, Obama found himself forced to publicly concede that in listening to the American people, he heard their 'deep frustration' with the lack of progress in alleviating poverty (Council of Foreign Relations website, www.cfr.org, consulted 10 November). But even as early as 2009, scepticism was taking hold of hope, making Obama's rhetoric sound naive at best, hollow and deceitful at worst. *The Economist* expressed doubts as to Obama's capacities in an article entitled 'The Quiet American' on 26 November 2009:[1]

Does this president have a strategy, backed if necessary by force, to reorder the world? Or is he merely a presidential version of Alden Pyle, Graham Greene's idealistic, clever Quiet American who wants to change the world, but underestimates how bad the world is – and ends up causing harm?

The journalists of *The Economist* berated Obama for being 'faint-hearted' and for having 'dithered, not deliberated' on Afghanistan (*ibid.*). Criticism is all too easy, though. *The Economist* moves with the wind, sniffing the breeze, before whistling a tune it feels fits the times. By the end of 2009, it had taken up the punching gloves once more, and was pummelling Obama. As we shall see in our final case study on war, *The Economist* had taken exactly the same tough-man pose in 2002, when it promoted the war in Iraq. Yet it was to denounce that war only a few months after the invasion, when it became obvious that the supposed weapons of mass destruction were a fiction invented by the warmongering parties. Unlike the President of the USA, the journalists of *The Economist* take the liberty of moralising, but feel themselves to be under no compunction to remain true to any particular moral or political stance. Obama's dilemma is of an entirely different nature and scope. And, as a statesman (worthy of the term), at least Obama appears to display a sincere desire to be held accountable for his acts and for the impact his country has upon the world. The question is: how much manoeuvring space does he have to change policy?

At a time when the US economy is faltering and many American citizens are suffering from a combination of the economic crisis and a welfare service which proves incapable of protecting them against unemployment and destitution, is it likely that Obama can risk going against US corporate interests in foreign policy? Leaving law and order in Iraq is certainly the aim of Obama, but what 'law' does that mean, and what form of social and economic 'order' are we speaking about? The neoconservatives did much to obscure their aims and desires, but their policies leave little room for doubt. *The Economist* called the regime-change project 'a capitalist dream' (quoted in Harvey 2003: 215). As Harvey, an anthropologist and specialist of geographical economic development, put it:

Paul Bremer, the head of the Coalition Provisional Authority, promulgated a series of decrees which included 'the full privatization of public enterprises, full ownership rights by foreign firms of Iraqi businesses, full repartition of foreign profits ... the opening of Iraq's banks to foreign control, national treatment for foreign companies and ... the elimination of nearly all trade barriers'. The orders were to apply to all areas of the economy. Only oil was exempt (presumably because of its special status and geopolitical significance). A flat tax (a regressive taxation system much favoured by certain neo-conservatives in the US) was imposed. Strikes were outlawed, and rights to unionize much restricted. (213–14)

Iraq's interim trade minister denounced this strategy as a flagrant display of 'free market fundamentalism' (*ibid*. 214). Chomsky was arguing, by 2010, that this free-market utopia had ended in failure, and that American corporate capitalists had failed to extract the right to set up permanent military bases in Iraq and to gain full control over energy rights. But it was Iraqi nationalism, not goodwill, that prevented America from exploiting Iraq, in his opinion. And the massive disappearance of artworks from Ancient Babylon has done little to reassure critics who cry out against the 'looting' of the country. Nobody questions the desire of Obama to believe in America and in the American people. Few people doubt his desire to be honest. But, in stepping into Bush's shoes, what kind of foreign policy does he 'truly' desire?

Words of truth

Again and again, we will return to the question of telling the truth in this book. Taking up the 'lies' of the neoconservatives is only one aspect of this philosophical question. But the question of bad faith is much vaster, much more profound. Ultimately, what is 'lying'?

If lying were restricted to failing to tell the truth, then truth would be a relatively simple matter: it would be difficult to discern, but easy to determine, once the hidden intention was compared to the pretence. But manipulation is more complex. Truth can involve hiding things from yourself, i.e. bad faith. And bad faith is a great generator of words and pretexts. As we have seen, the resentment against political obfuscation led to the coining of neologisms such as 'iraquet'. But the build-up to the war involved moving beyond individual isolated words: the representation of invasion was transformed. Warmongering was presented as a quest for a peaceful solution to a problem that must be solved. Bill Clinton was reproached for leaving business 'untended'. The 'irresponsibility' of Clinton was to be followed by the earnest assuming of 'responsibility' by the neoconservatives: the shoulders of George W. Bush were large enough to bear the burden. At one level, this involved passing war off as something else. Invasion became 'regime change': it became 'liberation'. Civilian casualties were considered to be the inevitable collateral victims who must be sacrificed for the greater good of 'saving' the Iraqis. And if the USA and Britain did engage in war, they were simply taking up the challenge forced upon them by a dictator who had 'ignited' the war by refusing to comply with investigators looking for hidden missiles (despite affirmations to the contrary by the chief inspector, Hans Blix). Grammar was enlisted in the 'selling' of the war in Iraq. The USA became a passive party upon which war was imposed. The Iraqi ruler was portrayed as provoking the USA. He was challenging them. Ironically, there is a lack of symmetry here, because it was not Iraq which was represented as forcing the war upon the USA, it was Saddam himself. Personification was enlisted as a strategy of propaganda. It was crucial to focus upon the person. Saddam became the personification of tyranny and evil. And logically, it was he that was bombed, not the Iraqis. The USA went in there 'to take him out', to catch the 'outlaw', to bring him to justice. He was a 'serial offender'. This served to distract attention from the bombing of schools and hospitals, the deaths of civilian men, women and children who were burned alive or crushed under collapsing buildings. Images of such events were not shown in the USA, and were carefully tailored even in countries such as France, which had come down in opposition to invasion. Such images were, however, watched throughout the Arab world thanks to internet journalism.

The reason that US propaganda was so successful at home was that the neoconservatives managed to metaphorically transform war into something entirely different. This transformation will be taken up in detail in the chapter on war. But it is necessary to stress here that the metaphors used to make war palatable managed to do two crucial things. Firstly, they managed to activate the myths of the frontier, so fundamental to American identity. The sheriff was coming to sort out the wild world after having sorted out the Wild West: and he would stop at nothing. Secondly, the neoconservative rhetoric managed to transform the perception of the war throughout the world and most importantly throughout the media of the USA. Whether journalists were advocates for or opponents to the war, they adopted the fundamental premises upon which neoconservatives had based their arguments. The 'war against terrorism' refused the status of soldiers to those opposing US will and US firepower. At the same time, the insistence that this 'war' against terror, was truly a war and must be waged as such both at home and abroad, was used to justify the suspension of civil rights at home and the detention and torture of persons who, 'in peacetime' would have been considered innocent until proven guilty. The neoconservatives shifted the debate, and everyone sang along with them in tune, however much they chanted their disaccord.

Linguistic patterning

Despite the impression these opening pages may have given, this book is not intended as a political treatise. This is a book about language and worldviews. This is a book about linguistic communities, the worlds they live within, and the way their worldviews interact, and the way they seek to impose themselves on one another when they come into conflict. Specialists of the Middle East exist, and their works are numerous. Marxist scholars such as Harvey and political critics such as Chomsky are far more qualified to discuss the future of New Imperialism and what is at stake in American foreign policy. Nevertheless, ethnolinguistics has something to bring to political debate. And ethnolinguistics itself is fundamentally political. The study of the worlds that linguistic communities construct for themselves and sustain by their communication cannot simply restrict itself to the construction of exotic, static, apolitical models of worldviews. Worldviews exist in time and space: historical, social and political space.

People live in language, and language is inherently and inescapably political. A discourse-based ethnolinguistics, an ethnolinguistics which takes on board discourse analysis and metaphor theory, will have much to say about politics, since all politics is carried out with words. Diplomacy, coercion and declaring war, all entail words, and even attempts to justify and render 'acceptable' the most brutal and brutish forms of action take us back into the sphere of speaking. Words are not innocent. They must therefore be weighed carefully, in order to allow us to see what they are 'worth'. Words are used to hide strategies as much as they are used to explicate them. Manifest destiny, building democracy, winning the peace, bringing law and order, terrorists, insurgents, enemies, rogue states, defenders of democracy, are all concepts which must be treated with suspicion. Moreover, words turn out to be only the tip of the iceberg when it comes to language and propaganda. Because, however complex individual concepts turn out to be, they remain, nevertheless, relatively easy to understand, to analyse and critique, when compared to the more surreptitious forms of rhetoric and manipulation. Using personification to diabolize the enemy, holding up Saddams and Bin Ladens, serves to consolidate a 'we-against-him' scenario, a seductive narrative in which we are all invited to play the 'good guys' who set off to lynch the miscreant. Meanwhile, the inevitable civilian casualties must pay the price of our self-glorification.

Conceptual metaphors and discourse strategies are enlisted to frame our understanding and focus our attention on one aspect of the question, while effacing the implications of strategies and 'solutions'. Indeed, given the anarchy in Afghanistan (which was predicted by generals of the Russian army, many of whom had fallen from grace during their own occupation of the territory), it now seems ludicrous that the occupations of Afghanistan and Iraq were presented as 'problem solving'. Blair, however, argued that war would, in fact, be a solution. The one-time pacifist Mussolini had justified his own declaration of war in similar terms: according to him, the Second World War would be the war to end all wars, the war that would bring peace. In the war against Iraq, pacifism was used once more to drive warmongering. Looking back, many of the arguments used to justify the invasion of Iraq appear shoddy and tasteless. Yet they were mortally efficient, and many of our respectable newspapers adopted those arguments.

Concerns over the cost of the war in Iraq were framed in terms of the 'price tag' of invasion. Such expressions reveal the grotesque commercial reasoning behind the war. But they succeeded in transforming the war itself from an active experience of disaster and destruction into a 'product'. Such rhetoric transformed the citizens of the USA and the UK into consumers deciding whether to buy or not.

What this propaganda shows, of course, is that language is political. And this involves a challenge to linguistics in general and to ethnolinguistics in particular. A linguistics which hides from politics is an amputated crippled science incapable of approaching language in all its full and complex dimensions. The essentialist forms of ethnology which concentrate upon the distinct nature of linguistic communities tend to downplay or even ignore this political dimension. But, as we shall see, as soon as we move beyond the most basic and fundamental forms of conceptual paradigms (often the preferred spheres of ethnologists and anthropologists), involving founding myths and kinship systems, actual speech takes us into power struggles, shifting hierarchies and attempts to defend identity. For this reason, ethnolinguistics cannot ignore the shifting influences of worldviews upon each other. Philology cannot escape politics.

Using words and phrases, using the active or the passive form, using metaphor and personification, we strategically situate ourselves in relation to others. All words circulate in society and, to a great extent, many of our fundamental everyday expressions derive from the strategies of interested parties, and are used to consolidate their position in society. An aristocratic regime will coin representations of a royal nature. God will be represented as the 'King' in the heavens, and his believers will be represented as his subjects and his servants. This metaphysical dimension serves to consolidate the legitimacy of the existing order. And our own largely post-aristocratic societies have not escaped the conceptual dominance of such thought patterns. We continue to speak (using politically charged hierarchies) of 'upper' and 'lower' classes (concepts which reaffirm the existing social order). We can 'put someone in their place' because we believe everyone, ultimately, 'has their place' in the existing order. Consequently, it is unacceptable for someone to 'get above their station'. An 'upstart' belongs down below in the 'gutter' with 'the dregs of society'.

We may abhor such ideas, as thinkers and individuals, and we may struggle as thinkers against the implications of such ways of thinking, but language continually provides us with existing linguistic patterns and encourages us to follow their logic unthinkingly. Resistance is possible: Obama struggles to resist the rhetoric he has inherited. And in the same way, as we translate American news, French and German politicians resist the patterns of thought and the rhetorical strategies inherent in US politics. And yet, resistance itself forces us to engage with existing patterns of thought. Ultimately, we can never fully break out of existing linguistic patterning.

In considering four key cultural concepts, truth, love, hate and war, this book will investigate the ways in which people play a part in constructing world-views. This takes us beyond the linguistic anthropology of the neo-Whorfians which will be briefly discussed in the overview of ethnolinguistic approaches. The individual will not be considered as the inhabitant of a thought-world, which confines him or her.

At the same time, our ethnolinguistic approach will also take us beyond critical discourse analysis. In contrast to much recent scholarship written in English and inspired by two great French thinkers, Foucault and Bourdieu, this book will not restrict itself to the political dimension of language. That is to say, in the ethnolinguistic approach that we will embark upon, we will not limit our consideration of the relationship between mind and language, to the power struggle between individuals and the reigning discourse they are subject to. Throughout the investigations of these key cultural concepts, individuals are never represented as the passive victims of dominant discourse. Language is no prison house, and we are no prisoners. Each one of us takes his or her place within language and within the social relations in which we live.

In terms of existing scholarship in English, this book owes a debt to Raymond Williams, whose *Key Words* (1983) did much to inspire critical theory and crit-ical discourse analysis. Williams, however, was a thinker rather than a phil-ologist, and like most thinkers, he tended to focus upon words. Thinkers know what words are, and they know they are crucial for any serious discussion. The serious thinker sets out by defining his terms. But words are, as we have seen, the most obvious expressions of rhetoric. Grammar and metaphor prove to be more subtle. It is for this reason that readers will find the present work is often closer in spirit to the work of Andrew Goatly, who in recent years has taken up the analysis of conceptual metaphor in political discourse. The essential contri-bution he makes is to take us beyond the study of individual concepts in isola-tion (William's approach): Goatly invites us to study the underlying patterning of discourse. This involves tracing the 'patterns of metaphors' (Goatly 2007: 4). Goatly's project is ultimately a moral one. He aims to 'remove harmful ways of thinking' (*ibid*.: 2). This does not mean we are in for a moralistic rant. Goatly proceeds by painstakingly analysing the forces that generate discourses and the forces which obscure reality. Ultimately, his rhetorical project resembles Aristotle's: he seeks to unveil the strategies of pernicious sophistry in order to allow us to see the world more clearly. Following Lakoff, Bourdieu, and most of all Gramsci, Goatly examines the way 'hegemony manages the mind in covert ways to construct a consensus about the social order which benefits those in power. Hegemony depends upon the naturalization of ideology as commonsense, and thereby makes ideology latent or hidden' (*ibid.*: 1). By studying metaphor and discourse, Goatly hopes to uncover the defining concepts which drive our social practices and reinforce social patterns of inequality.

Beyond ideology

In one sense, it is absurd to speak about moving 'beyond' ideology. We are all culture-bound creatures, and cannot escape the socio-historical context in which we think and breathe. And yet, a reductive concept of politics induces us to bring everything to the level of the powerplay of social forces, and such an approach leaves little room for personal life. The very division between the private and the public, the personal and the political, is itself a political construct, one which varies from culture to culture and which evolves over time.

The Spartans, for example, did not value very highly private life, feeling that each one realized himself or herself in the glory of public projects. Spartan women assumed a very different role than the traditional one ascribed to middle-class women in Western democracies until recent years. They were taught to bear arms rather than simply being relegated to bearing warrior-sons, and they took their participation in sporting events very seriously and considered the culture of the body as an important part of their social role. The traditional Western stereotype, with the division of the sexes and gender roles, attributing the woman to the household and the man to external social relations, would not, therefore, be of much use in trying to understand the public and private worlds of the Spartans.

The communist states show our own 'Western' separation of private life and public life to be absurd in certain cases. Such states, for example, assumed the responsibility of structuring working life in order to facilitate the private sphere by ensuring women could take time off for pregnancy. The state organized working hours for women by taking into account school hours, a fact which obviously facilitated their careers. Such harmonisation was, moreover, greatly appreciated by West Berliners, which explains why the system of kindergartens was preserved after the Wall came down. It also goes some way to explaining why the fertility rate of Berlin is remarkably high by German standards today. Capitalist societies leave such fine tuning of social relations to the free hand of the market (with the predictable confusion and stress that this lack of coordination provokes within the family). What the examples of the Spartans and the communists prove, is that private life does not stand outwith the public sphere. Private life exists within society, and is subject to politics. Private speech also takes place within the sphere of social relations and cannot be divorced from public language.

Nevertheless, society cannot be reduced to politics and neither can language. For this reason, literature and everyday social interaction highlight something which is pushed to the side and into the shadows by the focus of much discourse analysis. Though language is important, politically speaking, and though politics is one essential dimension of language, politics cannot account for other dimensions of language. And this book is about language as a whole, about the relationship between language and worldviews. The 'personal world' transcends the political domain, just as the political domain transcends the sphere of the individual. This book will investigate political manipulation in the case study of war. The case studies of truth and hate will also have some bearing upon the question of political integrity with which this book opened. To what extent Obama 'speaks the truth' (where Blair and Bush 'lied') depends upon our definition of truth. But one of the major contributions of this book is to go beyond politics and to reach into the deeper levels of linguistic patterning. By doing so, and by comparing the ways different languages construct 'truth', truth will be shown to be both elusive in nature and relative to the language system in which the concept emerges. Truth turns out to be a chameleon-like concept, which changes from language to language.

The case study of hate is by far the longest of the four studies. This does not necessarily mean that negative emotions are being attributed the limelight. The very question of the negativity of hate is questioned. After all, most cultures appear to find hate essential. Hate is often celebrated. Hate is at times considered to be a force which invigorates us and defines us in relation to others. How are we supposed to feel about crimes, lies and 'sins'? Would it not seem logical and natural to hate them?

This study concentrates on English, though it is essentially philological in that it seeks to understand the roots of our concept of hate as it has emerged in the traditions of other languages which have contributed to our own linguistic tradition. The starting point is the promotion of hate and war in neoconservative rhetoric. A critique of Bush's religious rhetoric justifies a close analysis of the development of hate in the Bible. But to speak of 'the' Bible is to efface the existence of two very different Bibles, the Old Testament and the New Testament. So it becomes important to trace the way the notion of hate evolves and is transformed throughout these two volumes.

This book will move on from the promotion of hate by the neoconservatives, to reflect briefly upon the ways Obama is trying to promote a discourse of love. But in philological terms, it will be of interest in that it will take us on a tour of the etymological, historical and metaphorical roots which have enabled us to draw on diverse traditions of hate to form our own meaningful concept in English. The latter part of the study will lead us back from discourse analysis to ethnolinguistics, by considering two forms of French hate (*haine*). The first form concerns a confusing form of apathetic hatred which entails an aimless, unmotivated form of hate, which neither engages others, nor involves real enemies. The second form of hate is an amusingly complex and surprisingly adaptable form of aversion, anti-Americanism. This sentiment will be studied, not in order to criticize the Americans, but in order to demonstrate that hatred expresses as much about the hater as about the hated. In this example, hate simply serves to reflect the state of French society at any time, and the aspirations and frustrations of the French people. As a result, the case study on hate should also be of political interest in that it makes a contribution to the way in which hate is represented, generated and harnessed in politics.

But neither the case study on hate nor the one on truth are intended as political projects. Both truth and hate are human experiences. As such, the investigation of these two concepts in different languages aims to elucidate something about the universal nature of people, but also something about the specific means by which each language system generates its concepts and offers them to its speakers to accept or adapt as they communicate with each other. This takes us back to the spirit of language study found in the work of Herder, Hamann and (most of all) Humboldt. The ethnolinguistics of this book will not aim to define the essence of a 'primitive' or 'exotic' worldview which exists in isolation, as much twentieth-century anthropology sought to define the worlds of the peoples it studied. Nor will it aim to uncover the universal underlying cognitive unconscious, the goal animating much contemporary cognitive research. This book will consider the ways different cultures develop, in their own particular ways, similar rhetorical strategies and similar forms of linguistic patterning. And in this sense, each study of the specific nature of one particular worldview should shed some light upon the evolving nature of humankind.

This book was written over several years, almost a decade. Within that decade, American foreign policy was radically transformed. War, truth and hate became, more than ever, concepts at stake in civil society and in world relations. But the latter two are, of course, equally important in the intimate relations we have with others. In this sense, this book is also a very personal book. And the harnessing of the private and the public, the political and the personal, constitutes, in itself, a stance. The contemplative study of society cannot afford to forget the individual in his or her most intimate dimensions. Philosophy, when it forgets people, is of little use. Political regimes which defend principles, but fail to defend human lives, are grotesque.

Similarly, a linguistics which aspires to objectivity and to scientific abstraction should never forget why words are important for people and the reasons why we speak to one another. A philological project such as this one, in investigating the concept of worldview and the way language and thought shape worldviews, must never lose sight of the thinking-feeling-human-being. Ultimately, the individual is our unique object of study in any rigorous approach to language. For this reason, it is important to question the most fundamental concept for the individual, the very bond which links the individual to others: the concept of love. A lengthy case study has therefore been devoted to exactly that subject.

The study of love resembles the study of war in two ways: it focuses upon the metaphoric structuring of the concept, and it does so by relying upon a corpus-based study. But unlike the study of war, which focuses on ideology and the transformation of a collective cultural mindset, this study seeks to determine the metaphoric patterning at work in the construction of love at the most intimate level of expression. In order to avoid the pitfall of imposing my own conception of love upon the idea, I sought a corpus and – as a man – I felt obliged to investigate the way women spoke about love, in order to avoid a biased viewpoint. This led me on a curious (and not altogether enchanting) adventure, which involved struggling to interpret the ways in which French, Czech and British women expressed their ideas about love in the feminine press.

This study of the way this key cultural concept is constructed is, as we shall see, perplexing. Love, we are often told, is eternal and essential. And yet, love turns out to change over time and to change from language to language. The love of which Czechs speak as they move from the communist worldview into the worldview of the democratic market economy entails an increasing objectification of sexual relations.[2] The sexual act becomes increasingly represented in terms of a mechanical process, a machine. This explains why Czechs began to adopt the language of user guide instructions: articles on sex and sexual performance offered advice on how 'it' 'works'. Such attitudes were apparently widespread in English and in French before such patterns began emerging in Czech.

In France and Britain, third-generation feminism has opened the way to a new enslavement of the male, in reducing him to the sexual object which serves only to fulfil the fantasy desires of erotic scenarios. Men are 'tried out' and collected as 'trophies' in French. In English, men are frequently reduced to FWBs (Friends With Benefits) capable of fulfilling the sexual requirements of their partners, when and if the women can fit them into their busy romantic 'agenda'. Breaking with traditional representations of love as 'fusion', which involves 'the coupling of two souls', or, at the very least, 'attachment', the writers of the feminine press in English spoke irritably of 'bolt-on boyfriends'. Clinging men (who inevitably introduced obligations and expectations) were in particular disparaged by DCDs (Don't Care Daters).

Like all corpus-based studies, this study of love metaphors was limited in scope, and it would be unwise to draw conclusions as to the nature of Czech,

French or British women from a study of women's magazines. Nevertheless, the study will certainly allow us to ascertain the means by which one particular form of media highlights existing traditional metaphoric paradigms and transforms them or negates them. This should remind us that though many concepts are resilient, they must be constantly reaffirmed and reinvented, and each era will reinvent them in ways which reflect the ongoing transformation of culture and society. Furthermore, this study reminds us (more than the other three studies) of the degree to which individual speakers and writers contribute to the transformation of worldviews. In the context of cultural criticism, which often represents language as a tool of power (the manifestation of class-based interests in dominant discourse), we must not allow ourselves to forget that, ultimately, worldviews do not exist outside of the individual. Only in individual speech are worldviews expressed. They exist only within the individual mind, the mind capable of discerning the coherent and meaningful patterning of concepts.

This discussion of love and sex has taken us far from our initial concern for Obama's redirection of American culture. If this is so, it is because the central focus of this book is worldview and not ideology. This book is about ethnolinguistics first, and politics second. Politics may be pervasive, even ubiquitous, but politics forms only one dimension of the philosophical project which aims to uncover what concepts reveal about a culture's mode of perceiving and understanding the world around us. All of the studies in this book are concerned with the way worldviews are linguistically patterned, and about the way individuals take their stand in language in relation to worldviews. This stress on individual discourse does not contradict the implicit aims of ethnolinguistics, but it does stand at odds with many of the forms of ethnolinguistics and linguistic anthropology that have evolved in recent decades in English-speaking countries. It also distinguishes this approach from much mainstream linguistics and from those forms of cognitive scholarship which would like to occult the individual, and which increasingly focus upon the 'brain' at the expense of the study of the 'life of the mind', a fact which alienates them further and further from the study of culture and the adventure of humankind as a meaning-making communal endeavour. For this reason, it is worth defining more clearly the place ethnolinguistics might hope to take up within linguistics as a whole: not least of all, because many scholars working within and outside of the field are content to see linguistic anthropology as a part of the social sciences, anthropology, rather than a part of linguistics or philology. Before proceeding to the case studies, the following section should go some way to clarifying where ethnolinguistics stands in relation to linguistics and to society as a whole.

2   Ethnolinguistics

Linguists and their problem with ethnolinguistics

This book is a defence of ethnolinguistics. But this begs the question: does ethnolinguistics require defending? Certainly, no one is condemning ethnolinguistics. But a problem does exist, nonetheless. The problem is that ethnolinguistics, the study of the relationship between languages and the communities they help to define, is often marginalized and forgotten about in mainstream linguistics. According to the American linguist Palmer (1996: 13), the tradition in anthropological linguistics inspired by Boas and continued by Sapir and his student Whorf, found 'few active followers during the thirty-year period from 1950 to 1980, a time when formal and mathematical approaches grabbed everyone's attention'.

For Palmer, a wave of publications since the 1980s has enabled us to return to the study of the relationship between language, culture and thought. He outlines three traditions in anthropological linguistics:

1. Boasian linguistics, which received impetus from Madeleine Mathiot, when she published her *Ethnolinguistics: Boas, Sapir and Whorf Revisited*, in 1979, and was consolidated by neo-Whorfians such as John A. Lucy in his work *Language, Diversity and Thought: A Reformulation of the Linguistic Relativity Hypothesis* (1992)
2. Ethnosemantics, a mode of study which 'emerged as the favored mode of linguistic analysis in anthropology during the 1960s and which remained a popular mode of interpretation in the 1970s' (Palmer 1996: 18–19). 'Ethnosemantics or ethnoscience [as Palmer explains, 19], is the study of the ways in which different cultures organize and categorize domains of knowledge, such as those of plants, animals, and kin.' Palmer cites Tyler as an exponent of ethnosemantics for whom this particular field of study remained a part of cognitive anthropology. As far as Tyler was concerned, the question was to discover 'how different peoples organize and use their cultures', and to uncover 'the organizing principles underlying behavior' (Tyler, quoted by Palmer, *ibid.*)
3. The ethnography of speaking, which 'assumes that purposeful speakers apply linguistic resources toward social ends in culturally defined

situations'. This tradition, which developed in the 1960s and 1970s, takes us closer to discourse analysis. Palmer quotes Dell Hymes (1974) as one of its major exponents. Hymes, arguing against the background of Chomsky's generativist linguistics, affirmed that linguistic competence involves using language pragmatically in specific social and cultural contexts. Rather than hoping to provide an explanatory theory of language, Hymes advocated that we should aim for a descriptive theory in which the ethnographer should record settings, participants, ends, act sequences, keys, instrumentalities, norms and genres. Such an approach would allow us, Hymes believed, to open up to and account for many forms of language use which mainstream linguistics has little time for and little aptitude for understanding. He quoted as examples, speaking to stones in Ojibwa culture, Indian concepts of time, black street talk, ritual language, wailing, and forms of performance and poetic activities which Hymes himself studied in Chinookan narratives.

More recently, and closer to home, Carmen Fought has defended an ethnic approach to linguistics in her *Language and Ethnicity* (2006), in which she gives accounts of 'ebonics', African American Vernacular English, French creoles, and Latino dialects of Spanish. Joshua A. Fishman's *Handbook of Language & Ethnic Identity* (1999) covers a vast array of ethnolinguistic questions, from linguistic diversity in Canada to European linguistic policy, the development of Swedish in Finland, ethnic identity in the Maghreb and the Near East and the linguistic modes expression of migrant workers. Indeed, linguistic anthropology is increasingly becoming a discipline with defenders such as Alessandro Duranti (1997), Foley (1997), Salzmann (1999), Marcel Danesi (2004), Ottenheimer (2006) and Riley (2007).

Nonetheless, this impressive list of thought-provoking scholarship might lull us into a false sense of security, and lead us into believing that the study of language and culture is central to linguistics. If this were the case, how are we to explain the fact that ethnolinguistics finds so few entries in introductions to linguistics and linguistic encyclopaedias? R. L. Trask, in his *Key Concepts in Language and Linguistics* (1999) attributes only a brief entry to 'anthropological linguistics' and has no entry for 'ethnolinguistics'. Jean Aitchison finds space for neither term in her *Glossary of Language and Mind* (2003). Among the more established references, Kristen Malmkjær's *The Linguistics Encyclopedia* (1991) lists neither ethnolinguistics nor anthropological linguistics. David Crystal in his *Cambridge Encyclopaedia of Language* (1997) is one of the few linguists to list the term ethnolinguistics in his index. And he discusses the term's significance in various sections of his encyclopaedia. This is, sadly, the exception rather than the rule.

To be fair to Malmkjær, Trask and Aitchison, they are simply representing the current state of affairs. In modern and contemporary linguistics, ethnolinguistics has little place. And if we look to the language system itself, we find that the term rarely appears in spoken English. The Corpus of Contemporary American (COCA) 410-million-word corpus provided only one reference to 'ethnolinguistics', a reference, predictably, to Amerindian language study, whereas 682 references were found for 'linguistics'. Ethnology proved to be a minor term, but one which is, nonetheless, firmly anchored within the language system, with 188 references. The evidence suggests, therefore, that though ethnology exists within the English-speaking imagination, ethnolinguistics does not.

The adjective 'ethnic', in contrast, seems to be highly active in contemporary speech and writing in American English. The term collocates most commonly with 'group', a fact which tends to show that 'ethnic peoples' are most commonly considered to be minorities. But minorities are invariably associated with others: with them, not us. There is little evidence to suggest that English speakers in America, Britain or elsewhere in 'Anglo-culture' are capable of taking on the ethnolinguistic challenge which consists in seeing themselves as the exponents of a language culture with its own frameworks of thought and conceptual and cultural limits. To put it bluntly, we perceive other world-views, but we appear to be incapable of imagining that we ourselves inhabit a worldview, and that the limits of our views and perspectives might be clearly discernible to those who inhabit different 'worlds'.

The other collocations for 'ethnic' (background, race, origin, encounter, identity, codes, traditions, distinctions, affinities, niche, enclaves, cleansing, separatism, cleavages, homeland, body art, gender, origin) certainly seem to lead us to such a conclusion. And of those 'groups' referred to, the most common ones were 'minority ethnic groups', 'immigrant ethnic groups', who were supposed to achieve successful 'integration' to various degrees. In contrast to 'ethnic minorities', 'ethnic majorities', though they did exist, were, predictably, rare.

Are we blind to our own limits? Are we deaf to other languages? Perhaps. Yet, it would furthermore be unfair to overtax English-speaking scholars for this deafness when it comes to hearing the claims of ethnolinguistics. Curiously, this insensitivity is not culture specific. Throughout the history of Western thought, there has been a strong disinclination to consider the foreign. Among philosophers (even the greatest of them, Aristotle included), foreigners were often considered 'barbarians'. And apart from rare exceptions, such as Michel de Montaigne (1533–92), ethnology could hardly be said to figure at all within the preoccupations of philosophers. The French philosophical tradition since Montaigne can hardly be said to be aware of ethnological questions. Michel Blay's *Dictionnaire des concepts philosophiques* (879 pages), published in Paris (2006) has no entry for *ethnologie, ethnolinguistique* or *anthropologie*. The *Vocabulaire européen des philosophes Dictionnaires des intraduisibles* (1531), edited by Barbara Cassin, and published in Paris in 2004, finds space for entries for obscure terms such as the German concept of *Anschaulichkeit* (meaning intuitive character, transposed from the English term 'visualisability'), but finds no space for *anthropologie, ethnologie,* or *ethnolinguistique.* The conclusion is inescapable. For philosophy, man exists, but men do not. And despite what is increasingly known as 'the linguistic turn in philosophy', languages, in their own right, as living thought-worlds, do not exist for philosophy either. Philosophy deals in models, but in constructing models of the world, philosophers have little patience for individual men and women expressing themselves in their own particular language. While Wilhelm von Humboldt (1767–1835), that great philosopher of language, dealt always with the man in the middle of interactive exchange, the speaking individual, philosophy when it does consider human beings, considers them in abstraction. And when it does not exclude language from discussion and reflection, philosophy relegates it to an abstract model for 'reflecting' or 'translating' thought.

Anthropologie fares somewhat better with psychoanalysis in French. In the two volumes of the *Dictionnaire international de la psychanalyse,* which he edited in 2002, Alain de Mijolla finds space to discuss the relationship between anthropology and psychoanalysis. No doubt psychology was, from the outset, better fitted to consider ethnology, thanks to Freud's and Jung's contributions on culture. Alain de Mijolla perpetuates this tradition, and quotes Malinowski and Margaret Mead in his bibliography. There is no entry for *ethnologie* or *ethnolinguistique,* but there are entries for *ethnique* (2002: 549–51) and, interestingly, for *ethnopsychanalyse* (including an intriguing discussion of the importance of holding together the universal psychic nature of mankind and the cultural 'context' or 'framework' (*cadrage*), and the influence of frameworks upon 'psychic contents' (*contenus psychiques*)). According to Georges Devereux, 'ethnopsychoanalysis' is constructed from a complementary method which excludes no valid theory: approaches are combined and 'coordinated' (de Mijolla 2002: 551).

Perhaps because psychoanalysts such as Devereux, Jung and Freud, and psychiatrists such as R. D. Laing, are dealing with real people, they are more inclined to challenge the abstract categories of understanding upon which the Enlightenment is founded. Psychiatrists are less likely to speak of the 'universal man', considered in abstraction. But from the ethnolinguistic perspective, psychology, psychiatry and psychoanalysis have their limits. The problem for the psychiatrist will be to understand the group. Splitting up sociology and psychology is legitimate at one level, but it does tend to deepen the schism which separates and opposes individuals and their contexts. Although the two disciplines regularly attract 'bridge-builders', the sociologist is, in both theory and practice, poorly equipped for dealing with the thinking, feeling, acting individual, just as the psychologist finds it difficult to speak convincingly about groups and the socio-historical forces which act upon them or the way they anticipate and handle those forces. That psychology is partially aware of its own blind spots is encouraging. It remains insufficient, however.

Linguistics should by rights force us to return to the context of communication, to the study of individuals taking their place in groups. Ethnolinguistics, for its part, must move beyond the essentialist reflex in anthropology and ethnology of seeking to reduce the individual to the expression of his or her culture. Though individuals do indeed 'carry' their culture, and reflect the worldview of the group, they cannot be circumscribed to this sole role. If they are to be considered as 'individuals' then their specific individual nature, their personality, must be taken into account. This concern will be taken up in the analysis of discourse in the case studies. At this stage the importance of the personal world in worldview studies becomes crucial. For the moment, we are concerned only with the place of language within ethnology and anthropology, however. Where does language stand within these fields of study?

It is disconcerting that no ethnolinguistics entry can be found in Pierre Bonte and Michel Izard's *Dictionnaire d'ethnologie et d'anthropologie* (1991). We might like to believe this was a simple oversight. This does not, however, appear to be the case. No reference can be found to ethnolinguistics in either the contents or the indexes of Marie Odile Géraid's *Notions clés de l'ethnologie* (Key Concepts in Ethnology, 2000), or in Gerard Gaillard's *Dictionnaire des ethnologues et des anthropologies* (1997).

Where are we to find defenders of ethnolinguistics, then? If ethnolinguistics is to be defined as the study of the languages of various different peoples, on the one hand, and of the study of peoples defining themselves through their languages, on the other, then we might be inclined to look to linguists such as the much-celebrated Claude Hagège, who sees himself very much as a defender of language. Hagège, however, does not tend to speak of *l'ethnolinguistique*, but has, for the past twenty-five years, been speaking about *l'écolinguistique* (1985: 328, 2000: 125, 215), a term which translates into our English term, 'ecolinguistics'. His *Halte à la mort des langues* (2002) is literally a rallying cry for us to 'halt the death of languages!' And his discourse has increasingly developed into an 'inspired' lyricism. But this lyrical celebration of language and Hagège's defence of dying languages allows little space for close analysis in the ethnolinguistics vein. His concern is very different from that of Humboldt's linguistic anthropology.

In his celebration of the 'vital' and 'vivacious' nature of languages, Hagège takes on board the stock conceptual metaphors of ecology and the biosphere, but he transposes them to the field of linguistics with a surprising lack of lucidity. Whether each language is vital for the interactive fertilising force of the human adventure in the same way that each plant and animal has its place in the food chain and the environment, is far from certain. But what does, at least, appear to be certain, is that linguistics in France has tended to fork off on a route which leads to the celebration of languages and worldviews from afar. Crystal (2000) takes a similar course, and that fact that Crystal and Hagège are famous mainstream linguists whose works have become greatly influential, tends to point to a move away from the study of speech and texts, in order to pursue this well-meaning attempt to protect endangered communities from economic and linguistic extinction.

All in all, this state of affairs is disappointing. Linguistics, for Herder, Hamann and Humboldt, was about peoples. But it was also about people. That is to say, it was about the way individuals, binding together, made sense of the world and gave meaning to their own shared expression of the world. People take their place in the world and in social relations in language. We think in language. This makes us not prisoners of language, but rather, to some extent, the artisans of our own destinies. Language provides us with the means to take the world into our own consciousness. Within the scope of our own intellectual endeavours, and within the shared communion of speech, language allows us to reach out to others and bind them to us, as we act within our relationships.

Humboldt understood 'ethnies' in this sense. His study of 'nations' was the study of the linguistic communities which were born together and developed together thanks to the 'work of the mind', which was always a 'thinking-within-language' (*Sprachdenken*). But despite being frequently cited, Humboldt's conception of speech finds little echo in modern linguistics. There is a double blindness involved in eclipsing ethnolinguistics in the French- and English-speaking authors we have considered. On the one hand, we downplay the specificity of language systems in the concept of language we are setting up. This is, of course, convenient for cognitive scholars who are involved in the quest for universals but are often impatient with the details of the hundreds of thousands of existing linguistic systems known to mankind. On the other, it betrays an insensitivity to personality. Indeed, the study of individuality in language has been railroaded into 'stylistics' and cut off from mainstream linguistics. And Sapir (1949; 1985) is one of the few modern linguists to attribute a primary place to the study of personality in his concept of language.

In recent years, ethnology has moved towards a more complex analysis of culture and subcultures. Following Fredrik Barth, ethnology has begun to deal with the strategic ways in which ethnic groups in modern multilingual societies define themselves and assert their interests as groups. In such a context, ethnolinguistics must pay more attention to both individuals and the groups they form within different contexts. Ethnolinguists cannot remain complacent: they cannot continue to describe languages as fixed worldviews, reduced to a series of underlying views held by all members of the group. They cannot continue to conceive of a language's worldview as a set of core beliefs awaiting discovery like a nut that has to be cracked. They cannot continue to present worldviews as essences, undisturbed by internal conflicts and external influence.

This is a part of the ethnolinguistic challenge. And it is very much a challenge to linguistics as it is conceived in the modern university. But are linguists capable of hearing this challenge? This is far from clear: because modern linguists do not draw their inspiration from Humboldt or Herder, who were arguably the first 'ethnolinguists'. Disappointingly, even those linguistic anthropologists who are animated by a reappraisal of Whorf's work (see Lee 1996; Duranti 1997; Danesi 2004) seem wholly ignorant of Humboldt's project, though linguistic anthropologists do at time make reference to a supposed 'Humboldtian tradition'. Modern linguistics as a whole derives from an entirely different and more modern conception of language which has imposed its constraints upon the linguistic project. At this stage, it is important to consider Saussure and the way he has shaped our thought. But this will also lead us to consider the context within which (and against which) he was thinking, since the currents of thought of his period inevitably shaped the course he took in developing his own conception of language. This should allow us to extract ourselves from the Saussurean tradition, without doing an injustice to that great linguist, who cannot be reduced to the tradition which his adherents set up and bequeathed to us.

Linguistics following Saussure

Linguistics, in West European university departments, at least, usually begins with Saussure (1857–1913), as though that great thinker of language was 'the unmoved mover', whence all linguistic élan could be traced. This is, of course, very much a fairy tale. As the case of Humboldt shows, philologists had long been occupied with thinking about the importance of language for culture. Philosophers such as Locke and Leibniz, writing around a hundred years before Humboldt, were far more at home in discussing the way languages carve out different concepts for their speakers than most contemporary philosophers are. This is clearly demonstrated, for example, by Locke's consideration of the ways *hora* and *hour* are used differently in Latin and English. Locke knew perfectly well that words do not refer to things but to the objects of understanding, 'ideas', and that a great many words refer to complex constructs with multiple meanings held together in the word as in a 'knot' (Locke 1964: 279–81). But linguistics rarely begins with thinkers of language such as Leibniz, Locke and Humboldt. If we are to understand the ways in which ethnolinguistics is conceived (or pushed out of sight) in the English-speaking community, then it will prove worthwhile to begin with Saussure's conception of language in general and his reflections on *éthnie* in particular.

Saussure has, to some degree, been reduced to a caricature. The oppositions which shaped his conception of language, the oppositions between 'the language system' (*langue*) and 'speech act' (*parole*), between diachrony and synchrony, were explored and consolidated by linguists who tended to focus upon one of the terms, and then found themselves obliged to assimilate the opposite term into their field of vision. These oppositions were modes of conceptualisation for Saussure, not rigid divisions, and though he himself focused upon the language system, disregarding the individual was certainly not what he advocated. The idea of making the individual the unthinking automaton which simply activates the templates of linguistic patterning would have appeared to him a bizarre and absurd notion. The idea of an abstract language (a language divorced from socio-historical, linguistic and individual situation) – the very model with which many neuroscientists and cognitive linguists are working today – would have seemed to him a pale reflection of language, a non-empirical 'scientific' phantasm, an 'objectification' with very little weight in terms of objective reality.

Speech implied individuals for Saussure. The necessity of focusing on the individual nature of speech is something he took pains to highlight when he gave his example of a man crying 'War! I'm telling you war!'(*La guerre, je vous dit, la guerre!*, Saussure, quoted by Tullio de Mauro in his introduction to Saussure's *Cours*, 1994). Saussure insisted that each one of us has our own concept of 'war'. In this sense, Saussure was speaking of what would today be termed 'idiolect'. But he was also making a second point: that words intervene in space and time, and that even the same person using the same word would give it a different meaning in a different context. The repetition of the word 'war' does not function, nor is it interpreted, in the same manner in the two consecutive instances. The intonation with which the word is uttered is different. The emotional resonance, the impact upon the interlocutor is different.[1]

Saussure's concern for the individual use of language did not greatly animate the linguistics of the twentieth century, however. De Mauro seems to be ignorant of the linguistic anthropology of Sapir and the philology of the Prague Linguistic Circle when he affirms: 'Only Wittgenstein, and only forty years later, attained a similar clarity in his vision [to Saussure] of the radically social character of language' (1994: xiii). This is clearly overstating the point. But here again, it is not Saussure himself, but his interpreter, who is at fault. De Mauro's remark reveals all of the formalism of twentieth-century linguists. When confronted by a true thinker such as Wittgenstein considering how the individual mind grapples with words, linguists who have been educated within a tradition which has little time for philosophy and speculative thought, find themselves disarmed and in awe. They are unable to handle questions of a philosophical and speculative nature, questions which the contemplation of language use and the construction of reality in language necessarily force us to face up to. Having said this, de Mauro is certainly right, however, in affirming that Saussure was sensitive to the social nature of speech and capable of speculating about the historical and interpersonal forces acting upon it. And it is, indeed, important to stress the point, since the Saussure which his students tended to bequeath to us, is the Saussure of the language system operating, or so it would seem, in and of itself, outside of time.

We may appear to be taking a rather roundabout route in defining ethnolinguistics, but it is important to stress that modern linguistics has tended to marginalize the question of groups because Saussure himself thought of the relationship between people and language as the relationship between 'man' and 'language'. He either described the 'structure', or he shifted positions and considered language from the perspective of the individual evolving within the structure and taking his place within it as he communicated with others. In fairness to Saussure, two points must be made. The group was not the focus of his study, and his *Cours* did indeed contain a eight-page chapter on linguistic groups (1994: 305–12). This study of linguistic groups was considered by Saussure to be a part of *Ethnisme*, by which he meant 'the unity residing in the multiple relations between religion, civilization and common defence' (*l'unité reposant sur des rapports multiples de religion, de civilisation, de defense commune, etc. ibid.*: 305, my translation, as in the following quotes).

Indeed, Saussure's sensitivity remains very much in harmony with the understanding of ethnolinguists of our own times for a number of reasons:

1. Saussure did not fall prey to the social Darwinism which was taking hold of linguistics in the second half of the nineteenth century. Like his contemporary, the great German-American anthropologist and Amerindian specialist, Boas, Saussure disparaged the illusion of a link between race and language. He pointed to the great variety of hair colour, complexion, and craniums among people speaking Germanic languages as evidence of the absurdity of such a hypothesis (*ibid.*: 304).
2. He argued that 'the social link tends to create the linguistic community (*communauté de langue*) and impresses certain characters upon its shared idiom' (*ibid.*).
3. He posited that 'it is the linguistic community which, to a certain extent, constitutes the ethnic unity' (*ibid.*: 305–6).
4. He believed that the study of other ethnic groups and the origins of people must necessarily begin with the study of language, as this testimony stands above all others.
5. He affirmed that 'the language system (*la langue*) is a historical document' (*ibid.*).
6. He affirmed that 'language reflects the psychological character of a nation'.

As an observer, and as a thinker, Saussure did not forget these points. Nevertheless, the system of the language, whose description he was so anxious to define and interpret, tended to eclipse this intuitive sensitivity. And for this reason, Saussure at times formalizes linguistic transformation, extracting it from the minds and mouths of speaking men and women. When he speaks of the influence of certain Indo-European associations, for example, he speaks of them as occurring 'outside of the mind (*hors de l'esprit*) in the sphere of sounds' (*ibid.*: 311). These associations, he argues, can form the 'absolute yoke' in relation to thought (*joug absolu à la pensée*). The model he is working with here is therefore one in which thought is 'forced to enter into a special path which is opened up to it by the material state of signs' (*ibid.*). This takes us close to a linguistic determinism, however, and it is essential to disengage ourselves as ethnolinguists from such a mode of thinking.

Linguistic determinism is a form of interpretation which, in contemporary debates, is often wrongly attributed to Whorf and Sapir, and which is so vehemently condemned by contemporary American linguists such as Pinker. Pinker (1994; 2007) caricatures the positions of 'the neo-Whorfians' who, he claims, believe that language determines thought. This is no innocent gesture. It enables Pinker to play the defender of freethinking and creativity. In rejecting the idea that different linguistic communities think fundamentally differently and think with different conceptual means, Pinker is playing the party game which consists in parading himself as the defender of the 'psychic unity of man'. This is not altogether honest. That human kind can be considered to share certain underlying cognitive capacities is a postulate Humboldt, Boas and Sapir, as defenders of the Enlightenment, would not have contested. Pinker, however, uses the defence of the psychic unity of man as a strategy. It allows him to play the defender of language. Because language cannot, Pinker rightly believes, be reduced to a cultural version of Orwell's Newspeak. Language cannot dictate thought.

Public debates and university politics tend to encourage antagonistic oppositions and simplifications. This situation is not helped by the fact that Pinker's knowledge of other languages is invariably taken from second- and third-hand sources. Certain of the 'neo-Whorfians' in the States whom he criticizes are, it must be admitted, often no better equipped for entering into the worldviews of the languages they study. Defenders of linguistic determinism can be found. And attempts to demonstrate the degree to which language 'conditions' thought are often erected on rather superficial arguments and on secondary sources. In other words, the debate itself which opposes 'freethinkers' such as Pinker and those who consider language to be conceptual spaces from which we cannot escape is a misleading debate which sets up caricatures that are of very little real interest for ethnolinguistics.

Debates of this kind make it difficult to convey the true scope, aims and foundations of the ethnolinguistic approach. The debate on linguistic determinism is, in fact, only one of the obstacles standing in the way of explaining the importance of ethnolinguistics, and those obstacles should not be underestimated. Six principle obstacles can be discerned.

Six obstacles on the road to understanding ethnolinguistics

1. Many linguists follow a formalist tradition in interpreting Saussure, and tend to avoid considering the relationship between thinking individuals and linguistic patterning.
2. The opposition *parole–langue* tended to stress the interaction between the individual and the collective linguistic 'instrument', at the expense of the social group, whose collective and interactive contribution to maintaining and modifying existing structures, patterns of understanding and concepts was neglected.
3. The study of the worldviews and the languages of ethnic groups requires an enormous investment of time and energy, and a scrupulous attention to both detail and to the role the individual part plays within the language and the culture as a whole. This effort is not always made by those who support and promote linguistic anthropology, and it is invariably neglected by those who contest the idea that consciousness and language are linked in any fundamental way.
4. The generative linguistics of Chomsky privileged the search for linguistic universals. The implicitly religious impulse of this 'quest' for universals and for a psychic origin for mankind has tended to downplay difference. And the overwhelming scope of 'universalism' makes detailed linguistic study of thinking-in-language and discourse analysis impossible.
5. Defenders of linguistic diversity often erect radical models of language specificity based upon grammar. Whorf's conclusions about the Hopi conception of time is one case in point. And the lack of linguistic proficiency makes such theses all too easy to criticize and debunk.
6. Finally, ethnies are associated with 'others', not 'us'. COCA provides various references to 'ethnic Georgians' and 'ethnic Albanians', but not to 'ethnic English individuals'. And would George W. Bush or Tony Blair consider themselves as members of an 'ethnie'?

Before we can return to a positive definition of ethnolinguistics, and to see how foreign schools of thought might bring fertile ideas to English-speaking scholars, it is first necessary to deal with this last difficulty. And to do so, we will need to plunge into the definition of ethnology and the forces that have moulded this field of study.

Defining and redefining ethnology

To understand the importance of Saussure's rejection of a relationship between blood and thought, between race and language, it is important to enter the spirit of his times. What context was Saussure working in? What constellation of ideas of thought and culture was he thinking within?

The publications of Saussure's times might enlighten us. The sixteenth volume of *La Grande Encyclopédie*, published between 1885 and 1902 in Paris, offers two terms to which any theory of language related to ethnies might logically be linked: *ethnographie* and *ethnologie*, which are, however, defined under one single entry (647–9).

Deux termes qui se rapportent au même genre d'études s'occupant des « groupes humains » ou groupes ethniques (peuples, peuplades, tribus, etc.). Malheureusement, on n'est pas bien d'accord, non seulement dans les différents pays, mais même entre les savants d'une seule et même nation, sur ce qu'il faut entendre exactement par l'un et l'autre de ces termes. Le mot ethnologie a été employé pour la première fois, semble-t-il, par un chercheur français, W. Edwards, qui s'en est servi pour désigner l'objet et le but de la Société de l'ethnologie crée par lui en 1839. Ce mot correspondait à cette époque à l'ensemble d'études qui relève aujourd'hui de l'anthropologie. Quant au mot ethnographie, il signifiait au commencement du siècle tout simplement le classement des peuples d'après leurs langues: c'était un terme linguistique introduit par Balbi (1826). (648)

Two terms which refer to the same kind of studies dealing with 'human groups' or 'ethnic groups' (peoples, tribes etc.). Unfortunately, we are not altogether in agreement, either in various countries, or among specialists of a single nation, as to what we are to understand by either of these two terms. It would seem that the term *ethnologie* was used for the first time by a French researcher, W. Edwards, who used it to designate the objective of the Society for Ethnology, created by himself in 1839. At the time, the word corresponded to the related studies which now form anthropology. As to the term *ethnographie*, at the beginning of the [nineteenth] century, it designated the classing of peoples according to their languages: the term was coined by Balbi (in 1826).

What is remarkable is that despite definition and redefinition, the terms remain obscure and ambiguous in interdisciplinary debate today. The double irony is that the confusion as to their meanings within specialist discourse and in various languages persists. *Ethnographie*, according to the *Grande Encyclopédie* should have rendered ethnolinguistics and linguistic anthropology superfluous. And indeed there is something deeply pleonastic about the terms which attempt to 'import' into language study a dimension which should by rights be considered inalienable to it, the importance of culture and linguistic difference. The term *ethnographie* has not taken root in French culture. Few French people have an inkling as to what ground is covered by the term.

Language and culture were of great importance to nineteenth-century thought, but coupling them in reflection proved problematic for a series of reasons. During the nineteenth century, a period of great effervescence in linguistic study, a series of dynamic forces was acting upon the conceptions of culture being promoted. And these forces concern our conception of ethnolinguistics directly. What transpires is interesting if we investigate the way this confusion was ordered along political and ideological lines. Although the *hommes de lettres* of the eighteenth century were still fascinated by the study of man in all his diverse forms, a curiosity which was manifest already in the sixteenth-century writings of Montaigne, who saw the discovery of the New World as a wonderful opportunity to discover different forms of cultures, this spirit was not to live untainted long into nineteenth-century France. If anthropology at the outset was interested in *l'homme*, the representative of Mankind, *les hommes et les femmes*, men and women, would soon be displaced by a concern for 'races'. By the middle of the nineteenth century, Prichard was already affirming that 'ethnologie is the history of human races (*races humaines*, *La Grande Encyclopédie* 1885–1902, vol. XVI: 648). By 1886, Broca was affirming that: 'Anthropology is the natural history of man: it can be divided into two great branches. One is related to the human species, excluding its varieties, is known as general anthropology. The other, related to varieties referred to by the term human races, is known as "special anthropology" (*l'anthropologie spéciale*) or ethnologie (*ethnologie, ibid.*).'

This is not an innocent distinction. Already by the second half of the nineteenth century, the French were separating the study of man (which logically entailed the study of men as 'a people') and the study of races: groups of 'others'. *La Grande Encyclopédie* stresses the relation to the German branch of *Völkerkunde* represented by Peschel and Fr. Müller. France, for its own part, had already produced a prodigious racial (or racist) thinker in the much-celebrated Comte de Gobineau, whose long *Essai sur l'inégalité des races humaines* was published in several volumes between 1853 and 1855.

From our perspective, the crucial change in the course of the nineteenth century is that colonial nations such as Britain and France were moving towards the consolidation of a dynamic opposition between 'civilisation' and 'primitive savagery'. Culture and nature were being opposed, and other cultures were increasingly being set on the side of nature: foreign peoples were being identified as primitive savages, animals. The logic was the logic of second- and third-generation colonial experience. Explorers and colonials of the first waves of imperialism encounter a culture. As the invading army devastates the country by war, and as famine and disease inevitably follow up on war to decimate the local population, as the structures and institutions, schools and cultural organisations break down, a chaos resembling anarchy asserts itself. Anarchy and savagery does indeed flourish under such circumstances: and the absence of civilisation appears to beg for order and governance. Thus invading armies create the need that 'justifies' their presence. The grotesque Iraq misadventure in recent years is only one more chapter in this inevitable and predictable scenario.

As far as cultural studies is concerned, nineteenth-century ethnology increasingly becomes associated with 'primitive savages'. Racial connotations still cling to the term. Affirmative action in both the UK and the States has tended, on the whole, to consolidate this association. That this is so is made obvious by the very reluctance of dominant cultures to accept themselves as an 'ethnic group'. Dominant groups consider themselves to be 'normal', just as they consider their worldviews to be 'natural'. Though they are capable of understanding that other cultures exist, these cultures either appear to them 'strange' and 'exotic', or 'perverted'. Their worldviews are inevitably perceived in the same terms. This blindness to the limits of one's own cultural and linguistic group is not restricted to English speakers of course. This reaction is typical for any ruling elite. The same reaction can be observed when the tenets of any ruling ideology or cultural mindset are questioned. Asking communists of the Cold War period to entertain the idea that the 'truths' of the Party were merely 'opinions' and 'ideas' provoked the same irritation and anger.

Where does this leave ethnolinguistics? Modern-day ethnology has integrated the critique of colonialism that I have briefly outlined above, but the history of the school of thought and the practice of this discipline is not innocent, and its definition, like the division of races and their treatment, remains a highly charged political issue.

Repercussions for linguistics as a tradition

Linguistics tended to follow the colonial mythologising of primitivism in the nineteenth century, the century from which Saussure and Boas were to emerge. Gobineau and Spengler and Hovelaque were all to make attempts to prove that certain cultures were inferior and others, superior. Just as Gobineau (a disillusioned impoverished aristocrat) believed the cultures of the white race of Germanic descent were the heralds of progress who were born 'to reign', so Spengler would argue that the Amerindian languages were inferior. They were formally 'too complicated', and full of superfluous forms, he argued. In his opinion, they were inevitably destined to regress and to become extinct (Hagège 2000; 2002: 28).

Have we made any 'progress' in ethnolinguistics since? Answering this proves tricky, because linguistics as a discipline is essentially positivistic. As a science, it would like to see itself moving forward, taking us deeper and further into modernity, shining light upon the shadows of our ignorance. In this scenario, doubt and superstition are eradicated by the illumination of the Enlightenment which transports us from the Dark Ages into the clarity of modern understanding. The history of linguistic thought proves this to be a fairy tale, however. After all, just as Montaigne was more open-minded than Gobineau, Humboldt, writing fifty years before Gobineau, was already one hundred years ahead of Saussure in understanding the relationship between language and thought and between speech and culture.

The linguistic anthropology of Humboldt (the thinker who wrote over thirty grammars of Amerindian languages) was the thought of someone who breathed the clean air of intellectual curiosity, not the stifled and stifling atmosphere of that arrogance and contempt which infects colonial thought (and which Spengler and Holevaque espoused). Humboldt's linguistic anthropology bears little in common with the linguistics and ethnologie quoted by *La Grande Encyclopédie* (1885–1902). And this sense the nineteenth century – a period of undisputed innovation and of technological and scientific enlightenment – did regress into its own 'dark ages' in the field of linguistic anthropology. If we are to make any 'real progress' in ethnolinguistics, we will have to reach back into the enlightened curiosity of Humboldt and escape the introverted and perverted misrepresentations of linguistic otherness which emerged after he died. That contemporary scholars (Trabant 1992; 1999; 2003) are taking on this task is encouraging, but their marginal status in the linguistic project should leave no doubt as to the difficulty of the task they are undertaking.

Humboldt, Bartmiński, Wierzbicka and the ethnolinguistics project

The influence of 'colonial' Eurocentric thought during its gestation period explains to some extent 'the road not taken' by modern linguistics, the road to ethnolinguistics. However, it is now time to define more clearly the ethnolinguistic approach which is to be adopted. Three contemporary scholars represent the varying ways in which the different strands of Humboldt's project can be interpreted and furthered in their own distinct brand of linguistic anthropology or ethnolinguistics: Meschonnic, Bartmiński and Wierzbicka. Henri Meschonnic (1932–2009) and Jerzy Bartmiński (born 1939) rely heavily on Humboldt and the minority-tradition in German linguistics which maintained a concern for worldview in the face of an Indo-European tradition which was to impose a largely formalist approach upon language study. Meschonnic has written widely on Humboldt and sought to extrapolate his thought in his own poetics of language, a linguistic anthropology which explores the way in which the individual invigorates language, transforms it, bestowing upon it greater potential for expression as an instrument for thinking. Meschonnic is primarily concerned with literature, and with poetry in particular. But his conception of poetry accepts only 'poems' which transform life. His critique of modern linguistics takes the form of an attack on the linguistic sign, the signifier–signified paradigm, which reduces language study to the interpretation of meaning, a hermeneutics of understanding. The problem with such a paradigm, as far as Meschonnic is concerned, is that it fails to perceive the importance of many elements of language and linguistic patterning (which he includes as a part of his cardinal concept of 'rhythm', *rythme*). For Meschonnic, the organisation of words cannot be considered to be mere 'form': the forms of organisation, from accentuation to rhyme and phrasing, influence the way ideas are engendered and the way they move us as we listen to speech or read works of literature. Language is dynamic, it is a 'process of doing', an activity, not a content, awaiting discovery. Hermeneutics treats language as the expression of static meaning which can be injected into words and extracted from texts. But ultimately, Meschonnic feels that hermeneutics can teach us little about what we do with language: hermeneutics occults formal aspects, fails to understand the phatic function of small talk and other ritualistic forms of communication. And worst of all, it entirely fails to understand poetry or translation, aspects of language which any serious theory of language should be able to account for. As for languages, hermeneutics tends to posit the existence of essences existing in reality, without offering an account of the different frameworks of understanding which languages employ in dividing up reality.

Meschonnic's linguistic anthropology bears little in common with Whorf's concern for the deeper structures of other houses of consciousness. What interests Meschonnic is the radically subjective nature of language. But unlike exponents of modernist and post-modernist aesthetics, he will not reduce this radically subjective element to a poetics of rupture which breaks with usage. This is because Meschonnic refuses to make a straw man of language: he refuses to set language up as the foil for revolutionary romantic expression. Ultimately, all language is subjective for Meschonnic, all 'real' expression which perpetuates the language system and consolidates its force and its élan. While Sapir represents one of the few examples of an English speaking linguist capable of hearing personality in language, Meschonnic is one of the main exponents to insist that the personal inscription of the subject in language is the basis of language itself. This allows him to escape the reductive and sterile opposition between the individual and the structure. For Meschonnic, the structure is dead, the subject lives. That is to say, the language system has no reality other than in the act of individuals expressing themselves. From this perspective, Meschonnic is not concerned with individuals. He is concerned with subjects. And the subject is not the individual who 'uses' language as a mode of expression: it is by engaging in speech and in writing that the 'I' who speaks becomes, thanks to communication, thanks to discourse, a subject defining him- or herself in terms of others. The subject 'becomes' through language. In this sense, his anthropology of language can be considered as an extension of Humboldt's project to investigate the sense of language (*Sprachsinn*). Subjects engage in what Locke and Humboldt both called 'the work of the mind'.

At another level, Meschonnic, as a translator, is concerned with the way languages influence one another. But here again his main concern is with poetics. What intrigues him is the way in which great translations such as *The King James Bible* (which, to some extent, he emulates in his own translations of the Bible from Hebrew into French) transform the linguistic system into which they come. This concern for translation, for form, for patterning, and for the individual impetus which keeps language alive, all make Meschonnic a Humboldtian. But while Humboldt maintains an interest in linguistic universals and is working towards a synthesis in his comparison of languages, Meschonnic is more interested in pioneering towards a greater understanding of the development of subjectivity in language.

Jerzy Bartmiński is less concerned with translation and the comparison of languages. What fascinates him in Humboldt's project is the concern for *Weltansicht*. This word was coined by Humboldt to designate the understanding of the world which comes to us through language. It is usually translated as 'world view', though I personally prefer to speak of 'world-perceiving' and 'world-conceiving' in adapting Humboldt's German term to contemporary English-speaking linguistics. Bartmiński finds inspiration for his project in Slavic ethnolinguistics, American linguistic anthropology and even in contemporary cognitive schools of thought in linguistics. But essentially, his vast and multifaceted project, as part of the Polish ethnolinguistics of the Lublin School, focuses upon the definition of the Polish worldview. This form of scholarship represents the antithesis of the reductive models of worldview bandied about in contemporary debates on linguistic determinism and ecolinguistics. Bartmiński's academic journal on ethnolinguistics and his work with the contemporary Prague School (and his collaboration with Irena Vaňková in particular) form the diverse threads of a tightly bound project to study, in painstaking detail, the elements of language which can be said to be constitutive of the worldview we attribute to a language.

Bartmiński's work focuses upon what makes the Polish worldview specific: and a great deal of his efforts have gone into establishing reliable constructions of the underlying 'stereotypes' shared by speakers of Polish. By stereotypes, he has in mind those cardinal concepts which have fundamental meaning for a linguistic community. It is in this spirit that Bartmiński attempts to define what is commonly understood by (*dom*) 'home' in Polish (Bartmiński 2009:149–61), or (*matka*) 'mother' (132–48). Such attempts have precedents, it is true. George Steiner liked to affirm that French had no word equivalent to *home* in English or *Heimat* in German. What is refreshing about Bartmiński's approach, though, is its rigour, and the vast nature of its comprehensive research into literature, popular idioms, discourse and etymology. In contrast to the linguistic anthropology of the States, and in contrast to the incisive but fragmentary studies made by Whorf, Bartmiński's studies give an infinitely more profound insight into the linguistic imagination into which he is reaching. The paradigms his study provides are inevitably both more detailed and more reliable (though of course it should be remembered that he was dealing with his own mother tongue, while Whorf, to his credit, was reaching into entirely different frameworks of understanding when he studied foreign languages).

Bartmiński's work also has the advantage of enabling us to consider the inter-relations between concepts. Rather than treating concepts such as 'mother' and 'home' in isolation within the linguistic system, he seeks to determine the ways in which these key concepts stretch out, organising related concepts with their patterning. Parenthood and home can be considered related concepts in two of the languages we have been studying. What is closest to us tends to shape the configuration of our ideals and our civic conduct. We might choose to fight for the 'fatherland' (*das Vaterland* in German, or *la patrie* in French, from the Latin, *patria*, 'the land of the father'). And the affection for our 'mother tongue' is almost inevitably linked to the mother who teaches it to us at her breast, a link that is borne out in French, German and Czech (*langue mater-nelle*, *Muttersprache*, *mateřský jazyk*, respectively).

Within the Polish emotional and psychological universe, linguistic patterns and trajectories can be traced between conceptual coordinates. 'Home' (*dom*) organizes the fundamental set of oppositions dividing the world into internal and external space. Intimacy, inevitably, remains within the circumference of 'home'. A deep mistrust of the world sets everything foreign and alien on the outside, far from 'home' in Polish. Our English expression 'there's no place like home' is rendered as 'let him who feels well at home not roam the world' (Bartmiński 2009: 52), for example. But the way our relationship to home is harnessed in language is culture specific. And this means we must struggle to understand many of the more complex or figurative uses of *dom* if we are to begin to find our bearings within the Polish worldview.

Dom designates both 'house' and 'home', and this will affect everyday idiomatic expression and the way we move from the concrete to the abstract. *Dom* (house/home) is projected upon the body. To 'open the gates', in the Body-as-House paradigm, means to open one's mouth. And in student slang, 'balconies' refer to a well-rounded bosom. In patriotic political discourse *dom* (home/house) becomes a politically motivated concept, as in 'Poland: the home of all Poles', the election slogan of the former Polish president, Aleksander Kwaśkniewski (Bartmiński 2009: 153). This shows the way the world-perceiving and world-conceiving of the mother tongue is harnessed and directed by the conceptual mindset of politicians. In attempting to manipulate and direct thought and sentiment, ideology reaches deep within the emotive links that have gone to form the fundamental concepts of home and homeland. The individual's sense of place is penetrated by politics, as political discourse sets off resonant conceptual echoes by recovering concepts within a given socio-historical situation.

In a similarly patriotic vein, the mother tongue becomes a home (*dom*) to be defended, a set of walls that protects its people (ibid.: 155). The disappearance of the Polish nation and the Nazi occupation inevitably continues to give great resonance to such a discourse. But at the same time, pro-European discourse in Polish sets out from the same principle of a link between home and homeland to promote the paradigm of 'Europe as *dom*' (*ibid.*: 154).

On a biblical level, the Polish Renaissance poet Jan Kochanowski translated the 12th Psalm (presumably from Latin), using the following phrase: 'Save me, oh you builder of the heavenly *dom*' (*ibid.*). He envisaged the world to come as 'home'. A whole nineteenth-century tradition supports this conceptual construct, and given that more than 90 per cent of Poles declare themselves to be practising Catholics, the importance of such a construct for the popular imagination should not be underestimated.[2]

The approach Bartmiński is practising is impressive in that it reaches back into the etymology of conceptual paradigms, rooting out their Indo-European origins, without neglecting to focus upon modern socially situated developments in usage. Bartmiński lists six types of public discourse, which situates *dom* within its own ideological parameters (2009: 158). Catholic discourse promotes *dom* as the patriarchal home. In patriotic or nationalist discourse, *dom* becomes the home and family, the stronghold of national identity, and implies the *Polish Mother.* For émigrés, *dom* becomes the focus of nostalgia. For the liberal, *dom* becomes the 'open house'. In left-wing discourse, *dom* (home and family) must be subordinated to community. And finally, in feminist discourse, *dom* becomes a 'prison'. It is the place to which woman is confined: *dom* entails an implicit threat or manifested domestic violence.

These are complex associations, the echoes of patterned discourse that has woven a deeply personal sense into the shared paradigms of a linguistic community. Unlike the French and the Slavic languages, which have remained closer to the Latin concept of 'home', we no longer hear *domus* in 'domestic' violence. The euphony of our language is, in this respect, truncated. Our language has split off on another course, connecting different coordinates. What it is important to stress, however, is not the richness of the Polish worldview and its creative and resonant links. What is important is the fact that all languages begin with logical, deeply ingrained, deeply felt links, which are then exploited as speakers tug at connections, oppositions and implications in their own personal fashion in order to project their personal world upon the language system which englobes them and in which they participate each time they express themselves. Bartmiński's ethnolinguistics constitutes a philological investigation into the psychology of the nation, but it also provides a map for the streets and routes we choose as we wander around the mother tongue. And it does not neglect the creative highways and scenic routes which writers and original thinkers take when they break out of standard usage.

My own work, in contrast to Bartmiński's, is resolutely comparative. Readers may well recognize a certain similarity between this comparative work and

Anna Wierzbicka's approach to language. Wierzbicka is a Polish scholar who was initially an exponent of the same school as Bartmiński, but she has been working within the world of 'Anglo' scholarship since emigrating to Australia in the 1980s. Wierzbicka is concerned with the key words in culture. In this respect, her work bears some resemblance to the work of Raymond Williams and the critical discourse analysis which Williams' work has inspired. The obvious difference between Williams' and Wierzbicka's approach to 'key words', though, is that the former adopted a unilingual approach, while Wierzbicka contrasts the way concepts emerge in different language systems. Williams is interested in 'language'. Wierzbicka is interested in languages. This does not dispose her to relativism, one of the hallmarks of less rigorous scholarship inspired by the Sapir–Whorf hypothesis. Wierzbicka's work is not only descriptive but analytical and critical. Moreover, it is linguistically informed.

Many linguists claim each language constitutes a worldview, without taking the trouble of analysing words, phrases and texts. Often such scholars do not actually have a direct knowledge of the languages they describe. Wierzbicka, on the other hand, is competent in several languages. Perhaps this goes some way to explaining why she is not interested in sweeping generalisations of a relativistic nature. On the contrary, Wierzbicka is one of the few scholars making an informed contribution to the theory of linguistic universals. One of her major works *Semantics: Primes and Universals* (1996/2004) investigates the underlying shared paradigms of language. Her approach is Humboldtian, though, not Chomskian. In other words, Wierzbicka does not posit an underlying deep structure which is shared by all languages and which explains linguistic competence as a learnable capacity. She works empirically, whittling down the concepts of existing languages to a few dozen key concepts which all the languages she studies seem to provide terms for. Her list of concepts includes far, near, big, small, I, you, someone, something, if, because, good and bad, for example.

However, when it comes to key cultural concepts, Wierzbicka is adamant: concepts may show a certain degree of compatibility in different languages, but each one is specific to the culture in which it circulates. And this prompts Wierzbicka to make the claim that 'cultures can be interpreted in part though their key words' (Wierzbicka 1997: 17). In her study of 'freedom' (a key concept for Americans), Wierzbicka comes to the same conclusion that I arrive at in my study of 'truth' in German, French, Czech and English, our first case study: that no universal concept exists. '*Freedom* [Wierzbicka affirms] does not stand for a universal human ideal. In fact, it doesn't even stand for a common European ideal, although European languages contain a family of related concepts centred on the idea that it is good for people to be able to do what they want to do' (*ibid.*: 152).

Over the past decade, Wierzbicka has been investigating the culture-specific nature of emotions, a field of scholarship to which the studies of hate and love in the following chapters will make a contribution. With the rising popularity of cognitive models for emotions and models provided by the neuropsychology of Antonio Damasio, who is attempting to 'situate' emotions in the body and the brain, finding the seat of 'joy' and 'sorrow' (2003), Wierzbicka's work is crucial. It reaffirms that 'emotions' such as love and happiness do not 'exist' in and of themselves, outside of language, they are constructed as concepts in order to define and denote complex emotional experiences which then become enrooted in language systems. Though it is possible to 'translate' our terms for emotions such as joy, anguish, fear and love, to forget the culturally specific nature of linguistic construction is, in her opinion, an unforgivable oversight. *Bonheur* (from French) is not 'happiness'. *Angst* in German is not 'angst', or 'anguish', and will invariably translate into English as 'fear'. Whether the speakers of languages actually feel the same emotions remains an open question, but when they speak of emotions, they are speaking of very different constructs, whose contours and complexities differ widely, and whose place in the linguistic system is not easy to translate from one language to another.

One essential aspect of Wierzbicka's work is that it exemplifies what I will call 'the ethnolinguistic challenge'. Wierzbicka forces us, the speakers of the world language, English, to face up to something which inevitably leaves us feeling uncomfortable, something which less prolific cultures feel goes without saying: that our language does not offer us direct unmediated access to the world and all that is in it, but rather provides us with a series of concepts which construct reality along culturally specific lines. Language organizes our concept of the world, and that process of organisation implies limits, blindness and insensitivity, just as it is through the medium of language that we open up to the world, see it, feel it, and manipulate our conceptions of it in our conscious and unconscious thought.

For this reason, Wierzbicka is not content with an ethnolinguistics which restricts itself to the examination of alternative worldviews. She does indeed make an important contribution to this field of research in her consideration of the differences between largely analogous concepts such as 'homeland', in English, *Heimat* in German, *Ojczyna* in Polish and *Rodina* in Russian (Wierzbicka 1997). But she is equally interested in showing the specificity of the limits of 'Anglo' consciousness. And it is for this reason that she wrote *Experience, Evidence & Sense: The Hidden Cultural Legacy of English* in 2010. Experience, evidence and sense are key cultural concepts for the Anglo understanding of the world, according to Wierzbicka. They are, she argues, the products of a tradition of British Empiricism, and therefore culturally specific. For most English speakers, these terms appear largely unproblematic. But as soon as we try to translate them, we find that numerous philological and philosophical considerations come into play, and languages propose other solutions for forming ideas which we tend to conceive of in terms of experience, evidence or sense.

Sense, for example has spread its wings throughout the lexicon, giving such varied phrases as 'a keen sense of something', 'a sense of reality', 'a sense of history', 'a sense of obligation', 'a sense of freedom', 'a sense of what is happening' and 'a sense of self'. Many of these will translate into French or Czech by making use of words very different from the word which might be thought to be the direct translation (*sens*, *smysl* respectively). And the fact that our word 'sense' covers both meaning and feeling already testifies to the fact that a compounding of sensibility and understanding has taken place at the deepest level of our linguistic consciousness, or within what the cognitive scholars would call the 'cognitive unconscious'. Essentially, one of the great services Wierzbicka is doing is alerting English speakers to the underlying patterns of understanding and expression with which our language culture has equipped us for interpreting the world.

Wierzbicka's work tends not to concentrate on corpus-based studies as mine does, and she does not make abundant use of the conceptual tools of metaphor theory as Lakoff, Johnson, Eubanks and Goatly do, and as I do in adopting their analytical tools. In this respect, though my own studies will often overlap with her investigations of emotions and concepts, my discourse analysis and linguistic comparisons should enable us to reach into new dimensions of ethnolinguistics. Obviously, for reasons of space, no multiple approach can be systematically applied to various languages, and my own studies will limit themselves to exploring one mode of analysis at the cost of neglecting another, as the nature of the study and the subject dictate. The field of ethnolinguistics is potentially so vast that no one scholar can be expected to cover all of the aspects of linguistic use in a multilingual study.

Another important distinction is that my own work is perhaps closer in spirit to the work of Meschonnic and Williams, in that it is critical in a political sense. Wierzbicka, for her part, intends to play the role of the comparative philologist who strives for objectivity. This is a justifiable strategy, but one which was not open to me in this book. Because my own work often focuses on discourse, we will constantly be drawn into the subjective: we will be forced to conceive of the ways in which individuals perceive changing reality, and the way in which they vividly and meaningfully express their gut feelings

Love and hate will take us into the guts. Obama and Bush, on the other hand, will take us into politics. At both levels, objectivity is not an option: we are forced as individuals to take a stance in relation towards individuals jostling in the world of politics in the social sphere. This is obviously true of war, but it is no less true of truth. There have already been countless wars over truth, and for this reason we will begin with a comparative case study of the concept of truth in English, French, German and Czech. And we will end with war.

The approach I have adopted in this book is in many respects the same as the one I adopted in *Creating Worldviews: Metaphor Ideology and Language*, published in 2011. Both works combine Wierzbicka's concern for comparative linguistics with the discourse analysis of Williams and the metaphor theory of Lakoff and Goatly. The result is an ethnolinguistic approach which I would define as 'a cross-lingual discourse analysis'. This makes it a cultural project. Language will be studied in terms of the forms it takes within society and within culture, just as both culture and society will be studied from the perspective of language. Languages will be studied as worldviews. Following Humboldt, this approach will seek to investigate the ways in which concepts are 'patterned'. In this attempt, my approach coincides with the concerns of Sapir and Whorf, who introduced the term 'patterning'. But this approach takes us beyond the Sapir–Whorf hypothesis. My approach does not break with the spirit of either of those two great linguists, but it will require us to move beyond what has come to be meant by this hypothesis (as it is used by those who often turn out to be unfamiliar with the work of Whorf and wholly ignorant of the work of Sapir). Studying discourse, conceptual metaphor and linguistic creativity will require us to enter into a level of linguistic depth and into a level of complexity in political debate that will take us beyond the construction of formal models of foreign worldviews.

The ethnolinguistics which is espoused in the present book involves championing philology over linguistics. It involves an individual- and group-centred linguistics: one which is capable of both conceptualising worlds-as-models, in the way philosophers are accustomed to doing, but which does not forget that the source of both language itself and linguistic constructions of the world are to be found in people and only in people. That is to say, the activity of individuals and groups of speakers living together, thinking together and defining themselves, and their identities, and organising their worlds is the only place to look for worldviews. In contrast to mainstream linguistics and dominant paradigms emerging in contemporary research, the approach I am advocating will champion:

1. the mind over brain
2. the individual over structure in the study of linguistic forms
3. meaning over form in expression
4. the study of patterning and conceptual interaction over the study of isolated elements of speech or grammar
5. flux over stasis, a dynamic model of language cultivated and nurtured by humans over an oppressive overarching static model of language which directs or limits speech and thought

6. language as 'producing' over the conception of language as a fixed product – or tool
7. language as the defining force for community, over a conception of language as the possession of community or as an external force acting upon a community.

Bearing in mind these working principles should help remind us that language is 'we', and 'we' are language. The construction of 'we' and 'us' finds no other source, basis or stimulation other than in speech. If we understand this, then the ethnolinguistics which we espouse will not involve the sterile categorisation of comparative grammars, or the naive and uninformed celebration of otherworldly world-conceptions. It will involve a painstaking investigation into linguistic patterning. This will take us into 'peoples', into 'politics', and it will take us deeply into the personal life of individuals. It will force us to reappraise the frameworks of thought which have emerged and which continue to be consolidated in speech by members of the 'Anglo-culture'. It will take us into truth, love, hate and war.

3   The shapes of truth: a comparative study of converging and diverging tendencies in the construction of *truth* in English, French, German and Czech

In the ethnolinguistics of Wierzbicka and Bartmiński, an attempt to seize the full meaning of a concept (and in turn to compare it with its counterparts in other linguistic systems) will comprehend an overview of the dictionary definition of the term, an etymological account, an investigation as to its opposites and synonyms, its multiple definitions, and the way those various meanings are extrapolated and exploited habitually in idioms and, by creative revitalisation, in literary works. Such a study comparing even two languages would, of course, require a book-length study. That is not the objective of this chapter. The objective is both more modest and more ambitious. For reasons of space, unlike the chapters on love and war, no corpus study will be brought to bear here. This study will take for its methodological limits the paradigms of conceptual metaphor and metaphoric extensions introduced by Lakoff and Johnson and elaborated by second-generation cognitive linguists such as Turner, Fauconnier, Sweetser, Goatly and Eubanks. This approach proves highly fruitful for ethnolinguistic study: it provides evidence that the concepts of all languages are linguistically defined and formulated in metaphoric frames. Multiple and conflicting metaphoric frames enable us to speak of diverse forms of 'truth' in all of the four languages studied.

The comparative ethnolinguistics of Wilhelm von Humboldt has not become part of mainstream cognitive research. This study should do something to correct this fact by stressing the necessity of including the ethnolinguistic dimension into any model of language and language study. Moreover, it should achieve three complementary aims concerning linguistic anthropology, cognitive research and, more generally speaking, philosophical investigation. It should correct the sights of ethnolinguistic study, which since the linguistic anthropology of Whorf have tended to stress difference over similitude, by demonstrating that different languages often follow the same paths and create largely analogous patterns of metaphoric representation in defining 'truth'. It should force cognitive linguists to ask themselves questions which the discussion of language in English does not enable us to formulate: how does gender affect the representation of truth, for example? Finally, though this study is 'scientific' in that it aims to create a form of knowledge hitherto unknown, it will force us to question our very attempts to compare concepts in languages and even to translate words. The translator and the philosopher both try to find equivalents, but what the translator knows and the philosopher tries to ignore, is that concepts do not designate 'things' awaiting labelling in objective reality. Words create concepts. For this reason, the very attempt to find 'truth' in other languages proves, though worthwhile, somewhat perverted, if we allow ourselves to be duped into believing we will find, in other languages, the concept which we refer to by that word in ours. The accounts of the different ways in which 'truth', *vérité*, *Wahrheit* and *Pravda* extend throughout the lexicons of English, French, German and Czech should dispel this myth. This is neither an attack on philosophy nor on reality. But in stressing our dependency upon language for conceiving the world, it is necessary again and again to defend language against cynics and sceptics who see linguistic limits as barriers to comprehension and communication. Language successfully enables us to conceive of truth and to negotiate truth in the world, to recognize it, determine it and question it. But languages employ different means to cover different ground. It is in this spirit, in the spirit of the explorer, that we will set out to explore the geography of truth in our four languages.

Establishing the truth

In order to *establish* the truth, we first have to accept that truth can be *built*. Is it made of bricks, building blocks? So we seem to believe, if we contend that a truth must be *well founded*. If my argument is *ill-founded*, it may be *demolished*. I might reasonably be ordered by the one who has done the damage to start again from scratch by *building a more solid argument*.

On the other hand, if my argument is condemned as *untrue*, I may be indignant and cry out against the injustice: 'Perhaps I was wrong, but I acted in good faith, speaking my truth, as well as I could manage. I was *truthful!*' This introduces a crucial distinction to our definition of truth. I can be honest, but still be wrong. This is a common enough experience, which appears, at first sight, straightforward enough. Yet, it requires a fair amount of intellectual gymnastics to follow the symbolic or metaphoric architecture of such a proposition: I am not *in* the wrong, because truth is *in* me. Paradoxically, this is the only conclusion we can reach, if we accept that I spoke *truth-full-y*. Truth inhabited me. In speaking about truth, it would seem, we should first distinguish between falseness of heart on the one hand, and *truth* as an absolute objective reality on the other. *Truthfulness* belongs not to the world of facts but to the realm of honesty. Truthfulness is the cement that consolidates our relationships by allowing us to share interpersonal truths.

Does this bring us any closer to the essence of truth? Hardly. Yet we don't give up. We search on for truth. But where can we find it? If one truth can enter me (in the sense that I can be 'full' of it), I seek another truth outside of myself in the world. Yet, for more than a thousand years, the Church and Christian philosophy would have advocated doing just the opposite: Augustine and Bonaventure suggested we embark on the quest for truth by turning inwards. Given that the soul was considered the godlike part of the self, then it became natural to presume that the most likely place to find truth would be deep within our own souls. The deeper we delve into the soul, the closer we come to God, truth transcendent, truth itself.

For the sake of schematising (because all we can set up are models for truth), let us assume for the moment that we may find truth outside of ourselves. What would truth be? Certainly a precious thing. Why else would we search for it? For Plato, truth was the *summum bonum*, the greatest good. This was something that neither political leaders nor sophists had understood. The tyrant craved power: power over things, power over others. Ironically, his ignorance of the truth of himself, his ignorance of his own soul, his nature and his desires, meant that he could not even control himself. The tyrant became, consequently, ever more the slave to his own passions and a slave to the passions of those base kinsmen that he drew to him to share in his debauchery. The rhetorician fared little better, Plato believed: he could lead his listeners by the nose, as Faust led his students, but he himself could not find the way to truth, and (unlike Faust) he did not possess sufficient insight into himself to realize that manipulating and misleading others entails seducing oneself with one's own spurious arguments, losing oneself as one leads others astray. Plato believed that the purified soul, in stark contrast, inclines towards truth. Love of wisdom is its own reward because justice, the application of the good that truth reveals, is the best thing for the soul (Plato 1968, *X* 611e: 836–7).

If we follow Plato up to this point, the truth of which he speaks is surely worth more than all the riches any man or woman can accumulate. It is a *treasure*. But where shall we look for this *treasure*? Is it buried? Can it be *uncovered*? Is it the *grail* we search for in vain? Is it *shrouded*? *Hidden*? Is it *obscure* or *clear*? Is truth a tempting prize? Often the image of this illusive truth has taken this form. Can the prize be seized? Can it be *unveiled*? At times, chameleon-like, truth takes on a human form. We speak of the *naked truth*. We speak of the *pure truth*. Such a representation would seem to bring us back to women, if we assume our language shows traces of that age-old patriarchal prerequisite that 'women of value', objects of exchange, must be 'untouched' (by vice). On the other hand, perhaps truth is *pure* when it is unadulterated, like *pure whisky*.

We began by searching for truth, and found we could not even define what we were looking for. What does that mean? Will we be able to recognize truth even if we find it? Perhaps the truth has been staring us in the face all along. Or should we conclude that, until we find it, we can only have a faint inkling of what truth is? Do we glimpse only enough to inspire the quest; not enough to trace the contours of its shape and penetrate its essence?

These are philosophical questions, but they are also questions about language and representation. The philosopher stumbles in his quest to find truth. The ethnolinguist may not resolve the philosophical conundrum, but he proceeds differently, more lucidly, by defining the patterns and the paradigms which allow us to generate meaningful concepts of truth in context. Our study of the paradigms and patterns of other languages may instruct us as to the meaningful limits which our own concept of truth assumes as it takes its place in discourse in multiple and varying contexts. In this way, paradoxically, searching for *vérité* or *Wahrheit* might lead us back to a more lucid perception of 'truths' we construct and share with others. Such an approach does, however, challenge the very principle of philosophical investigation on two accounts. It assumes that concepts, however much they are useful for describing objective reality, are language specific. And it thereby brings into question the very existence of the 'essence' of truth.

Essence and family resemblance

Instead of pinpointing *truth*, limiting it to a confined semantic space and defining its configuration and its contours, our study of the language of truth unveiled for us a concept shattering into shards and splinters, leading us in very different directions. Yet, perhaps it is the very quest for an essence that is vain. The concept of essence is fundamental for the way we frame our categories and organize our experience of the world around us. As Lakoff and Johnson argued (1999: 347), essence forms part of a folk theory (a contemporary mythical narrative or collective mode of reasoning about and interpreting the course of events) according to which we define things in terms of substance, form and 'the causal source of its natural behaviour' (*ibid.*). This folk theory treats abstract concepts metaphorically as concrete things; things with an essential inner fundamental nature. But does truth have an essential inner fundamental nature? Or is truth more a composite concept?

Wittgenstein was a philosopher, but he was, nevertheless, more than a little sceptical as to the essence of concepts, and when Lakoff and Johnson argued that metaphors highlighted different facets of a concept, they were following in the footsteps of the philosopher who argued that time and time again we are led astray when we strive to formulate the essence of a thing. Searching for essences was, in Wittgenstein's opinion, no more than a crude striving towards generality. It was a theory fed 'on a "one-sided diet" of examples' (Schulte 1992: 113). Wittgenstein offered his famous example of 'games', which he argued could in no way be reduced to one generic catch-all concept. Instead of the one-sided model of understanding which was geared to search for a unique essence, Wittgenstein proposed his model of 'family resemblances' (*Familienähnlichkeiten*). In this model, concepts emerged as 'a complicated network of similarities overlapping and criss-crossing: sometimes overall similarities, sometimes similarities of detail' (*ein kompliziertes Netz von Ähnlichkeiten, die einander übergreifen und kreuzen. Ähnlichkeiten im Großen und Kleinen.* Wittgenstein 2001: §66, p. 27). He went on to explain:

> *Ich kann diese Ähnlichkeiten nicht besser charakterisieren, als durch das Wort 'Familienähnlichkeiten'; denn so übergreifen und kreuzen sich die verschiedenen Ähnlichkeiten, die zwischen den Gliedern einer Familie bestehen: Wuchs, Gesichtzüge, Augenfarbe, Gang, Temperament, etc. etc. – Und ich werde sagen: 'die Spiele' bilden eine Familie.*

I can think of no better expression to characterize these similarities than 'family resemblances'; for the various resemblances between members of a family: build, features, colour of eyes, gait, temperament, etc., etc. overlap and criss-cross in the same way. – And I shall say: 'games' form a family (*ibid.*: §67, p. 27–8).

This redefinition of conceptual meaning has been taken up by Cognitive Semantics, and cognitive linguists have tried to adapt the classical theory of categories 'according to which a category is defined in terms of a set of necessary and sufficient conditions for membership' (Taylor, 2003: 41). While the classical theory encourages us to believe that words can be reduced to sets of primitive semantic components, cognitive linguists have tried to develop a theory of 'prototypical meaning' in which one central ideal model will enable a concept to develop and grow into a conglomerate form of intersecting secondary meanings. According to such a theory, though, you might win a 'cup', if you win a marathon, though during a game of golf you might reach into the metal 'cup' that gives form to the hole. However, neither the trophy nor the metal cup form the prototypical category for 'cups'. A cup is something you drink tea or coffee from, and it is from this prototypical category that other designations are derived metaphorically or metonymically.

Towards a new universalism – a *languageless* linguistics

Although cognitive linguists were eager to adapt the classical theory of categorisation and though they have taken up Wittgenstein's definition of family resemblances, they have, on the whole, tended to focus on concepts in much the same way as philosophers do. They take one concept and strive to find its prototypical meaning around which all other meanings are considered to conglomerate. Though Lakoff and Johnson argue that there are various definitions of *the self*, for example, they tend to see *the self* as one composite concept with various forms or aspects. The idea of separate concepts inhabiting one word remains foreign to their mode of research.

Furthermore, since cognitive linguistics remains on the whole an Anglo-American adventure, this has tended to mean that studying 'language' means studying English. In practice this means that, for example, the *self* will be taken as a concept and any comparison with foreign languages will work from the hypothesis that it is possible to assimilate the concepts of other languages into the frameworks which the English definition of *self* opens up for us. Though such an approach does allow a certain amount of verification and can confront the researcher with differences which are incompatible with the frameworks of the English concept, it has the obvious disadvantage of not allowing us to formulate a definition of the concept in question from the point of view of the other languages under study. The different lexical structure of the language, the morphology of the word and the grammar of the language are difficult to assimilate into such an approach. For example, in studying the *self*, how would Lakoff and Johnson analyse reflexive forms such as those found in French (*se connaître*, 'to know oneself', for example) or Czech (*zdálo se mi*, translated as both 'it seemed to me' and 'I dreamed')?

Lakoff and Johnson (1999) show a sincere curiosity for alternative conceptual categories. Early cognitive projects (Paprotté and Dirven 1985) opened the debate on metaphor to multilingual studies. Sweetser and others have continued in this endeavour: but the implicit universalism, deriving from the foundations of Chomsky's generativist linguistics, has resurfaced in recent years. The danger is that we may return to a 'languageless approach', to concepts that Trabant warns against in cognitive linguistics. In such a context, the work of the metaphoric.de web journal, which is based in Hamburg and which has provided a forum for comparative philological study of metaphor, is an essential counterbalance to the universalist temptation. This style of scholarship coincides perfectly with the aims of Humboldt's ethnolinguistics and the contemporary form it has taken in the work of Wierzbicka. Comparative work of an ethnolinguistic nature fulfils three functions. Firstly, it allows us to ascertain the degree to which concepts in different languages converge along the same lines. Secondly, it allows us to trace the different trajectories concepts follow as they are elaborated by the speakers of each language in discourse. And thirdly, comparative studies generate questions related to structural linguistic form and its influence on semantic structure, questions which the study of English alone does not incite us to reflect upon.

Foreign languages force the mind into new patterns and frameworks. The mind strives to carve concepts for understanding language use. The role of the philologist was, Humboldt believed, to trace the different courses taken by a people in the formulation of its language. Contemporary Humboldt scholars such as Trabant continue to advocate that the comparison of concepts and worldviews in different languages represents the unfulfilled vocation of linguistics. The present study of truth should enable us to make a contribution along all three lines defined above as we verify the similarities and dissimilarities of the concept of truth in English, French, German and Czech, and as we are forced to take on board alternative and disconcerting extensions of truth.

Approaching truth

Verifying the truth

Before verifying whether analogous concepts of truth exist and whether the meanings attributed to those concepts 'coincide' in different languages, we should perhaps point out that *verifying truth* is, etymologically speaking, a pleonasm. *To verify* means *to establish the truth* of something. Indeed, it would sound strange to the French ear to say we will *vérifier la verité*. The English equivalent, *verity*, had difficulty in outlasting the nineteenth century, and we have all but forgotten that it formed the nominal root of *verify*. This may seem like a digression, but what it does indicate is that, intangible and elusive as the concept of *truth* is, the older word itself (*verity*) has been staunchly productive: it was able to form other words (*verification*, for example).

It would be interesting to trace the etymological evolution of truth throughout Indo-European languages. However, bearing in mind Humboldt's intuition that language study should base itself upon discourse, returning to the speaking individual and tracing the way individuals leave their impression in written discourse, I shall restrain my short tour of *truth* to languages which I speak and to examples provided from my own knowledge, from texts, expressions quoted in dictionaries and examples proposed to me by native speakers. This course has the disadvantage of limiting the study to a comparison of English, French, German and Czech. A second disadvantage is that the comparison offers a purely synchronic, ahistorical view of the concept of truth as elaborated in different languages. Nevertheless, a brief tour of the representation of truth in these languages should prove fruitful in three ways:

1. It should force us to integrate into our study of 'truth', a concern for the word itself and for its place within the lexicon.
2. It should demonstrate ways in which different languages coincide with and differ from our English models of 'truth'.
3. It should force us to reconsider linguistic constraints acting upon the elaboration of the concept of truth, constraints which will remain inconceivable if we remain within our own linguistic system.

Translating 'truth'

At first sight, the translation of the term seems to present no difficulties: 'truth' is *vérité* in French, isn't it? *Wahrheit* in German? *Pravda* in Czech? One word, one concept. This seems a little too tidy, though, doesn't it? Things become more complicated if you start from what must, culturally and linguistically speaking, be the furthest relation to English from our three examples from the Indo-European linguistic family. In Czech, the most obvious thing you can do with *pravda* is to have it. *Mám pravdu*, in English, however, means not to grasp or attain truth but *to be right*. Where Czech finds and possesses truth, English speaks of being *in the right*. The English expression is clearly related to *having the right to*, and this takes us, by extension, into a legalistic and moral context. German follows a similar path with *Recht haben*, though the transition of *being* into *having* reinforces this legalistic aspect. You can 'have' truth, just as you can 'have' rights, in German.

French reserves the expression *avoir droit* (literally, 'to have right') to the inalienable human rights, while the introduction of the article in *avoir le droit à quelque chose*, is used more widely to signify being allowed to do or to have something. On the other hand, it is not colloquial for French people to claim that they 'have' or 'possess' truth as Czechs do in everyday conversation. While the English speaker 'is right', the Frenchman *a raison*, he has (or possesses) reason. Reason, the faculty for finding truth, replaces the object towards which we reason (the truth), as the Czechs would perceive it, when they say: *Mám pravdu* ('I have truth'/'I'm right').

The gender of 'truth'

The second obvious thing about the translations is that all three of the foreign forms are feminine. Claims about the sexual associations of concepts have been widely covered in poetics. Obvious examples are the way in which *La Mort*, a feminine noun in French, becomes a temptress for lyrical and romantic poets such as Baudelaire. If death is feminine, then she tends to become seductive, a dark muse. Dying will become a union with the object of desire. German poets express a fascination for death at times. The German romantic poet Novalis even goes as far as representing it as a rejuvenating force. But force is masculine, isn't it? In the traditional English imagination, this would seem to be so (though *die Macht* and *die Kraft* are feminine in German). At any rate, the use of feminine forces which empower death does not seem to feminize it in the German imagination in either Novalis' poetry or elsewhere. For my own part, I have yet to come across a representation of a *temptress-Tod*, and this is perhaps partly explained by the fact that death is masculine in German. In the English-speaker's imagination, death is also usually personified in terms of a man: the Grim Reaper, an example studied by Lakoff and Turner (1989: 76–9). Hardly a temptress.

Does the gender of truth also contribute to defining it as a concept in different languages? Partly. The influence can be seen in the proliferation of verbs used to speak of truth in French (*dévoiler*, 'to unveil', *vêtir*, 'to dress', *dévêtir*, 'to undress', *pénétrer*, 'to penetrate'). On the whole an active male agent observes, investigates and manipulates a passive feminine object. Though it might be argued that some of the verbs associated with truth might be used for a man, in the traditional French imagination we are dealing with a truth that dresses herself up and a man who admires, seduces, undresses, penetrates and takes possession of her. Feminist critiques of language and conceptualisation would have much to say about this state of affairs. Indeed, this gendered conception of truth says as much about the frustrations of French philosophers as it does about the reasons why so few women have been tempted by the vocation of the philosopher, the lover of truth.

Do the other concepts of truth develop along similar lines? In German, we can *in die Wahrheit eindringen* ('penetrate' or 'pierce' truth). This is a rare example, however, and *eindringen* can also be translated into English as 'to force an entry' or 'to invade'. On the whole, metaphoric elaborations of truth as a woman seem to be rare, almost non-existent, in German. *Wahrheit* is not seductive and does not undress herself for us, nor, would it seem, does she allow us to undress her. The only two references of this kind, found using the internet search engine www.google.de, were both related to Nietzsche's remark: '*Vielleicht ist die Wahrheit ein Weib*' (Perhaps truth is a woman), and even that was presented as a novel hypothesis. It is also doubtful that this idea has gained any real currency in German. Given that Nietzsche was, among other things, both a philologist and a Francophile, his rumination might be attributed to the influence of French.

I have found few examples of a feminine personification of truth in Czech. In English we speak of the *naked truth*, and since voyeurism has been the prerogative of males on the whole until recently, in such a model, truth might reasonably be supposed to be feminine. In Czech, we can find examples of *naked truth* (*nahá pravda*), but a far more idiomatic expression is *čistá pravda* ('the clean truth'), and cleanliness can hardly be restricted to women. Consequently, evidence would seem to suggest that on the whole, the gender system does not influence the personification of truth in Czech.

It is also important to note here that most Slavic languages like Czech are not binary in their gender system: they employ a third gender, *neuter*. The neuter gender would seem to desexualize the concept. But the neuter gender does not necessarily impose one unavoidable representation upon a concept. This will become clear if we consider the following example. Several languages seem to opt for a binary gender pair when speaking about the sun and the moon. The larger of the two is (logically enough) attributed the masculine gender, while the smaller one is attributed the feminine gender. French follows this pattern: *le soleil* is masculine, *la lune* is feminine. German contravenes this trend by both feminising *die Sonne* and masculinising *der Mond*. Czech represents the two in a different manner, by neutering the sun (*slunce*) and attributing a masculine inanimate gender to the moon (*měsíc*).

Nevertheless, we must not fall prey to the English speaker's pitfall of conflating sex and gender: it is important to leave behind a naive and dogmatic conception of gender as a rigorous mode of sexual definition. Such is the creativity of speech that it can be used to contravene its own laws. There is a synonym for *měsíc* (moon) in Czech, a poetical word of Latin origin, *luna*, and *luna* is feminine. Unsurprisingly, when the twentieth-century lyric poet František Halas mused on the seductive moon that rose towards midnight undressing itself (*Luna se svlékla k půlnoci*) he opted for the feminine word of Latin origin. A butch moon stripping off in the night sky might warm the hearts of modern Czech women, bringing to mind associations of the Chippendale-style male stripper, but that, apparently, didn't fit into Halas' lyrical universe.

Languages can choose to confirm, exploit and deepen the sexual associations of gender. Individual writers may reinforce existing associations. The French *homme de lettres*, Fénelon (1651–1715), for example, exploits the feminized model of *vérité*, when he says: *La vérité est une reine qui a dans le ciel son trône éternel* (Truth is a queen who has her eternal throne in the sky, Littré 1962: 1638, my translation). He deepens this analogy by distinguishing between two facets of his feminized truth, a beautiful young one and an ageing one who may have lost her charms but nevertheless acquires a stately virtue: *La vérité n'a ni jeunesse ni vieillesse; les agréments de l'une ne la doivent pas faire aimer davantage, et les rides de l'autre ne lui doivent pas attirer plus de respect* (Beauty has neither youth nor agedness, the charms of one should not make her loved any the more, nor should the wrinkles of the other earn her any more respect. *ibid.*, my translation).

However, these are poetical innovations, novel extensions, and are received as such. They open up new paths within a language, offering new formulations for its speakers to muse upon. These are not the patterns of our subconscious thought, patterns that we follow *without thinking*. They are the divergent expressive explorations of inquisitive and creative minds forging new thought within the language system. In the same way that Halas operates a lyrical sex change on the Czech moon by opting for the Latin term, Voltaire has no problem in changing the gender of truth by metamorphosing truth (feminine in French) into a fruit (masculine): *La vérité est **un fruit** qui ne droit être cueilli que s'il est tout à fait mûr* (Truth is a fruit which should not be picked until it [he] is quite ripe, Ripert 1993: 422). In the same way, La Fontaine inverted heterosexual gender characterisation when he spoke of man's passion for the lie (*mensonge*, which is masculine in French) and his frigidity when it came to truth (feminine):

> *L'homme est de glace aux vérités*
> *Il est de feu pour les mensonges.*
> (Man is all ice towards truths / but lies set him on fire.)
> *Le Statuaire et la Statue de Jupiter*, my translation
> La Fontaine, quoted by Ripert 1993: 421

So what can we conclude concerning the semantic implications of the linguistic constraints of gender, then? On the whole, the feminisation of concepts can coincide with gender, but gender does not seem to dictate the degree to which a concept is *feminized* or *masculinized.* Gender invites personification along sexually defined lines. But just as these lines can be redrawn, nothing prevents a language such as English with no gender system (or the extremely impoverished remains of one) from formulating the same metaphoric expressions along sexually defined lines. The parallels in verbs used in English and French to speak about what we do with truth (e.g. *unveil it*, *dress it up*) would seem to support this claim.

Truth and right

In English, if our view is well founded, if our case is legitimate, we are said to be 'in the right'. But here once more, some languages will translate our 'right' into 'truth'. As we saw above, the Czech can 'have' truth. Similarly, the Frenchman can 'be in the truth' (*être dans le vrai*). German follows the same logic as English, using 'right', not 'truth' (*im Recht sein*: to be in the right). Czech offers the example of 'living in truth' (*žít v pravdě*). Nevertheless, though the same spatial metaphor is used in both French and Czech to represent truth as a space we can enter and remain within, the Czech example differs slightly in having religious connotations, implying a state of harmony between a person's conscience and his faith. Consequently, the Czech expression is generally restricted to the discussion of a certain range of subjects. The French and German expressions, on the other hand, are used widely in various everyday spheres of life.

Truth and honesty

In English we can be full of truth, 'truthful'. In German, on the other hand, 'truthful' is translated as *wahrheitsgetreu* (true to truth, faithful to the truth). Moreover, this term is used for things, such as a truthful 'representation' (*Darstellung*), while 'truthful', when applied to people, is usually translated as *ehrlich* (honest). In neither of the terms are we represented as a space or container which truth enters, or fills up. Truthful is translated into French as *véridique*. And though something in French can be full of truth (*une histoire*, a story, for example), a person is not usually represented in such a way. Neither can such a representation be found in Czech. A truthful person in Czech would be *pravdomluvný člověk* (a truth-speaking man). A truthful account or statement would be *pravý* (true or real) or *přesný* (exact).

Enlightenment

In all four languages, truth is associated with light. An *enlightened* man is a wise man of wide learning, someone who, as defined by the Enlightenment itself, draws close to the truth. This metaphor was not invented by the Enlightenment, however. Enlightenment philosophers borrowed the metaphor from biblical rhetoric. God creates light: God lights up the earth and enlightens man, who lives in darkness and ignorance. It was not to replace this version of truth with their own version that the philosophers of the Enlightenment enlisted the biblical metaphor, but rather to endow their own quest for scientific knowledge with the same lofty status as that associated with biblical revelations. A slightly less elevated rhetoric would enlist the metaphor of *clarifying truth*, and the verbs meaning 'to clarify' in French (*clarifier*), German (*klären, klarstellen*) and Czech (*objasnit*) all stress that clarification entails *shedding light*. If anything, this characteristic is more pronounced in these expressions than their English equivalent 'clarify'.

Truth as construction

Establishing the truth makes the concept into a building, as we said in the introduction. We construct it from putting things together. In the same way, we can say truth is a construction in German (*Die Wahrheit ist eine Konstruktion*). In English we might prefer the term *a construct*. In French, truth can be established (*établie*), it can be constructed (*construite*). But in all three examples from English and French, considering truth as a construct takes us into a philosophical discourse.

In both French and English, we are more likely to use the idea of *reconstruction* when it comes to verifying the facts and trying to understand what happened in the past, as in history or in a murder case. The analogous verb exists in German (*rekonstruieren*, no doubt borrowed from French), used in the expression *Geschichte rekonstruieren* (to reconstruct history, or to reconstruct a story). In Czech we do not reconstruct (*rekonstruovat*) the truth or the facts, we reconstruct a story (*příběh*). Neither do we construct truth (*vytvořit pravdu*). Truth, in Czech can, nonetheless, be conceived of in terms of a combination of two or more things. We say, for instance, that 'truth is the concord of judgement and experience' (*Pravda je shodou úsudku se skutečností*).

Though truth might be conceived as an assembly of different parts, fitted together, it can also form one unified whole which may be divided up: and this is not necessarily a contradiction. A house may be built of bricks, for example. In the same way, we speak of the whole truth, implying the truth can be divided up into various pieces or measured out in varying quantities. German, French and Czech follow the same pattern. In German, we can 'tell only half of the truth' (*nur die halbe Wahrheit sagen*). In French we speak of 'half-truths' (*demi-vérités*), an expression also found in Czech (*polopravdy*). We can also say in Czech: 'There isn't even a piece of truth in (on) that' (*Není na tom ani kousek pravdy*).

The taste of truth

Truth can be tasted, though usually the experience is unpleasant or painful: truth is said to be 'bitter'. This metaphor is found in Czech (*trpká pravda*) and in French (*âpre vérité*). The same phrase exists in German (*die bittere Wahrheit*) and it is used in two expressions, both equivalents of our expression 'to swallow the bitter pill' (*die bittere Pille schlucken, in den sauren Apfel beißen*). The former expression translates word for word into its English equivalent: the latter would translate into 'to bite into the sour apple'.

Though these are common expressions used in everyday speech, they were originally poetic extensions. In this instance, the translation of the abstract idea into the concrete experience with traits and characteristics is particularly poignant. Not only is the truth tasted and digested, internalized, the whole scenario invoked involves apprehension and overcoming repulsion. While a startling metaphor usually arrests our attention, often awakening our sensibility to a hitherto unsuspected aspect of reality, this example posits a prior knowledge of the experience, a long-standing aversion to what must finally be faced up to.

If the expression 'the taste of truth' does not surprise us it is because it has been fully integrated into our habitual modes of conceiving truth. The taste of truth has a long history, one that precedes the birth of all four languages studied in this chapter. In The Book of Job, Job had already experienced and expressed the taste of truth, or rather, he had refused to accept that his words of lamentation insulted God because he felt sure that he would be able to taste falseness and perversity if it came forth from his mouth: 'Is there iniquity in my tongue? [he asked] Cannot my taste discern perverse things?' (Chapter 7:29, *King James Bible*). This inverts the idea upon which our expression is based, however: while our truth is bitter, it is lies which would taste sour to Job. Truth would, presumably, taste sweet. Nevertheless, the same fundamental framework for understanding the act of facing up to facts is at work here. What the biblical example would seem to suggest is that languages such as the four under study, languages which arose out of fusions of other languages, were enriched by the borrowings of words, phrases and conceptual frameworks from those other languages. Creative speech coins expressions in all languages, and those expressions can survive translation and even survive the 'death' of the languages from which they derive. Creative speech within the language which receives such expressions will, in turn, go on to adapt and reconfigure the expressions generated by the creative impulse which manifested itself in the original language. In this respect, the story of Job is particularly pertinent, because it must be borne in mind that Job was not a Hebrew. His story is handed down to the Jews of the Bible passing from the language of a foreign nation into Hebrew, to be translated into Greek and Roman before entering the four languages studied here. Metaphors, flights of fancy, like birds, do not respect cultural or linguistic barriers when migrating.

The depth of truth

Truth can be 'deep' in English, French (*la vérité profonde*), in German (*die tiefe Wahrheit*) and Czech (*hluboká pravda*). The idea that something which is superficial, has little content or truth to it, is also to be found in all four languages.

Serving truth

As an ideal, truth can become a master. So what does that make those who are faithful to their ideal? Servants. We serve truth. In French we can work *au service de la vérité* ('in truth's service'). In German we can say of something that 'it serves the truth' (*Das dient der Wahrheit*). Only in Czech do we fail to find this expression. In Czech we don't serve truth, we serve the Lord (*sloužit Bohu*). Although the other three languages can, of course, translate this expression, thanks to the Christian heritage which has conditioned each language's development, only in Czech has the concept of truth failed to detach itself from the religious paradigm, for truth to come to stand on its own as an empirical verity of this world, worthy of service.

Innovations

The expressions we have been considering are commonplace in everyday speech. However, figurative expressions can of course be used with imagination. In a Czech online debate concerning the best way to bring up children, one person suggested that: 'Truth is the best guide when it comes to education' (*Pravda je nejlepší průvodce výchovou*, www.rodina.cz). I have yet to come across the conception of truth as a guide in English. The meta-phorical framing of truth as a goal we move towards may have prevented us from conceiving of truth as a guide. Something leads us to truth, or so we seem to understand truth in English. The conception of truth as a guide is not to be found in either German or French, but to my knowledge, it is not a common expression in Czech either. That is to say, it does not form part of those subconscious metaphorical frameworks with which Czechs think. For this reason, it seems reasonable to consider it as a novel invention. If it is worth considering here, it is because we continuously redraw the contours and frameworks of metaphorical expression. Though this construction is not widespread throughout a given linguistic system, it is important to remem-ber that language derives from discourse, as much as discourse derives from language. Here a conscious effort has been made to break out of conven-tional conceptual patterning, in order to elaborate an idea on education and childcare.

Truth's semantic structure in the lexicon

Thus far, we have been trying to establish whether the metaphors which are enlisted to define our concept of truth in French, German and Czech coin-cide with those found in English. If we have managed to *verify* whether they do, we will not only have taken a step in the right direction towards under-standing how metaphor works in constructing the concepts we live within, we will also have established that concepts such as truth and verification are themselves useful and meaningful. Though our first steps led us into poly-semy and uncertainty about the core definition of truth, the expressions we have been considering in all four languages have allowed people to conduct meaningful conversations and establish, verify and define more precisely the questions they are concerned with. If 'truth' remains a philosophical prob-lem, it remains, nevertheless, a highly effective discursive tool which allows us to take strategic steps towards well-defined objectives. Whether we are establishing whether the criminal was truly where he said he was, whether we are comparing someone's posture with their 'true nature', or whether we are contrasting the seductive dream with the 'bitter truth' that must be faced, our discursive strategies enable us to adopt truth as a concept and pinpoint its definition within the fabric of discussion and the dynamics of the relationship we find ourselves in.

Nevertheless, the reasoning which has led us to these meaningful conclusions remains somewhat perverse. Although it has allowed us to contrast the ethno-linguistic approach to meaning with the philosophical quest to define concepts, our study thus far has, ironically, adopted a philosophical mode of approach. That is to say, we have posited the existence of a supra-lingual concept, 'truth', and we have set out to track it down as it takes form in each of the languages. But do abstract concepts exist outside the realm of language? Can all the overlapping concepts related to truth (right, justice, precision, validity, authenticity, etc.) be considered to be parts of one conceptual whole 'truth'? This is far from clear.

For this reason, it will perhaps prove more interesting now to look at things the other way around. This engages us in what I have called the ethnolinguistic challenge. We might begin by considering the way the semantic root for truth proliferates throughout the language systems of French, German and Czech to form related concepts. Do these languages trace the same trajectories as those that branch out through the English lexicon? This forces us to do something which jars with our own worldview. It forces us to open up to different courses in linguistic, metaphoric and conceptual patterning. And it forces us, thereby, to accept that our own modes and paths of reflection and contemplation are themselves framed in such a way that must be loosened if we are to come to understand what *pravda*, *vérité*, and *Wahrheit* are capable of meaning for speakers of Czech, French and German.

French

In English, work of the kind we are engaging in forces us to synthesize findings derived from the study of traditional dictionaries and dictionaries of etymologies. French linguists have facilitated this arduous task. *Le Robert Brio*, edited by Josette Rey-Debove, which came out in France in 2004, is groundbreaking in that it takes a radically new approach to ordering the description of the lexicon: 33,000 words are explained in terms of their morphology; 1,856 roots, prefixes and suffixes are listed, and the different developments of words throughout the lexicon are considered under the same heading. This allows us to re-establish the link between words which seem to us to belong to very different groups, and which, until now, have never been found side by side in a dictionary of etymology for the simple reason that the first letters of the words themselves are not the same.

It would seem strange to link many words which are, in fact, linked, etymologically speaking, by the use of the root, *préc*, which, curiously enough, derives from *pretium* (price). This link allows French to create words like *apprécier* (to appreciate), *inappréciable*, (priceless/inestimable), *déprécier* (to depreciate) and *précieux* (precious). All of these have some relation to money or value, and their association does not surprise us. But in French, 'to despise' is translated as *mépriser*. The root, *prix* (price) remained hidden in the word and in dictionaries, until Debove, reorganised it in her morphological dictionary, listing the roots and not the first letters in alphabetical order (Debove, 2004, 1348–1351).

Rey-Debove's project is one that it would profit us greatly to copy in English. And ethnolinguistics would benefit from a comparative morphological approach. Her approach proves equally revealing when it comes to re-establishing the flowers that have blossomed forth from the root of the word *vérité* (from *véri*, meaning 'true'). The word *vérité* came into the French language as *veritiet*, borrowed from the Latin *veritas, -atis* (meaning 'the true', 'the truth', 'reality', see Rey 1998: 4033). The root of these words, which derives from *verus*, meaning 'true', and *verax*, meaning 'he who speaks truthfully', has given the following offshoots: *s'avérer* (to transpire), *verdict* (verdict), *veracité* (truthfulness), *véridique* (truthful, veracious, genuine), borrowed from *veridicus* in Low Latin in the middle of the fifteenth century, *verifier* (to check or to verify), which had been borrowed from the same language in the form *verificare* almost two centuries before, *vérifiable* (verifiable), *vérification* (verification), *vérificateur* (checker, inspector, verifier), which did not come to be used until the late seventeenth century, as well as *contrevérité* (falsehood, Rey-Debove 2004: 1802–3; Rey 1998).

Véritable is usually translated as 'genuine' or 'real', and so is *vrai*. This explains why the French colloquial expression *un vrai cowboy*, would be translated as 'a real cowboy'. When we do things in earnest, we do them 'for real'. In everyday spoken French, we say we do something *pour de vrai*. An actor in a tragedy who actually has a heart attack on stage can be said 'to die for real' (*mourir pour de vrai*).

Branching off in the same direction, the equivalent of our term for 'really' derives not from 'reality' in French but from 'truth' (*vrai–vraiment*). More surprising for English speakers is the link forged in French between truth and the French word for 'likely' (*vraisemblable*) and 'probably', which, though it can be translated as *probablement*, is equally translated as *vraisemblablement*. *Vraisemblance* (likelihood) also derives from *vrai* in French: a parallel development can be found in English in one possible translation for *vraisemblance*, 'verisimilitude', which derives from 'verity' in English. But the latter word is elevated in English, as are many of the words we borrow from French. For this reason, more common translations for *vraisemblance* would be 'likelihood' or 'plausibility', in which the morphological and sonorous link to truth is lost.

As is often the case, the traces of morphological links are effaced when words are borrowed from another language. This weakens what we might call the 'semantic resonance' of the language which takes on the fragments of conceptual networks from other languages. The failure to transmit the network as a whole disrupts the orchestration of semantic values that play within the original language. As we borrow fragments, we leave behind the meaningful links which forged them and gave them vigour and force. Borrowed metaphors often fail to resonate within the imagination and the memory of the speakers who adopt them. The orchestration which was replayed when metaphors organized the thoughts of native speakers falls on deaf ears once those metaphors are dislocated from their context.

This was what Wilhelm von Humboldt had in mind when he spoke of the euphony of language. Euphony for Humboldt was not simply a formal harmony which is pleasing to the ear, it was a harmonious concordance of semantic links in the sonorous organisation and classification of meaning. In exploring morphology and etymology, we are listening to the euphony of language. *Vérité* reaches out throughout the French consciousness sparking off and lighting up related meanings.

German

If German sounds very different to the English ear, then the euphony that structures the semantic links of its lexicon 'sounds' just as different. True and truth have a prodigious destiny in the German lexicon. *Wahr?* is used to form the reflexive questions which are formed with *n'est-ce pas*, in French, and for which English uses a more complex system which entails question tags (repeating the auxiliary verb, as for example, in sentences such as: You like fish, don't you? You aren't planning on coming on holiday with us, are you?). In German, both of these tags would be replaced by the expression, *nicht wahr?*

The verb *wahren* means 'to preserve', 'to maintain' or 'to keep', as in to keep the balance. *Wahrung*, though rare, means 'preservation'. Used primarily in the negative sense, the verb *wahrhaben* (literally, 'to have truth') means 'to admit'. *Etwas nicht wahrhaben wollen* means 'to not want to admit something'. *Wahrhaft* means 'true' or 'genuine' and is synonymous with *véritable* in French, which also makes a direct morphological and sonorous link between truth and authenticity. These are the unconscious melodies that play within our imagination, rising to the surface in creative expressions. *Wahrhaftig* (truthful) and *Wahrhaftigkeit* (truthfulness) play the same tune.

Wahrheit is itself polysemous in that, besides 'truth', it also means 'accuracy'. This opens the door to *Wahrheitsfindung* (the proof of truth) and *wahrheitsgemäß* (truthful, accurate or reliable), as in the expression 'reliable information'. *Ein wahrheitsliebender Mensch* is not a pedantic man, though, but 'a truthful man' (a lover of truth).

The adverb *wahrlich* ('really') follows the same pattern that creates *vraisemblable* from *vrai* in French. A more curious creation is *wahrnemen* which, though one might suppose it to mean 'to take the truth', is actually translated in English as 'to perceive' or 'to discern'. This maintains our primary, original relationship to truth: we believe what we perceive is real or 'truly' there. But *wahrnehmen* is also used to mean 'to take advantage of', 'to exploit' or 'to use'. It can mean 'to look after' in the sense of looking after someone's affairs. It can also mean 'to perform' or 'to fulfil', as in 'to perform a function' or 'to fulfil a responsibility'. The nominal form derived from the verb reflects all four meanings of the verb. *Die Wahrnehmung* can mean: 1. perception or awareness; 2. the exercise or exercising (of your rights, for example); 3. representation (of someone's interests); or 4. performance, fulfilment (of an obligation), or execution (of an order).

Stranger still (for the English imagination) is the link that is forged between truth and fortune-telling: *wahrsagen* (literally, to tell the truth), means 'to tell fortunes'. A fortune-teller is a *Wahrsager* (m) or a *Wahrsagerin* (f). 'Prediction' follows the same logic, becoming *Wahrsagung*.

This takes truth on a metaphysical adventure and transforms it into something of questionable 'veracity'. The path from truth to probability has also been opened up in German: *wahrscheinlich* ('probable' or 'likely') follows the same route as *vraisemblable*, by deriving from *wahr* where the French word derives from *vrai*. Similarly, *vraisemblance* takes us on the same trip as *Wahrscheinlichkeit* ('probability').

Czech

Pravda is known to many English readers because it was the name given to the daily newspaper in Soviet Russia. In this name (which means 'truth' in Russian just as it does in Czech), Westerners saw a dark irony of the Cold War. The metaphoric origins of our own press (*The Guardian* and *The Independent*) go largely unnoticed, so common to us are these newspapers, though those names once affirmed their paper's adherence to a political and moral stance. The 'gutter press', on the other hand, has never pretended to be a vector of truth. In true capitalist spirit, the tabloids only seek to entertain, and that means bringing a little 'light' into our lives (hence, *The Sun* and *The Daily Star*).

What are the origins and the morphological trajectories of the Czech word for truth? Holub and Lyer's dictionary of etymology (1978: 360) traces *pravda* back to Old Slavic, from which Russian, Bulgarian, Czech, Polish and other Slavic languages derive. The word has remained unchanged in both Russian and Czech, and in the latter its morphological creativity is as prodigious as its German counterpart.

The four prototypical meanings of the Czech word *pravda* are: 1. truth; 2. veracity; 3. reality; and 4. axiom, a self-evident truth or universally received principle. Of the four, English speakers will only have difficulty 'getting their minds around' the third one (reality). In Czech, there is the reality of this world and the ultimate reality of the next world, 'God's truth' (*pravda Boží*). 'To be in God's truth' (*být na pravdě Boží*) means to have departed this world for the next. The soul returns to its divine source.

Czechs will use *v pravdě* where we would be likely to say *indeed* (though the fact that we can also say *in truth* testifies to the same channel of thinking). *Nicht wahr?* in German (isn't it, aren't you, etc.) translates directly into Czech using the word truth in the expression *není-liž pravda?* As in colloquial French, *Quoi?* meaning 'what?' can be used in Czech (*co?*), though it is considered somewhat vulgar (while in French it is merely familiar). Most Czechs prefer a more polite term with the same meaning: *cože?*

As in French and German, truth forms the root of 'probable' (*pravděpodobný*), 'probability' (*pravděpobnost*) and 'likely' (*pravděpodobně*). It forms the root of *opravdu?*, the equivalent of our 'really?' A truthful person is one who speaks the truth: he is *pravdomluvný* (literally, 'truth-speaking'). If he speaks the truth because he has a 'love of truth' (*pravdymilovnost*), we call him 'a lover of truth' (*pravdymilovný*, Poldauf 1986: 586).

Holub and Lyer (1978) affirm that *pravda* also forms the root of the adjectives 'real' (*opravdový*) and 'fair' (*spravedlivý*). *Spravedlnost* (fairness) derives grammatically from 'what is with truth' (*co je s pravdou*). This links the word semantically, morphologically and phonetically to the word for 'right' in Czech, *právo*. Indeed all words related to justice, jurisprudence, fairness and rights are etymologically linked to truth. It would probably be unfair to see *pravda* (truth) as being the root form from which all these expressions are derived, but the form and sound of the words reinforce the link between these related concepts within the Czech imagination (or what might be called the Czech *cognitive unconscious*). Where an English speaker would say: That's not **fair**, You're not being **honest**, What you say is not **true**, all three of the highlighted words would be derived from or related to the word *pravda* if this were said in Czech.

This is not an isolated case. In Czech, the concept of truth lies behind other words which remain unharnessed to 'truth' in the English speaker's imagination. The Czech word *pravý*, meaning 'direct' in the physical sense of moving forwards, for example, also relates to truth. This becomes a little easier to understand if we remember the expression 'My aim is true', which dates from a time when an analogous semantic link existed in English between directness and truth. The same link forged the Czech expression *právě*, which can mean 'at this precise moment' in the expression *právě ted* or 'That's exactly it!' in *Ano, právě!*

Metaphoric paths

We can derive three conclusions from our short ethnolinguistic study of the way the links in the semantic chains related to the word for 'truth' resonate within the imagination:

1. Truth cannot be reduced to a single core meaning in the traditional sense according to which a category is defined in terms of a set of necessary and sufficient conditions. Neither can it be confined to a prototypical meaning. A cup may have a prototypical meaning, from which all other meanings are derived, but truth appears to cover multiple distinct semantic spheres. This proves to be 'true' of other languages as well as English. The Czech 'equivalent' for truth, for example, also coincides with our concepts 'veracity', 'reality' and 'axiom'.
2. For this reason, Wittgenstein's theory of family resemblances would seem a far more adequate concept for describing the term *pravda* and for describing the relationships between *fairness*, *honesty* and *truth* within the Czech lexicon.
3. Despite striking resemblances in metaphoric patterning, the structuring frameworks of the imagination and the resonance of euphonic patterns differ from language to language.

Some of the examples we have been looking at ('truthful', *Wahrsagerin*, *vraisemblance* and so on) are not metaphors, but everyday expressions. On the other hand, examples like constructing truth imply an underlying analogical reasoning. And this is the case of much of our supposedly 'literal' language. Living in truth implies that truth is a space, a container. Being truthful implies that truth is something which we can contain within ourselves, our own intimate space. Expressions like 'truthful' and 'truthless' are morphological extensions of root forms: but morphology must be understood to be a dynamic process, an ongoing process of creativity. And creativity often turns out to be metaphoric in nature.

We like to think of the 'root' as the 'fixed' origin of other words, but origins themselves have origins, and the more we trace words back in time, the more we see they are the 'fruits' as much as the 'roots' of other words. Words are formed by association in two senses: they are formed by making an imaginative leap as in a figurative expression, or by associating different suffixes and prefixes to make new words. In both ways, associations constitute the links that bind words together in the imagination.

In the first instance, the relationship between truth, justice, fairness and precision has been strengthened by associative jumps, the traces of which are left upon the morphology of the words. In the second instance, the addition of suffixes can introduce or crystallize new metaphors: a person can be a 'lover of truth' in German (*wahrheitsliebender Mensch*).

Just as the association of concepts can surprise us (linking truth-telling to fortune-telling, in German, for example), so can it appear strange that certain patterns do not emerge in a language. Why did German opt for *wahrhaftig* instead of *wahrheitsvoll*? After all, *wundervoll* exists, an innovation which follows the same pattern that created our word *wonderful*. Is the suffix *–voll* less dynamic in German than in English? Likewise, why can't we say *wahrheitslos*? We can say *lieblos* (loveless or unfeeling). Is it because the suffix *–los* implies being deprived of something? Is it because Germans cannot conceive of 'having' *Wahrheit* that they cannot conceive of being deprived of its possession? This hypothesis seems plausible if we consider examples which take the suffix (*kinderlos*, 'childless', *elternlos*, 'parentless/orphaned', *sorglos*, 'careless/carefree'). Accordingly *vaterlos* ('fatherless') is far more common than *mutterlos* in German, because one might not 'have' a father, whilst being 'motherless' is far more rare.

The links between words and the metaphors which can either form those links or exploit them to form new metaphors are clearly logical and motivated. Their logic can be traced and documented. But they belong to the logic of the creative imagination. Those links are the signposts that show the direction thinking men, women and children have taken as they struggled to give a form to their thoughts in language, by not only 'using' that language (as we 'use' a pen or a spade), but also by pushing back its frontiers. When it comes to language, speakers are artisans, not labourers. They weave the fabric of the imagination.

Languages not only sound different to the ear, their euphony, the semantic links in the frameworks of the lexicon resonate and resound differently. Language offers up patterns to us: they are like games to the thinking person. We can choose to play the game according to the rules, taking the grammar and associations inscribed in the language as constraints that must be observed. But that essentially personal and subjective mode of expression, speech, is continuously repersonalising and reinvigorating the language system. Rules are bent, transgressed. Patterns break out into new directions, as the mountain streams which break their banks with the thaw reach out into new grooves, and cut fresh gullies into the mountainside. We do not live in a prison house of language: we create space in language.

But let us not take ourselves for romantic revolutionaries who sweep down upon language to create a clean slate by sweeping the past aside. Our new adventures do not efface the history of the language. In reshaping language, the organ of speech, we can hear within that creative space we open up for ourselves the jangling of chains, the echoes of the links between words.

Defining truth

Has this investigation into morphological and metaphorical patterning served to define truth more faithfully and more perspicaciously? Perhaps. But it is worth pausing to question the motivation which hides behind the desire to define truth. Defining truth can be seen as two different projects depending upon whether one takes a philosophical or a philological approach. The philosopher seeks the essence of truth: the inner truth of truths. Whether this inner truth is in fact held within truth, or whether it hides elsewhere, waiting to be discovered or uncovered, it remains, for the philosopher, a situated truth. It is fixed, stationary. And if it appears vague or shaky, then the work of the philosopher becomes the struggle to pin it down.

What transpires from this short exploration of the morphological and metaphorical study of 'truth', *vérité*, *Wahrheit* and *pravda* is that these terms do not form one fixed meaning which can be circumscribed by a philosophical definition. Rather than sharing one transcendental and translingual essence, these words appear to be composite constructions. In 'truth', *vérité*, *Wahrheit* and *pravda* various related concepts converge and overlap.

Our study has discovered that the paths these concepts have taken coincide to a certain degree as they serve to define related concepts in the language system and as they themselves are further refined in contradistinction to those concepts. This involves semantic rapprochements and setting up meaningful oppositions. We are often surprised by the similarities between our language and foreign tongues, when it comes to the links between words and metaphoric expressions. And this is because there is in fact nothing inevitable in these rapprochements and oppositions. Similarities and distinctions grow.

In defining truth, the philosopher resembles an archaeologist who tries to unearth it, or an architect who plans to build it. The philologist, on the other hand, resembles the horticulturalist who studies the way concepts grow from seeds into plants. He observes the plants which, on reaching fruition, can be crossed with other plants to form new variations. The work of the philosopher is of course legitimate: in order to think with words, we must circumscribe the definitions we give to those words, when we speak to others, and when we write. This legitimate struggle to pin words down, to anchor them in thought, in theories and in dictionaries, may help the architect-philosopher to build a theory. Nevertheless, this struggle cannot ultimately situate truth within reality. Nor can it situate truth within language. It can only situate truth within the circumscribed limits of discourse, within the scope of the argument. The philosopher seeks to establish a contract with his partner according to which they will agree to respect a given definition of truth so as to enable them to go on to investigate related questions.

However truthful, real or useful the philosopher's theory may prove to be, it will only reflect one facet of the way concepts work upon us and the way we work with them. It will only help us to catch a glimpse of how we live with and within concepts. While the philosopher builds, speech spins off new inventions and unearths hitherto unrecognized relationships. Language keeps on growing: like oaks overshadowing tenements, the roots of speech dislodge the paving stones that lead up to the doors of definitions. Like ivy climbing up the walls of philosophical edifices, language will not be cut down to size.

4   Love

Is it true that we *look* for love? Can we *find* it? Or do we not rather *find* our-selves *in* love, overcome by it, awash in an ocean whose boundaries we cannot perceive or even conceive of. Certainly love, for most of us, means an encoun-ter that both energizes us and expands us, while, at the same time, belittling us. We feel in awe of love. And this feeling of the sublime grandeur of love, its overpowering passion, is something that will always be craved for by those who have never felt it (or who have known it but lost it). Love is obviously the most personal, and probably – for most people at least – the most deeply felt of the concepts that we have chosen to study in this ethnolinguistics of key concepts.

But studies of love are, of course, nothing new. Philosophy, beginning with Plato, has made a deeply meaningful contribution to love. Religion, from the Old and New Testaments to Augustine and Aquinas has enabled us to reflect on the diverse dimensions of love. And as we shall see, other religious traditions (the Hindu tradition and Arab philosophy) continue to inspire reflection on love and contemplation upon the complex warring emotions that take posses-sion of the lover. In more recent years, linguists (such as Kövecses) have made an effort to catalogue the metaphoric paradigms of emotions related to love.

This ethnolinguistic study of love is a response to these three approaches, philosophy, religion and linguistics. It is not a question of abandoning or rejecting these approaches (which will continue to animate debate for years to come). It is a question of determining the limits of these approaches from an ethnolinguistic perspective. Philosophy looks beyond experience and beyond language for a concept of love. This already leaves both language and lovers behind. Ethnolinguistics is more empiric. Love, from the ethnolinguistic per-spective, will remain closer to Saint Peter, who believed you can only love through loving other people. Turning to love or to God, if it means turning away from others, is not love. Just as Aristotle believed we learn to form an idea of the grape through studying grapes, ethnolinguistics will look at real expressions of love to form an idea of the complexity and the universality of love. Just as Martin Buber, the Jewish German religious philosopher, believed that we only exist by existing with others, and that the only real 'being' is the 'meeting' of 'I' and 'you', the ethnolinguistic approach will begin with asking how 'I's and 'you's express love, demand love, reject love and express their incapacity for love.

This will take us into language. Our 'love' will not be 'otherworldly'. This will take us into people speaking in space and time. In one respect, this study relies upon the work of Kövecses, who outlined various categories and subcategories of metaphorical frames used in expressing love. But this study expands upon that work in two significant ways, and these fundamental changes will seriously modify both the scope of the study and its findings. Cognitive scholars such as George Lakoff, Mark Turner and Zoltán Kövecses tend to rely upon common usage in planning their schemes for conceptual metaphor: they work with dictionaries, texts and everyday expressions. There is something arbitrary and superficial about this approach.[1] It both fails to situate speakers, to distinguish between age, sex, class, perspective, and so on, and it inevitably downplays the way we creatively manipulate conceptual love metaphors. The fact that Kövecses' study of love focuses upon English alone is unfortunate, too, in that it fails to define the culture-specific nature of our concept. What we first perceive on engaging upon a multilingual study are the 'limits' of our own culturally patterned perspective of love and loving.

This trilingual ethnolinguistic corpus-based study should achieve seven aims which the philosophical, religious and linguistic approaches we have mentioned do not allow us to discern (even as questions to be pondered). It should enable us:

- to define more clearly our own concept of love and loving by contrasting it to alternative conceptions of love and loving
- to engage in questions of gendered conceptions of love, by focusing on expressions of love by women, in contrast to philosophical and religious traditions which have induced us to consider love from a male perspective
- to understand that love is always privately 'situated': that expressions of feelings of love are always attempts to justify a personal stance in a given situation, a relationship
- to understand that love is always subject to socio-political forces: the fall of communism and the rise in post-feminist rhetoric are engendering new conceptions of love and loving at all levels of discourse
- to discern the omnipresent nature of creativity in speech: conceptual metaphoric frames for love are constantly being challenged, adapted and inverted
- to appreciate to what extent humour is fundamental to discourse on love and desire
- to open our minds and to reawaken our senses to other dimensions of love and loving which have been more strikingly circumscribed by the metaphors

of other languages, or which have been preserved in other linguistic systems, but which have fallen into disuse, or 'gone out of fashion', in our own conception of love.

The languages of love

The relationship between love and language is a long and complicated story. It is often said that passion, lust and devotion transport us to a plane upon which words lose their meaning. The coupling of hearts, souls (and let's not forget bodies!) opens up for us a new dimension and forces us to seek other fresh forms of expression: language is left behind. Following a diametrically opposed trajectory, poets, the master wordsmiths, throughout the ages and in a vast variety of languages, have channelled an immense amount of energy into uncovering each facet of love and fathoming the depths of each of love's dimensions. When love has been considered as a unified whole, poets have sought to bring out the gleaming individuality of each facet. When love has been considered as a mysterious collection of unrelated fragments, they have arranged and rearranged those fragments, seeking each one's internal logic and *raison d'être*.

Whether we see love as something which lies on the boundaries of language, defined negatively as something which cannot be described in words, or whether we see it as something which is, conceptually speaking, woven from the findings of one of the most prolific and most inspired poetical quests of language, love, the real lived experience, and 'love' the term we use to designate it, is without doubt one of the great cultural questions of Western society. Both the word and the concept seem to invite and necessitate an ongoing – even endless – redefinition. Nevertheless, for the most part, the exploration of the language of love has inevitably been limited to ruminations, inspirations and studies which are confined to one single language. Baudelaire explores *amour* in French; Shakespeare explores 'love' in English. Paradoxically, the great élan which has inspired our poets and startled and reawakened their enamoured readers by promising to take them beyond the here and now has rarely ventured beyond the confines of the language system in which those poets and their readers think and feel.

And yet, the limits of a monolingual investigation into the concept of love become obvious as soon as we compare languages. The first unavoidable fact which imposes itself is that languages do not tend to share the same unified concept of love. Indeed what we call 'love' is often split into various closely or more distantly related concepts in other languages. Love in foreign languages seems to engender different relationships between the sexes, parents and children. Above all, different conceptions of love implicitly posit that men and women have a different relationship to society, space and even to time and to the cosmos.

This study of love will take us into a metaphysical study of prepositions. Even in criticising the prepositions we use to structure, divide up and situate love, distributing its dimensions and consigning its aspects to different coordinates in space, we cannot escape spatial metaphors. Asking ourselves what we see 'in' love, and investigating 'into' love, are formulations which posit love as one unified space into which we can (or cannot) enter. But does love exist outside of ourselves? Is love one?

The idea of reducing our complex and diverse experiences and relationships to one essential and unitary form would have seemed strange for the ancient Greeks, for example. Any attempt to read Aristotle or Plato embroils us not only in the complex struggle of trying to enter into the elaborate thought of those two great philosophers, it also compels us to try to come to terms with at least four concepts which are rendered by using the word 'love', namely, *eros*, *filia*, *agapē* and *storge*.

Eros is that passionate physical attraction, associated with romance, but which is better rendered as 'erotic love'. For us, 'romantic love' is inextricably bound up with the paradigms of love which gained currency throughout centuries of celebration of chivalrous courtly love, paradigms which were modified by the Romantic poets and the neo-Romantics. The concept of 'romantic love' today has been further modified by the paradigms explored, extended and endlessly rehashed in twentieth-century films and pop songs. The erotic longing and the sensual pleasures of love expressed in such films and pop songs, nonetheless, all form part of the concept to which the ancient Greeks gave the name *eros*.

Philia is usually translated into English as 'friendship', though this is inevitably a problematic translation since the meaning of 'friendship' is ever subject to debate and discussion in English or any other language. In Greek, *philia* designated a virtuous form of love in which the 'lover' experienced and displayed, a dispassionate love for those he was familiar with. This familiarity embraced friends, family and community: it involves a binding loyalty to those we feel attached to. In his *Nicomachean Ethics*, Aristotle used *philia* to define the sense of love and comradeship felt by those men who came together as friends to work together and organize their lives in shared projects carried out within the *polis*. The active nature of the relationship was essential. It was in shared activity, group projects, social and work-related associations that this love was cultivated, nurtured and expressed; doing and loving were intertwined and inextricable, feeding and fuelling one another. In Aristotle's conception of *philia*, group activity (what American commerce and industry celebrate as 'team spirit') serves to structure the feelings of companionship. If we transplant this concept of friendship into contemporary society, we can express this in the following terms: friends are not people you see for a drink or a meal after work, friends are people you 'work' with. Because work (activity, meaningful self-defining social action) is a fundamental prerequisite of *philia* as Aristotle understood and celebrated it.

In contrast to this form of familiarity, and in contrast to the passionate nature of erotic love, *agapē* was used in ancient Greek to refer to a general affection, a disposition of goodwill towards others and to the world in general. It could be used to denote a high regard felt for people with whom one was not intimate, but it could also designate a general attitude towards things such as good food, for example. This kind of love is unlikely to flatter those of us who are eager to see ourselves as the object of desire and the centre of their lover's affections, because *agapē* was also used to refer to the feeling of dispassionate goodwill a man felt towards his spouse.

Storge seems to have overlapped this last usage of *agapē*, but while the latter emotion referred to a general disposition of goodwill, *storge* referred to the specific bonds that held family members together. *Storge* was used principally to speak of that natural love felt by parents for their offspring. *Storge* refers to the selfless concern and thoughtfulness that binds married couples together, whether passion has died or not. *Storge* is the emotional bond which comes into play when a wife puts up with her husband's endless pointless passion for DIY, or when a husband reluctantly puts up with washing the dishes or putting the children to bed in order to allow his wife to go out with her girlfriends for a drink.

Animated by the neo-Platonic drive to find first essential principles (the forms from which all things are derived), it was Christian thought which reduced all these diverse and linked forms of affections and passions into one general concept of love. Christianity championed *agapē* (*caritas*, in Latin). And English-speaking Christians have, ever since, been forced to dance an awkward jig as they strive to find a safe footing when speaking of feelings of affection, intimacy and responsibility for others by skipping from 'charity' to 'love'. By 'love', or what is often more precisely referred to as 'brotherly love', we mean the obligation to feel a general goodwill towards all people (who are, by Christian definition, both our 'brothers' and our 'neighbours') irrespective of our own relationship to those persons and irrespective of their attitudes towards us or the actions they subject us to. Ever since the conversion of the European peoples to Christianity during the Middle Ages, there has existed a strong pressure in literature and in language to see other forms of love (passionate erotic love and love for family and for friends) as subordinate forms of one unified concept of 'charity' or 'love'.

This may seem to misrepresent (or even pervert) the essential nature of each emotion brought under the harness of 'love', and, of course, poets such as Blake have rebelled against the limited, stilted and insipid form of love which emerges in this Christian refinement or distillation of love to one unique and fundamental essence. Once the force of erotic passion, on the one hand, and the unquestioned natural bond linking us to our children, on the other, have been reduced to a feeling of general companionship or a favourable disposition towards friends and strangers alike, what is left of the energy of love? How much of the tug of love's current is left, once the river reaches the delta and reaches out into the shallow channels stretching out towards the sea? Love as bond, love as immediate impulse, is drained of much of its animating force once it is 'spent' on all of mankind.

We can all resist or reject the moulds of thought that language provides us with in the form of cultural paradigms. Words and concepts are not prisons which enclose our thoughts; they are habitations which we can move into, live and feel within. In this respect we resemble hermit crabs more than prisoners. Words are places we can also choose to leave in order to explore alternative conceptual and linguistic constructs. This choice is subject to one crucial constraint, however: the exploration of those alternative constructs will always take place with and within language; we cannot escape using words and concepts. To some extent, therefore, the trajectories of our creative inspirations and our rebellious struggles against existing forms of symbolic thought remain language bound. They transcend the 'language' which gives form to conventional thought, but they make use of the language system as the springboard from which to launch themselves into new elaborations of thought and feeling.

This is the 'work of the mind' of which Humboldt spoke. It is a work which frees the mind from existing language, but it is a form of spiritual and intellectual activity which extends the language system. This lucid reflective thought is indeed an essential element of language, it is the activity which reanimates and invigorates the expressive potential of language. This is *Sprachdenken*, thinking and feeling 'in' language.

Love exists simultaneously, then, within the spheres of life, the spirit and language. 'Love' is not a fact of objective reality which transcends languages and cultures: love is a complex English-bound concept. This should not devalue love as a concept in our eyes. 'Love' helps us to organize experience: it helps us to understand, describe and explore a wide variety of emotions, relationships and desires. Comparing Greek to English makes it obvious that, in defining love, we are constructing a paradigm: but 'love' remains a meaningful paradigm, one which helps us give form and content to our thoughts and feelings.

The essential point we should bear in mind – and here both passion and language combine to enchant and confuse us – is that when we refer to 'love' we are not uncovering a 'truth'. Though we may love 'truly', and though we may find 'truth' in the expressions we give to our feelings, the shapes that emerge in our concepts and in the patterns in which those concepts are arranged are, nonetheless, linked and arranged in culturally specific and historically situated forms of symbolic thought. This implies no denigration of love. Love has outlasted dictatorships and the end of dynasties. Love as a concept retains its power within language and within culture. If it were 'merely a word', bearing no relation to reality, if it were incapable of embracing and giving expression to our thoughts and feelings, it would have fallen into disuse and been abandoned. The central place 'love' has acquired and retained in our language testifies, on the contrary, to the vigour of the concept and the capacity of thought to harness this complex conceptual construct to penetrate the reality we live within and which we share with others.

Love inclines us towards fusion, and often towards confusion. But we must be careful to make distinctions when we approach love. There is an implicit and inescapable tension between poetry and philology when it comes to approaching love. While the poet's soul opens up to embrace the lover and the heavens, when the poet celebrates Creation and his or her lover as the incarnation of the beauty of Creation, the philologist limits, divides and defines the various dimensions and aspects pertaining to the concept of love. In exploring other languages, the ethnolinguist will be forced to reinterpret the scope and limits of the concept of 'love' as it is used to define the diverse sentiments and experiences that can be grouped under that heading. The definition of the four forms of 'love' used by the ancient Greeks is only one example among others which forces us to reappraise our own concept, though the influence of ancient Greek upon the development of the consciousness of what are called the 'Western peoples' is self-evident. In Greek, we find a part of ourselves, but we are also forced to look for new bearings as we move into the constellation of concepts, distinctions and vibrant relations that we begin to perceive as we look into those Greek ideas and the worldview which engendered them. Each time we enter into a foreign language, we find ourselves entering into a new mode of world-perceiving and world-conceiving. Looking for 'love' in other languages will impose upon us the task of grappling with the complex conceptual threads which hold the language of love in place within the language system as a whole. This becomes all too clear as soon as we begin to grope our way towards an understanding of the concepts inherited from non-Western cultures.

Alternative formulations of 'love' can be found in the Hindu tradition. The *Kama Sutra* is far more often quoted than it is read by Westerners, of course, but patient readers find in this ancient work an elaborate form of ethics and codes of conduct which structure erotic and marital relationships. Unsurprisingly, the concepts used differ greatly from those of contemporary culture. Erotic passions and marital obligations do not spring forth, fully formed, from erotic physical dimensions or from heavenly spheres: they exist within given cultural constraints and are subject to socio-historical conditions. How much pleasure should be given to a water-bearing servant during sexual congress? What are the terms of binding obligations between courtesan and client? The answers to such questions depend upon conceptions of class and caste. And these social realities are underpinned by a spiritual conception of urges and desires that only begin to become comprehensible once we understand the nature of the society's gods and goddesses and the way that culture's narratives of Creation englobe the actual physical conception of the foetus. Language is, of course, part of this cultural conceptualisation of love, because language is fundamental to the evolution of symbolic forms of thought, offering words and patterns of thought to adopt, refine and resist.

The Hindu example is only one obvious one. In the Arab world of the thirteenth century, the Sufi mystic, 'Ibn Arabî, proposed one of the most elaborate and most penetrating philosophical treatises on love, inventing an ingeniously rigorous vocabulary for defining the different forms and states of desire, passion and affection. One thing which he shared with Christian thinkers was the desire to subordinate the diverse manifestations of feelings and passions to one supreme form of love. 'Ibn Arabî held divine love to be supreme. He was a poet who is said to have inspired Dante. His erotic spiritualism had little in common with the sterile frigidity we sometimes associate with conceptions of love espoused by the Catholic Church and Puritan Protestants. 'Ibn Arabî was always alive to the sensual pleasure of passionate erotic love. Love was not the insipid, curtailed passion promoted by the parish priest; love was not repressed or stifled, but uplifting and overflowing. And in this respect, 'Ibn Arabî rises above the commonplace expression of love in Christian ritual and the institutions which maintain the faith. The philosopher-poet rekindled something more akin to that animating fire that inspired Christianity as a living, loving worldview, a vision of the world which grew out of biblical scripture and Jewish allegories. 'Ibn Arabî defines a form of love which echoes the celebration of erotic passion found in texts such as *The Song of Solomon* in the Old Testament. All forms of love are related in 'Ibn Arabî's philosophy.

This makes this Moorish philosopher infinitely strange to us. Encountering him, we are faced with someone who is difficult to understand and to place within the framework of our own cultural mindset. He stands before us as a form of transcendental otherness. 'Ibn Arabî could not have been produced by our Western traditions, which from the early Christian neo-Platonic philosophers to Descartes, and down to this day, tend to oppose the body and the mind, the flesh and the spirit. Consequently, his holistic and conceptually ordered conception of love contains an implicit critique of our own attempts to represent the emotion and experience of love. At a conceptual, linguistic, philosophical and spiritual level, we live within the schism that dissects body and mind. Finding our way back to unity, the unity of experience as both a spiritual and a physical presence in the world, proves difficult for Christians and for English speakers as a whole. We are attracted to the opposite poles of sensuality and spiritual (or intellectual) pursuits, but these two attractions drag us apart. Sensuality and spirituality were, for example, the two forces which energized the opposite poles of John Donne's early erotic poetry and which continued to animate his later religious verse, but Donne was never capable of fully transcending the schism, and his poetry oscillated between the two poles without uniting to find the harmony which was disclosed by and celebrated in 'Ibn Arabî's conception of love, a conception which enacted the synthesis of what we would tend to consider opposing, incompatible, or paradoxical forms of love. Rather than a 'metaphysical poet' (like Donne), or a 'poetical philosopher' (like Plato), 'Ibn Arabî represents something more akin to the whole man, cultivated to the highest point in terms of sensitivity and consciousness of love. He reveals to us something of humankind's thinking-feeling potential.

Divine love, in 'Ibn Arabî's philosophy, is God's love for himself and His creations (which form part of Him). Spiritual love is man's love for God and His creations. Natural love is the love that is born between God's creatures as they celebrate (in a diluted form) God's own love for His creations by loving them in and for themselves. In order to extrapolate the diverse forms of inter-related love 'Ibn Arabî is led to define, for example, *hiyâm*, distraught or frantic love, the love that wanders aimlessly from object to object, frantically animated by a dissipating passion which is incapable of insight, true appreciation and permanence ('Ibn Arabî 1986: 147–8). In contrast to this, he describes *Al-Hawâ*, the sudden passionate love that awakens in the soul at the sight of someone (*ibid.*: 118). For the philosopher, the intensity of this moment is an echo (a fragment, a splinter of light) of the Divine impulse to create.

This sudden revelation is the love that is found in Dante's celebration of Beatrice, the love of God's creations and the love of beauty. But while Dante is considered as a great and original poet for having established a link between erotic and divine love, 'Ibn Arabî posited this link not as an original or provocative counterpart to the love promoted by his religion, but rather as one of the basic inalienable elements of religion. To fail to be touched by desire and amazement when faced with a young woman's beauty would have supposed a lukewarm and inadequate capacity to love God Himself in 'Ibn Arabî's conception of love.

The Greek definitions for what we call love and 'Ibn Arabî's philosophical theory and poetic ruminations on the forms and states of love offer only two alternative conceptions which force us to question the nature of, and the coherence of, our own concept of love today. If they strike us as profound and meaningful models, then that is perhaps because they light up the nooks and crannies of our own souls and trace some of the contours of the encounters and relationships we have with others. But if we are to understand how love is felt and how love is lived today in different cultures, we must leave the philosophers and the poets behind. We must come down to the level of everyday representations of love. What do *we* mean when we talk about love? What does our language reveal about the ways we define desire, about the sexual act and relationships? What does the linguistic representation of love and desire show about the ways we feel about our 'lovers' or about how we treat them? For the worldview project, the question will be to discover whether those representations change from language to language. This is an ethnolinguistic question. For metaphor theory, the question will be to establish the conceptual frameworks from which coinciding and differing patterns of representation are woven.

Love metaphors in English

Working with the Lakoff–Johnson approach to metaphor, the Hungarian Zoltán Kövecses was the first cognitive linguist to make a lengthy and detailed contribution to the analysis of 'love' in English back in 1986 (Kövecses 1986: 61–105). While he admitted that 'Romantic love is commonly thought of as a mysterious emotion which it is difficult to pin down', Kövecses claimed that the lexical approach employed in his study 'enables us to come up with a fairly clear definition of the concept of LOVE' (61). His lexical study consists in interpreting a great number of commonly used everyday phrases and expressions in terms of a limited number of root metaphors or conceptual metaphors from which they are derived and which enable us to understand each extension. Kövecses, for example, argues that we are able to understand the two phrases 'We were *made for each other*' and 'We *are one*', in terms of the conceptual metaphor, 'Love is a unity (of two complementary parts)' (62). He affirmed we could understand both, 'She *was filled with love*' and 'He *poured out* his affections on her' in terms of a deeper conceptual construct; love is a fluid in a container (82). Love could equally be represented in terms of a fire (He *was burning with* love), a natural force, a flood, for example (*Waves* of passion *came over* him) or a great wind (It was a *whirlwind* romance). Kövecses found love could also be represented as a force which interferes with accurate perception (e.g. He *was blinded* by love).

The object of love, Kövecses argued, was also metaphorically constituted. He or she could be designated in terms of 'appetising food' (Sugar, Honey, Sweetie-pie). Kövecses even found novel extensions of this conventional conceptual metaphor, e.g. 'She's the *cream in my coffee*' (67). The object of love could, on the other hand, be conceived of in terms of an object of veneration or devotion. This conceptual metaphor (which equates love with faith) is used by what cognitive linguists call our 'cognitive unconscious' to interpret 'He *worships the ground she walks on*' (72).

Most of these expressions are commonplace, and the explanations Kövecses offers are not particularly revealing since the conceptual metaphors upon which they are constructed are self-evident. But the linguist's findings should not be underestimated. Kövecses' contribution consists in ordering and arranging seemingly unrelated phrases and expressions which spring up in our speech. 'Love is insanity' and 'Love is a form of magnetism' are straightforward conceptual equations which all of us work with in everyday speech, but Kövecses' work does rigorously show the scope of these equations by cataloguing the diverse expressions we use to give form to our thoughts and emotions. We are not always instantly aware of the equation which allows us to interpret some of our metaphors. We may all find it easy to understand the following sentences:

- I *gave* her all my love
- I *didn't get* much in return
- She *rewarded* his love by taking care of him (95).

But are we lucid about the underlying equation upon which such phrases are based, i.e. that love, thus conceived, is a valuable commodity in an economic exchange? This would seem unlikely, since certain US expressions, such as 'She's *invested a lot* in that relationship', have a jarring effect on the ear for many English speakers, bringing home the thought pattern which has generated this phrase. British English has a whole host of expressions based upon the same conceptual metaphor ('enriching relationship' 'give and take in relationships'), but it is only when we find ourselves faced with a novel or foreign expression that the economic foundations of this representation of romance are felt, leaving a bad taste in the mouth.

Kövecses' study shows the pervasive importance within our language system of several conceptual metaphors which we do not immediately associate with romantic love. Love is a hidden object we seek for in the wrong places. It is a captive animal that can get out of hand. It is an opponent we sometimes have to fight off.

Nevertheless, his study does not exhaust the love metaphors found in English. Kövecses does not define a given corpus for study, but rather proceeds (like Lakoff) by listing commonly used expressions. This has at least two disadvantages: it limits the discussion to well-known and often largely unproblematic expressions, and it downplays the creative play involved in using metaphors ironically, in contradicting commonplace metaphorical expressions and in refining and redefining them. These are all common discourse procedures, but the methodology adopted by Kövecses and Lakoff tends to obscure and marginalize this element of speech. In this respect, their methodology resembles the generative linguist's practice of inventing sentences for study. Discourse analysis and corpus-based studies brings us back to speech and to strategies. As Eubanks (2000) showed in his study of Trade-is-War, real speech is invariably richer and more personal, because the speaker tugs expressions in one way or another, and remoulds phrases in ways that suit his or her intentions in any given situation. This situated, personal (or rather interpersonal) aspect of metaphoric expression makes any real speech infinitely more challenging for the interpreter than the catalogue of conventional expressions which, Kövecses seems to claim (somewhat naively, perhaps), exhausts our representations of love.

The last disadvantage is the most important, from the ethnolinguistic perspective. It is regrettable that Kövecses limited the scope of his study to English love metaphors without exploring other language systems (such as his own mother tongue, Hungarian). A comparative study would have allowed him to contrast the formulations of love in English with other forms and thereby highlight the specific nature of 'love' for English speakers. Admittedly, Kövecses does treat other languages in his later work *Metaphor and Emotion: Language, Culture and Body in Human Feeling* (2000/2003). And he does integrate aspects of Wierzbicka's ethnolinguistic concerns in his introduction. His analysis and methodology remain, however, much the same as in his work of the 1980s, as can be seen in his treatment of 'desire is hunger' (*ibid.*: 45).

Trilingual case study

The following study of 'love' situates the question within the framework of the ethnolinguistic project of worldview. How do we think and feel about love? And how does our language culture offer us the paradigms, categories and the expressive resources which give shape to our diverse creative expressions of love and loving. Ninety articles were selected from women's magazines in English, French and Czech. Thirty articles were selected from six or seven different magazines in each language to allow a considerable degree of variation in the scope of the corpus of each language. The articles were between one and six pages in length with an average length of two and a half pages. As the average number of words per page was around 700, this allows us to establish a corpus with the following statistics:

Average no. of words per article:	approx. 1,750
Number of articles per language:	30
Total number of words per language:	approx. 52,500
Total number of pages:	approx. 225
Total number of words studied:	approx. 157,500

The following magazines formed the corpus of the study:

English

OK, a woman's magazine concerned with gossip about stars, fashion and lifestyle, written for a wide readership of moderately educated and largely unprofessional women probably aged 30–50 (10 articles, May 2007)

Glamour, a woman's magazine concerned with fashion, love, sex and lifestyle, written for a wide range of women probably aged 18–30 (7 articles, June 2007)

Elle, a woman's magazine similar to the one above, though *Elle* probably attracts more educated readers and addresses women's issues likely to appeal to women of up to 35 (1 article, September 2002; 6 articles, November 2005)

Cosmopolitan, a woman's magazine with a readership similar to that of *Elle* (3 articles, June 2007)

Easy Living, a woman's lifestyle magazine written for women aged probably 30–45 (3 articles, June 2007)

French

France Dimanche, a woman's magazine similar to *OK* (3 articles, 25–31 May 2007)

Glamour, as in English (4 articles, October 2005; 4 articles, November 2005; 4 articles, November 2006)

Cosmopolitan, as in English (5 articles, September 2002; 4 articles, October 2005; 4 articles, May 2007)

Marie-Claire, a woman's lifestyle magazine with a readership which overlaps that of *Cosmopolitan* and *Easy Living* in English, probably addressing women aged 25–45 (2 articles, May 2006)

Czech

Katka, a specifically Czech-centred woman's magazine concerned with love, sex, fashion and lifestyle written for a wide readership of women probably aged 18–45 (5 articles, 27 August–2 September 2003)

Moje Psychologie, a woman's magazine concerned with love, sex, relationships, culture and lifestyle, which contains interviews with psychologists and psychoanalysts and which represents their theories in layman's terms (3 articles, May 2007)

Cosmopolitan, as in French and English (4 articles, May 2007)

Elle, as in French and English (1 article, May 2007)

Skvělá, a woman's magazine which is at times Czech-centred, but which is similar to *Elle* and *Cosmopolitan* in terms of themes and readership: *Skvělá* is concerned with love, sex, fashion, relationships and lifestyle, and addresses a wide readership of women probably aged 18–35 (5 articles, May 2007)

Bazar, a woman's magazine similar to *Glamour* in French and English, concerned with love, sex, fashion and lifestyle, which addresses a readership of women probably aged 18–30 (7 articles, February 2007; 5 articles, May 2007)

These articles were selected because they spoke explicitly about love, desire, the sexual act and relationships. As the case study made use of the printed page and not the computer, no attempt was made to quantify the exact number of times a metaphor or symbolic form of representation appeared. Metaphor study does not lend itself to word searches as lexical study does, and this too conditioned the nature of the study and the methodology followed. The objectives of the study were:

• to extend the field of study opened up by Kövecses by investigating a defined corpus of authentic English
• to analyse, interpret and categorize new and original metaphors
• to determine whether the French and Czech languages share the same conceptual metaphors which generate our concepts of love and desire in English
• to open up to the English speaker's mind the different dimensions of love and desire explored by French and Czech in a given linguistic context.

Love, *amour* and *láska*

All three languages showed a rich and varied network of metaphoric constructs which allow the formulation of creative and flexible paradigms of love in everyday life. Paradoxically, these metaphorical constructs turned out to be contradictory but complementary. That is to say, metaphors could not be assimilated into one coherent whole, a single structure with integrated and interacting parts. The metaphoric expressions found in the corpus allowed a series of opposing and mutually exclusive models of love to emerge. This neither proves problematic for the English speaker, nor is it particularly surprising. Back in 1980, Lakoff and Johnson were already explaining that the contradictory nature of conceptual metaphors, rather than demolishing a concept, as philosophers might suppose it would, enriches it.

For many people, the malleable elusive nature of 'love' will be perplexing, because they are looking in vain for a direct definable counterpart to the linguistic signifier: a tidy terminological definition. Many people like to think of words as terms: each one is supposed to designate a reality. Inevitably they are disappointed: words are not labels. At this stage, the ambiguity of words is confused with obscurity and inefficiency. Disappointment gives rise to the sentiment that language as a whole is a dark shadow of objective reality, a shroud or veil, which comes between us and the world.

Viewed from such a perspective, 'love' becomes the disappointing signpost to a transcendental plane of feeling and experience. This is a tradition which has its exponents at all levels of society, from the love-crazed adolescent to the philosopher. For such people 'language lies', 'language deceives us': at the very best, such people feel language is insufficient. Such people are what Ernst Cassirer called 'the modern sceptical critics of language [who deny] any alleged truth content of language' (Cassirer 1953: 7). Those who adopt this stance will inevitably find frustrating the complex and contradictory nature of language about love because they would like to reduce the complex patterns of experience, which have been elaborated in language, to one simple refined essence. Since the Middle Ages such people have been known as 'realists'. As Cassirer put it:

The realists always assume, as their solid basis for all ... explanations, the so-called 'given,' which is thought to have some definite form, some inherent structure of its own. They accept this reality as an integrated whole of causes and effects, things and attributes, states and processes, of objects at rest and of motions, and the only question for them is which of these elements a particular mental product such as myth, language or art originally embodied. (1953: 12)

As Cassirer, Sapir, Whorf, Lakoff and Johnson all knew only too well, words describe attributes, states and processes: metaphors introduce representations of motion and motionlessness, and language allows us to understand and describe both causes and effects. But those linguists also knew that such representations were simply modes of apprehension, strategies which language instils in consciousness in order to allow it to deal with experience, to organize and express it. Viewed from their perspective, words and metaphors do not encapsulate a phenomenon or truth of objective reality, they form the focal points or organising principles around which a supra-subjective meaning is generated. If metaphors entangle us in contradictions, then they are simply alerting us to the fact that our concept is a complex one, a network of frameworks which are superimposed on various planes or juxtaposed, one against the other, and offered up to us as options for orchestrating meaning.

Contradictory metaphors strengthen the concept which we know as 'love' by highlighting certain of its aspects or facets while downplaying others. Those downplayed facets will, in turn, seek their place in the limelight by shoving other constructs into the shadows. Metaphoric models always highlight and hide aspects of experience, and what emerges as a complex and contradictory whole reflects all the more accurately and all the more penetratingly the reality of our love and loving.

For this reason, it should not be surprising that love in English can be conceived of as both a space and as a force that penetrates a space. Love *enters* our lives: we fall *in* love. In metaphoric terms love can be both a container and the content of a container. Neither should it be surprising that in Czech love can be both conceived of as a means and an end. In fact, speakers of all three languages negotiate contradictions of such a nature with no apparent problem.

English love

The English concept of 'love' can be conceived of in the following terms:

Journey In this conception, love has its ups and downs. This paradigm also allows us to speak of difficulties, break downs and the act of resuming loving in terms of stopping off and moving on. In such a model, infidelity is conceived of in terms of 'straying' from the path. One woman spoke of her love for her husband, her divorce and her subsequent remarriage as 'a bittersweet journey' (*Glamour*, June 2007). This introduces a synaesthetic representation of pleasure and pain (as sweetness and sourness) into the representation of love as a journey or trajectory: for Fauconnier and Turner (2002/3) a 'complex blend'. When love becomes the object of the journey, its destination is conceived of in terms of a 'quest'. This can develop into hunting metaphors.

Elemental physical force One of the most obvious types is the fire metaphor. One journalist from *OK* asked a reality show actor about his love life in the following terms: 'Have the fires of that romance burned out for good?' The Love-is-Fire metaphor is obviously closely linked to the idea of passion as heat. Another common metaphor that is used is the earthquake, suggesting a dramatic transformation of the life of the lover: his or her 'world is shaken'. These metaphors confirm Kövecses' findings, and form parallels to his 'whirlwind' metaphor.

Harmony Lovers are said to be in tune with one another. This would imply that they could also be out of tune or discordant, but these extensions were not explored in the English corpus though they are common in the works of the Metaphysical Poets. This musical metaphor is closely related to the traditional metaphor of lovers being two parts of a unified whole. Lovers can be said to be 'at one with' one another.

Transmission Closely related to the above metaphor, this represents lovers as being 'on the same wavelength'.

Devotion As Kövecses found, love is often conceived of in terms of devotion. In the English articles, this traditional metaphor lost all of its religious and transcendental connotations. Devotion was reduced to the animal metaphor of 'doglike affection'. Though this might seem demeaning and even repulsive to Continental readers, it must be remembered that the British love their dogs: and indeed the idea of 'doggy love' was presented in a warm light with no hint of scorn or contempt.

The centre of life The idea of love as the central principle or goal of life, the centre-pin of the family and the basis of the identity of married partners, is an old one. This metaphor underwent a rhetorical process which was fairly widespread in this corpus: it was negated. In one article (*Elle*, November 2005), the modern promiscuous woman, which the author dubbed the *DCD* ('Don't Care Dater'), refused to consider love and men as the centre of her life. As she considered herself as 'an integral whole without a boyfriend bolt-on', she saw no reason why she should not define her life and herself in terms of other things (work, family and friends). Rather than allowing men to take up too much space, the DCD, we are told, prefers to 'call up a compliant FBW (friend with benefits), flick on her reliable rabbit, or indulge in a carefully chosen non-drunken one-night stand'. The 'benefits' provided take us into the field of commercial metaphors, describing sex as an added bonus. The DCD herself seems to regard her sexuality as a machine which can be switched on and off. What exactly the 'reliable rabbit' is supposed to represent remains open to question, though (I am told) it may refer to the vibrator. This mechanistic representation of love was consolidated by the author of the article when she described the conditions which give rise to this form of promiscuity in terms of mechanical causality: 'DCDs are *made*, not born. DCD-ness can be *triggered* by a break-up or during a hectic time at work' (my italics).

Life While the place of love in life is at times marginalized, at other times love comes to incarnate life itself. In the same article that we have just quoted in which love was displaced from the centre of life, loveless life was considered 'lifeless': it was compared to 'suspended animation'. One reason for becoming a DCD was said to be 'a conscious decision to go through a phase of suspended relationship animation after many years of unsatisfactory relationships' (*Elle*, November 2005).

Theatre play This allows us to create and understand a wide variety of expressions concerned with 'dramatic situations', 'actors' and 'love stories'. It also allowed the corpus to generate some novel extensions. For example, a new lover was described as 'a new man waiting in the wings'. This metaphor parallels and overlaps the metaphors in which love is conceived of in terms of film and cinema. In such a light, 'loving' becomes 'acting', but this does not inevitably imply deceit, but rather posits a playful complicity.

Content Love was regularly represented as something that we could fill our lives with. This implies love can 'enter' our lives and 'fulfil' us. It also helps give meaning to the idea that a loveless life is an 'empty' life.

Space While love was the content in some metaphors, this formulation was reversed in metaphors in which love was represented as a space or trajectory to 'enter into' and 'live through'. Love was represented as something you can 'drift into', though the authors of certain articles criticized this behaviour in love, advocating it was preferable to maintain a distance between one's sexual partner until a conscious rational decision was taken to engage in love.

Possession Love was at times regarded as a possession in the English corpus. But as 'property', it was not always a 'reliable form of currency'. One famous girl group singer, who had recently been jilted, regretted that you couldn't count on love. As she explained in *OK* (May 2007): 'Money is more important to me than sex ... Ultimately, money lasts longer than love'.

Cooking This relatively rare metaphoric formulation is not linked to the idea of desire as eating. It appeared in the English corpus in the *OK* article quoted directly above, in which the disenchanted singer was said to have put men 'on the back burner'. Love, in this example, is reduced to something amounting to the leftovers that are being kept warm to be eaten later on when we are feeling peckish.

Gene-determined state or medical condition With advances in genetics, love is increasingly being understood in terms of genes, genetic make-up and hormones. Falling in love is explained in terms of 'oxytocin (the get close hormone)' (*Cosmopolitan*, June 2007). Men's behaviour in love is described as hormonally predestined: 'postorgasm, their hormone levels shoot up by about 500 percent. So after sex is when a man is best able to bond' (*ibid.*). In the same article, it was argued that, 'When it comes to sex and relationships, his behaviour may be predetermined by his DNA'. This dubious genetic reasoning was not very convincingly supported by attempts to draw palmistry into the genetic equation. The same author claimed: 'If a man's ring finger is longer than his index finger, it means he got a big dose of testosterone while in utero. As a result, he will have a higher sex drive ... and he may be more prone to straying'. The conclusion was: 'He may have been born to cheat'. Gene-determined metaphors inevitably lead us to 'deterministic' conceptions of love and loving. This takes free will out of the equation and reduces lovers to the passive playthings of their desires. They are 'driven' by their 'drives'. Fate will express itself through the highly sexed male's promiscuity.

Amour français

Amour is commonly represented by two conceptual metaphors which are so widespread that they might be said to be lexicalized metaphors, linguistic reflexes: these two conceptual constructs are the *aventure* and the *histoire d'amour*. The first might best be translated by 'fling' or 'affair', though there is nothing necessarily 'illegitimate' about the *aventure*.

Aventure This form of representation stresses the exciting, passionate aspect of discovering another person and living through a possibly tumultuous experience full of unforeseeable events of a romantic and sensual nature. Because the *aventure* belongs to such an automatic mode of conceiving love in French, it is often adapted in more complex forms. Women will then conceive of their affairs not in terms of lovers as living human beings, but rather as reified collector's items. Men are often transformed into *aventures* and those *aventures* join a long list of other collector's items. This, at least is how one young woman, Laetitia, described her sexual background: 'We tested our powers of seduction by collecting affairs' (*On testait notre pouvoir de séduction en collectionnant les aventures*, *Cosmopolitan*, May 2007).

Histoire d'amour The *histoire d'amour* represents love in the framework of a 'story'. This can coincide with film and theatre metaphors involving actors, exciting beginnings, dramatic twists, and happy or tragic endings. When young women look back on falling in love, they often recognize the unrealistic nature of their dreamy conjectures by saying: '*Je me suis faite un film*' (I set up a film for myself). Like the *aventure*, the *histoire d'amour* is regularly transformed into novel extensions. One vulgar extension which is used to denote a fairly loveless sexual relationship, encounter or 'sex session', is the *histoire de cul* (ass story). Like many vulgar expressions, this one is metonymic. In a two-stage transformation, the lover is reduced to an object of desire, the body, and that object of desire is reduced to one of its parts (the ass, *cul*).

Living organism In French, as in English, *amour* can grow and develop. It can also die. In one article, the common expression was quoted: 'Letting yourself go [to the dogs] kills love' (*Le laisser-aller tue l'amour*, *Cosmopolitan*, May 2007).

Person *Amour*, *histoire d'amour* and *aventure* can all be personified in complex metaphorical constructs. A woman called Myriam in the same *Cosmopolitan* article quoted directly above claimed: 'Me and love stories were not made to get on' (*les histoires d'amour et moi, on n'était pas faites pour s'entendre*). In a far more complex blend, infidelity was conceived of in one article (*Marie-Claire*, May 2006) as: 'a lightning quiver which chucks a love affair out the door' (*vacillement éclair qui flanque à la porte une histoire d'amour*). A relationship with a man is transformed into a love story: but though this implies reification, the reified object (the story) is in turn personified, becoming a rowdy or undesirable guest who is thrown out for bad behaviour (infidelity). This represents the space of intimacy in terms of a home, a house with a front door. The representation of infidelity itself involves a curious blend: it is both kinaesthetic and visual in that it superimposes quivering or shaking upon lightning. Elsewhere, the personification of love was not rare. Personification opens up considerable scope for metaphoric extensions. If love is a person then that person (like any living thing) can die: at this point a woman will 'go into mourning' (*faire la deuil*) over a 'dead' love affair.

Harmony As in English, the idea of being in harmony or in tune is common in representations of love in French. In the French corpus this harmony was evoked in terms of 'being at one with one another' (*être un*). However, the authors of the articles studied often used these metaphors in the negative form. Love was not always harmonious. Harmony was 'not an exact science'. The framework of cooking was invoked when one author explained there was 'no recipe' (*recette de cuisine*) for a harmonious loving relationship. Just as many tragic or dramatic Hollywood films begin with idyllic images of marital bliss, so the use of harmony metaphors often signalled the approach of disaster in the French articles. One woman, Camille, described the period before being humiliated and devastated by her boyfriend's infidelity as 'perfect osmosis' (*l'osmose parfaite*).

Transmission As in English, loving or getting on well with someone is frequently described in terms of 'being on the same wavelength' (*être sur le même longueur d'onde*).

Construction/habitation Love is frequently described in terms of a building in French, and loving a person seriously involves 'constructing something'. French women frequently discussed their desire to *construire quelque chose*, 'to construct something', an expression which would probably be best translated by English metaphors related to 'stability', such as 'a steady relationship', 'a stable marriage' and so on. In French, such a paradigm implies that problems can threaten the 'stability' of love, and rupture 'devastates' it.

Intimate space Intimacy is represented in terms of a shared space. Love can therefore become your 'territory'. Such representations arise particularly when fidelity is in question. We are told in one article (*Marie-Claire*, May 2006) that after discovering the infidelity of a partner, 'the rival haunts our living space, she consumes our air' (*la rivale hante désormais notre espace vitale, elle consume notre air*). But generally speaking, in French, love is often characterized as a space in which we can live and which we can shape. We can, for example, 'instal a routine' (*installer une routine*) in love.

Journey As in English, love is often represented as a journey (*parcours* or *voyage*). A woman can envisage 'going a part of the way' with someone (*faire un bout de chemin*). Unlike its counterpart in English, this does not refer to the stage of foreplay or congress a woman is willing to engage in. It refers to the amount of time she envisages remaining with one stable sexual partner. One woman, disillusioned by a failed relationship, described her hopes for a new relationship in the following terms: 'I hope I will make a beautiful journey with him, but who knows? (*J'espère faire une belle route avec lui, mais qui sait? Marie-Claire*, May 2006). Falling in love can be described as setting out on a marathon (*prendre le départ d'un marathon*). Love can 'go forwards' or 'make progress' (*avancer*). And difficulties encountered in love (such as infidelity) can be formulated in extensions such as 'accidents along the way' (*accidents de parcours*).

Discovery Love as a discovery is often related to the Love-Journey metaphor. Like travel, love can 'open up new horizons' for lovers in French.

Gift Loving, like the sexual act, is often represented in terms of giving yourself (*le don de soi*). Of course, it is possible to give your body without giving that part of 'you' which you consider to be your 'real' or 'intimate' self. A total divorce between the body and the self would imply that clinically neurotic state which R. D. Laing referred to as 'the disembodied self'. Some of the women seemed to have advanced to something approaching this critical phase in the manner in which they 'managed' their affairs by compartmentalising their lives into family, friends, work and sex. But many seemed to feel fairly at ease with giving only a part of themselves, while withholding another dimension of their being.

Sacrifice Giving implies not only the pleasure of offering something, it also implies depriving yourself of things which must be sacrificed (freedom, time, money). A more fundamental sacrifice is the sacrifice of yourself (or a bit of yourself). One psychologist who was asked to comment on the love stories recounted by a series of women commented: 'You have to be ready to sacrifice yourself a little if you want to give a relationship a chance' (*Il faut être prêt à sacrifier un peu de soi pour pouvoir donner sa chance à une relation, Cosmopolitan*, May 2007).

Receiving Just as love implies giving, it requires someone at the receiving end: the partners alternate or reciprocate in the giving and receiving (at least in non-exploitative emotional and sexual exchanges).

Gamble In order to love, we are told, it is necessary to learn to trust someone. As the same psychologist quoted above claimed, 'Love means betting on confidence' (*L'amour c'est faire le pari de la confiance*, *Cosmopolitan*, May 2007).

Machine Mechanical metaphors are common in French when describing, relationships, sex and the body, and even desire. They are somewhat rarer when it comes to describing love. Love was, however, at times conceived of as a whole with parts which could be 'disconnected'. Women who had become immune to the pain inflicted by infidelity were described as women who had 'disconnected their sexuality from all feeling' (*des femmes qui déconnectent la sexualité de tout affect*, *Marie-Claire*, May 2006).

Madness *Amour fou* (mad love) is a common expression, and it was consequently found in the French corpus (in *France Dimanche*, 25–31 May 2007, for example). Madness is also used to represent love in expressions which refer to passionate affairs: *faire une folie*, which in romance means getting involved in a mad love story. *Une folie à deux* is a common widely used expression implying that two people fuel each other's absurd or silly activities. In the field of love this expression takes on the meaning of a mad affair that two lovers embark on, exciting one another to the extent that they abandon their usual reasonable habits and behaviour.

Illusion Love, once it is over, was frequently represented in the French corpus as an illusion. When one man announced to his wife that a daughter, born of an illegitimate love affair seventeen years before, wanted to meet her father, the wife in question concluded: 'My relationship with him had only been an illusion' (*Mon couple n'avait été qu'un leurre*, *Marie-Claire*, May 2006).

Illness French and English women in these corpora frequently expressed their frustration with affectionate men. Though the art of seduction and the tactics that it implies were certainly held to be of paramount importance, and though seduction implied for these women not only stimulating their bodies but also their emotions, men who showed too much affection or made unreciprocated demands upon a woman's affections were disparaged in both the French and the English corpora. They were described as 'clinging', 'clingy' and possessive in the English corpus. In French, a similar metaphor is used, 'sticky' (*collant*), and this metaphor was indeed found in the corpus. When this aversion to affection and emotional attachment is particularly pronounced, women are said to be 'allergic' to love in French. One woman complained that it was in these terms that one of her girlfriends introduced her to her friends: '*Myriam, businesswoman, allergique à l'engagement*' (This is Myriam, a businesswoman, allergic to commitment, *Cosmopolitan*, May 2007).

Jigsaw References to children were almost non-existent in the French corpus and extremely rare in the English one. It would seem that love and the sexual act have come to be completely divorced from procreation. Even contraception came up very rarely as a subject in both corpora. Nevertheless, in one French article a mother spoke of the death of her only daughter aged 23, who had been suffering from leukaemia, and she attributed the break-up of her marriage to the failure of her and her husband to face up to the death and overcome it as a couple, joined in mourning. This led the woman to describe her love as a jigsaw: 'We were all very attached, and it seems to you like something has broken it up, like a jigsaw, when you take one piece away' (*On était tous très attachés, et on a l'impression que quelque chose a un peu disloqué le tout, comme un puzzle dont on enlève une pièce*, *France Dimanche*, 25–31 May 2007).

Česká láska

'Love' in Czech (*láska*) was at times represented in our corpus differently to *love* and *amour*. But *láska* also followed many of the metaphorical patterns found in English and French.

Unity of two complementary parts The conceptual metaphor for love that was described by Kövecses as the unity of two complementary parts was found in Czech, as in the other two languages. In Czech, the loss of a loved one is experienced as the loss of a part of oneself. One young Czech woman whose boyfriend had been killed in a motorbike accident, asked: 'How could I forget someone who was a part of me?' (*mou součástí*, *Katka*, 27 August–2 September 2003).

Possession The downside of the above metaphorical conception of love is that it makes each of the unity's parts indispensable to the other. This is not always how both partners experience their love, of course. One Czech man complained that his girlfriend was possessive, and the language he used suggested that she considered him as her 'possession', her 'thing': 'She wants me whole and for always' (*Chce mě celého a pořád*, *Moje Psychologie*, May 2007). A woman complained, more explicitly: 'He takes me for his mere thing'

(*Bere mě pouze jako svoji věc*) and as a thing, 'I have no right to leave him' (*Bazar*, February 2007). It would probably also be fair to interpret one woman's conception of love as a possession when she claimed: 'love got lost' (*Láska se vytrácela, Katka*, 27 August–2 September 2003).

Person Paradoxically, objectification does not exclude personification. While the boyfriend in the example above was reduced to the status of an object, love itself was often personified in the Czech corpus, as in the French and English ones. A German-speaking Swiss woman confided in the Czech nanny of her children that she had 'finally understood why love was avoiding her'(*jí láska vyhýbá*). The reason was somewhat surprising: the nanny's employer claimed she was a lesbian and she desired to live with her as her lover (*Cosmopolitan*, May 2007). This scenario took place in Switzerland and the words were spoken in German, so we can probably assume that in both languages love can be represented as a person. In this scenario, love is someone we encounter or fail to encounter. In another Czech example of personification, love with a dominant partner gave rise to a form of love which was itself described as 'someone' who could 'force you into chains' (*zatlačit do kouta*).

Conqueror One specific type of personification came in the form of the conqueror. The author of an article in *Bazar* (February 2007) described the golden age of first love as that special period in which it seems 'love can conquer not only all present problems but even all those that are to come' (*láska překoná nejen všechny současné ale dokonce i budoucí potíže*).

Organism Love in Czech was frequently represented as a living thing which could develop and grow. Love, for example, could grow out of friendship.

Madness As in both English and French, madness and love might be said to be 'bedfellows' in Czech. Consequently, when one Czech young woman said of her boyfriend 'I loved him to madness' (*Milovala jsem ho k zbláznění*), she was merely using a hackneyed metaphorical expression (*Katka*, 27August–2 September 2003).

Heaven When the Italian boyfriend came to visit the same young woman in Brno in order to ask her to marry him, the woman in the example above said she was 'in seventh heaven' (*v sedmém nebi, ibid.*). This expression is found in both English and French. In French a similar expression for expressing joy is 'to be with the angels' (*être aux anges*).

Giving yourself As in both French and English, loving is often understood in terms of giving yourself to your lover. In Czech, lovers are said to be 'given to each other mutually' (*jsou si navzájem oddaní*).

Bond In Czech, love can be conceived of as an 'emotional bond' (*emoční vazby*).

Magnet Both bonding and magnetism are familiar conceptions of love in the three languages. At times this metaphor was explicitly used in Czech. A woman claimed she was 'drawn to a man like a magnet'. In one article (*Bazar*, May 2007), which considered the means used to attract love, the author explored the dynamic possibilities that this metaphor opens up for expression. She argued that most people were unable to perceive a person's 'energy and auras' (*energie a aury*), but when you 'open up inside' (*vnitřně otevžete*) to the 'new possibilities of a partnership-relationship', your 'energetic configuration' (*energetická konfigurace*) is transformed.

Spark Another metaphor for love found in all three languages is that of the spark. One Czech woman described falling in love with her husband as 'a spark that flew between' the two of them (*mezi námi přeskočila jiskra*, *Katka*, 27 August–2 September 2003).

Ring The symbolism of the marriage ring is common to all three of these Western cultures and is therefore found in the three languages. The ring represents the ongoing cycle of love which knows no beginning and no end. This metaphor was explicated in one article (*Bazar*, February 2007), and though the author suggested the symbolism was increasingly forgotten, the idea of eternal love was, she claimed, still very active to the Czech imagination. In the same article, the author considered another symbol of eternal love, diamonds, which, she told readers, were known as 'tears of the Gods' for the ancient Romans.

Food The link between love and food is ancient in the three languages. In Czech, the authors of articles and the people they quoted spoke of being 'hungry for love' (*mít chut' na lásku*, which literally means 'to have a taste for love'). Similarly, one horoscope promised readers of the Aquarius sign that they would 'taste' (*vychutnát*) love most fully before the tenth of the month (*Elle*, May 2007). In French, lovers are said to 'live on love and fresh water' (*vivre d'amour et de l'eau fraîche*). In English, we say they 'live on the food of love'. These traditional metaphors were, in general, displaced in the French and English corpora. They were 'colonized' by an adjacent concept, sex. In all three languages *Sex-as-Food* was a conceptual metaphor which was frequently exploited and explored. In our corpus, this resulted in the exclusion of *Love-as-Food* metaphors in French and English, a trend that only Czech seems to have resisted.

Though the metaphors above often take different turnings and trajectories to those followed in French and English, they are linked to or grounded in shared conceptual frameworks. The following Czech conceptual metaphors are some-what more disconcerting for the English and the French imagination.

Means It is commonplace in all three languages to speak of using sex or one's body as a means of achieving or acquiring something. Nevertheless, neither the French nor the English articles came up with examples of love being conceived of as a means. The Czech articles, in contrast, offered several examples. Both the author of an article and one of the persons quoted described love as 'the best means of learning a foreign language' (*Katka*, 27 August–2 September 2003). The word for 'means' varied in Czech: two synonyms were used (*způsob/prostředek*).

Water The Czech corpus offered several examples of Love-as-Water. Love is something you can dive into (*ponořit se do lásky*). Similarly, you can 'dive into emotion intensively'. You can 'dive into faith in love' (*Elle*, May 2007). These seem like original representations to the French and English imaginations. However, the idea of being 'deeply' in love is commonplace in both languages and testifies to the presence of the conceptual metaphor of *Love-as-Water* in both languages. This conceptual metaphor appears to be far more active in Czech, nonetheless. One striking example was found in a Czech article in which love was said to have 'evaporated somewhere' (*laska ... kamsi vyprchala*, *Bazar*, February 2007).

Period Spring is naturally associated with love in all three languages. This metaphor has, however, a special resonance for the Czech imagination since it was explored by one of the major poets of the Czech National Revival, Karel Macha, in his poem, *May* (Maj), in which he gave an inspired romantic definition of the nature of the Czech people. Given the impact of his words on Czech culture in general, it is hardly surprising that his representation of love is found recurrently in conversation and in articles such as the ones studied in the Czech corpus. Like many poetic representations, Macha's is a complex one: 'the time of love' is personified (or animated) to become someone or some-thing which 'runs wild all around us' (*všude kolem vás bují lásky čas*, quoted in this corpus in the *Elle* horoscope, May 2007).

Thing It will come as little surprise that sex and the sexual act were often reified in all three languages (Underhill 2007). Somewhat more surpris-ing, however, is the reification of love. Paradoxically, while reducing sex to a thing (or a lover to a thing to be used) can be considered negative, the reifica-tion of love seemed conversely to glorify love. When love was said to be 'it' (*ono*), it designated the full, perfect or complete experience of love. Sex, in this scenario is distinct from love. In one article (*Bazar*, May 2007), it was said that though sex could not save a relationship, love without good sex 'will not be it' (*nebude ono*). Curiously, English also glorifies love by resorting to reification, as in the expression, 'the real thing'.

Work The everyday experience of work for professional women has influenced the conception of sex and relationships in French, English and Czech. Expressions such as 'partnership' have become commonplace in all three languages, and in the French and English corpora, prospective boyfriends were at times considered in terms of 'candidates' for 'interviews'. Relationships themselves, the workaday structures and routines that grow out of our loving bonds, are often considered to be 'work' in both English and French. But love and relationships are neatly separated in the French and English imaginations. Only in Czech were examples of *Love-as-Work* found (e.g. *Bazar*, May 2007). *Love* and *amour* seem to occupy an otherworldly sphere when it comes to work metaphors in French and English: such a representation is patently judged to be too prosaic to represent 'love', the object of desire. *Láska* seems to be somewhat more flexible: it is a concept capable of reaching for the skies while keeping its feet firmly on the ground.

Years of tolerance The prosaic reality of loving in Czech is made manifest in other metaphors which forge links that are surprising for French and English imaginations. Relationships are said to require tolerance in English in our corpus, but love is not said to require it. The exploration of the requirements of relationships was explored far more fully in the English corpus than in the French one, but the French corpus made it clear that relationships do have requirements and do make demands upon lovers. Love, on the other hand, seems to escape these requirements in French. For this reason claiming 'love is work and partnership; those are years of tolerance' (*Bazar*, May 2007), strikes a discordant note in English and would probably upset the French imagination.

Conclusions and reflections

As we have just seen, it is difficult to separate love and relationships. This will seem like a problem if we give ourselves the task of defining the 'essential nature' of the concepts 'love' and 'relationship'. But if we consider words such as love as polysemous constructs which reach out to cover various related fields of concepts, then this state of affairs will become clearer. Ultimately, love resembles truth, in that Wittgenstein's model of family relationships proves an efficient mode of representation when dealing with the way related spheres of meaning intersect and overlap. The metaphor of 'family relationships' must, nonetheless, be adapted and extended in order to introduce related families.

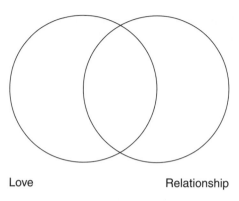

Love   Relationship

Figure 4.1 Overlapping concepts

If we 'marry' love and relationships, we should be able to come up with a plausible representation of two related spheres of meaning, neither of which possesses a core meaning or 'essence', and both of which proliferate in various related concepts. Think of those two sets of associated meanings as a marriage ceremony in which the two families meet and mingle. Whatever image is used, the essential point is that love and relationship as concepts are both varied and overlapping. Their intersection can, therefore, be represented in the most schematic form in Figure 4.1.

The philosopher and the realist will no doubt be dissatisfied with such a representation, since they both strive to understand the nature of things by dividing reality up into separate entities, extracting their fixed unchanging essences and disregarding all that does not contribute to that extractable essence. Such a drive towards understanding has the power of generating an abstract category of the mind, and this is of paramount importance to logic and the natural sciences. However, since Kant made his distinction between the phenomenon of objective experience and the noumenon of intellectual intuition (the idea we form which allows us to reason), linguistics has concerned itself with the way language reflects and directs perception, with the way it harnesses impressions as the resources that the imagination requires to construct abstract concepts.

We are not turning from the world and leaving love behind when we speak of its linguistic representation. Nevertheless, it is with 'love' as the noumenon (the object of intellectual intuition) that we are dealing when we compare the varying concepts that emerge in different languages. Only in leaving behind the naive belief in a 'love' that exists beyond language and awaits naming by language can we understand the place 'love' holds in each of the three cultures as one of the fundamental constructs of world-perceiving and world-conceiving.

Language does not so much define things of the phenomenal world as invent them as objects of consciousness, thereby enabling us to order our experience of the real world. Love exists for all of us, but exactly what English speakers,

French speakers and Czech speakers mean by 'love', *amour* and *láska* both varies from language to language and from context to context. This will seem unfortunate only to those who consider words to be labels rather than efficient means of defining and designating parts of a shared experience. This deeply philosophical question concerning the nature of being and the significance of language is not simply an abstract debate: it represents a fundamental antagonism concerning our faculty of understanding as a category-building consciousness, and this antagonism is consequently projected into everyday life. Among the people around us, we will find, on the one hand, realists who search for 'real love' or 'true love'. Though this may seem a laudable and 'romantic' ideal, this philosophy does have the disadvantage of inducing the realist to reject many forms of love and emotion which do not fit into his conception. On the other hand, we will find those who are arrested by experience, who are enthralled by encounters and engaged in ongoing adventures. Such people share the same faith that the Jewish philosopher Martin Buber spoke of when he affirmed: all being is meeting. For such lovers, love remains a complex experience, almost a mystery, anything but the simple ideal which the realist sets out on his quest to find. Such people are closer to the poets who see poetry as an investigation into reality, into the sensual world; the world that escapes the models and categories required by the objectifying mind of science that is concerned with absolutes and abstractions. The realist yearns to go beyond the here and now of kaleidoscopic experience, which he ultimately holds to be tiresome and inconsequential in comparison to the archetype of his own model-making understanding, and which he confuses with an underlying transcendental archetype of a higher, deeper or truer reality.

The nature of our concepts is not tidy. In all three languages, the symbolic forms used to conceive of and express the concepts of love lead us into contradictions. Obviously, love cannot be, at one and the same time, a person and an inanimate thing. And this contradictory representation cannot be simply explained away as 'a manner of speaking' that changes from situation to situation. Rather, this seems to be a contradiction which upsets and pains those living within it. Our study offered various examples of women who treat love and lovers as things, and yet who then find themselves frustrated by the meaninglessness of 'collecting' loves and lovers – things, objects. These women appear to crave for a warm and responsive love from a living individual rather than the non-response of a lover who becomes the object of a self-contained and preconceived desire. This trend was particularly pronounced in the French corpus.

The contradictory nature of these metaphorical frameworks hardly needs to be visualized. A wall separates the Czech conception of Love-as-a-Spark and Love-as-Water into which you can dive and which can evaporate. On the other hand, not all variations in metaphoric models lead to contrast and contradiction, and it is worth visualising the way related metaphors can congregate around one quality as if around a fixed point. In English, for example, the metaphors of fire,

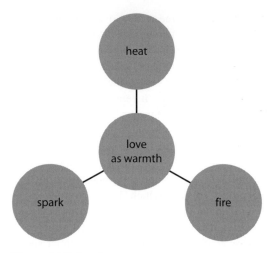

Figure 4.2 Related concepts

heat and sparks are clearly related, in that they can be said to share the same basic conceptual metaphor of love as warmth, as illustrated in Figure 2.

Symbolic frameworks such as these open up new possibilities to the imagination. Each conceptual metaphor exists in its own right, imposing its expressive potential by creating meaningful representations. The meaning of those representations is not undermined by the coexistence of mutually contradictory metaphors in the same language system.

Contradiction seems, on the contrary, to play an important role in structuring metaphorical forms and patterns. Each conceptual metaphor can be treated as a fixed point which permits negation. Often, traditional metaphors are quoted only to be debunked. The ring metaphor in Czech was used ironically to contrast modern relationships with traditional and historical conceptions of engagement and marital union. Setting up the past as a contrast to the present is a habitual process in conceptual representation. As Laurie Taylor, the contemporary sociologist, argued in his discussion with Pat Thane on her work on the history of the myth of the 'happy family' and government policy generated around this myth (*Thinking Allowed*, Radio Four, 1 November 2010, www.bbc. uk/programmes), the idea of a golden age of harmony in love and relationships is regularly invoked, but rarely borne out by research. Contemporary publications do, nevertheless, hark back to a period of stability in the boom years of the three decades following the Second World War, and research does seem to confirm this general trend when it comes to stability in marriage and relationships with children.

A whole field of metaphors has emerged in all three languages to explore and explain lack of love and desire in terms of the negation of Love-as-Heat.

Coldness, frigidity and cooling down are concepts common to all three languages in the field of love. Interestingly, it is by closing down a conceptual
metaphor that new meaningful possibilities are opened up through 'analogical
negation'. Instead of being offered a warm bosom we might be given 'the
cold shoulder'. The fire of passion can 'die down', though the 'embers' can
be 'rekindled'. Similarly, the desire for love, which in both French and Czech
is often expressed in terms of taste, can be negated, at which point the rich
conceptual resources used to express taste can be harnessed to help conceive
of repulsion in terms of disgust for food (*dégoût* in French, *nechut'* in Czech).
The English word 'disgust' does, etymologically speaking, derive from the
Old French (*desgoust*) and some of the links between desire and taste have
been preserved in such English expressions as 'gustable' and 'gustation', but
these are rare words and, generally speaking, the link has not been preserved
in the common imagination. What Wilhelm von Humboldt described as the
'euphony' of language (the meaningful resonance of morphological patterns
which allow the sense of one word to echo within another and reverberate in
harmony or disharmony with it) is often lost as individual words enter a new
language leaving behind their belongings, as it were, when they take the trip.

Desire, *désir* and *touha*

Desire

It would take us far beyond the study of love to investigate fully the symbolic
representation of 'desire' in all three languages. Nevertheless, it will be useful to outline the contours of this concept in the two other languages and the
coordinates at which their spheres coincide with our concept of 'love'. This
will then enable us to demonstrate the way language allows understanding to
generate concepts with which to deal with and act upon situations in real life.
How did the outlines of 'desire' emerge in our corpus of texts, then?

In English, desire can be conceived of in terms of an explosive force, a fire
(which can 'fizzle out'). It can be expressed as electricity. Desire can therefore
be 'turned on' or 'off'. Desire, like love, can be expressed as heat. It can also
be expressed as pressure. It can, consequently, 'peak' or 'spike'. In our corpus,
desire (rather than love) was conceived of in terms of taste, and this gave rise to
various metaphors of 'spicy food' and 'appetising dishes'. Desire also took the
form of a paralysing force. The object of a desire would paralyse the beholder:
the object of desire was 'stunning'. Desire was also a 'drive': and it could be
measured on a vertical scale. Both men and women spoke of desire in both sexes
in terms of 'having a high or low sex drive'. There is an implicit reification in
this. Desire, the attraction between two living people, enthralled and confused
by the force that draws them together, is slotted into a neat pigeonhole: desire

becomes a thing you have, a possession. You can therefore have more or less desire. The disadvantage of this representation is that it cuts the other and the relationship you have with him or her out of the equation. Your desire depends on your own quota of self-motivated and self-motivating energy. The sex drive paradigm also opens up the configuration of desire as a path. This allows perversions to be conceived of in terms of 'diversions' (though the 'normal trajectory' from which perversions deviate was not made explicit when this metaphor was used in our corpus). Desire was also, like love, conceived of in terms of the metaphor of the unity of two matching parts. This metaphor was negated in one text, however, in which the author spoke of 'mismatched libidos'.

Fantasy, voyeurism and appetite for sex gave rise to some curious metaphors in English. The most predictable one (and the one which was found in all three languages) was the concept of love of sex as 'addiction'. In the late 1970s, the punk band The Buzzcocks were singing of the 'orgasm addict'. This seems to be a common idea which takes various forms in the three languages. Addiction to sex, love and men was a commonplace form of representation in our corpus. And in the English articles, a man was at one point referred to as 'a quick-fix lover', someone (or something) who (or which) could relieve the suffering of a drug-hungry addict.

Elsewhere, men were regarded as consumer items. Women who perused such items without seriously wishing to get involved with the men physically, described their own behaviour as 'window shopping'. The visual nature of fantasy was very important in metaphors used to describe desire. Fantasies were, in one English article, described as a film 'unspooling' in the mind. This is a curiously apt metaphor in that it captures the paradoxical involvement of voyeurism. The voyeur is at once absorbed in desire while standing outside of or aloof from the sexual act. It also serves to emphasize that though films, like all fiction, pretend to show real experience, real experience itself tends to be increasingly perceived and experienced in terms of film and fiction. The culture industry shapes the imagination to some extent.

Perhaps the most curious English metaphor for desire was a tactile one. Being desired was conceived of as stroking. Flattery as stroking is a common metaphor which has been used in the field of behavioural psychology for the past couple of generations at least. In the example in question, being desired was described as an experience which strokes the ego. This tactile metaphor was then, however, brutally brought back to earth or *regrounded*. The author pointed out that those men whose desire for a woman strokes her ego are not necessarily those she would choose to stroke her clitoris.

Désir

If it might be fair to say that desire, like love, has a rich and varied symbolic patterning in English, the complexity and innovation of French metaphors for *désir* were no less rich. In French, desire or desires were at times personified: desires could speak to you. Desire in French, as in English, could rise (*monter*) and fall (*descendre*). The rich culinary metaphors used to describe desire in terms of taste have already been mentioned. Since sex is conceived of in terms of 'food', a woman can observe a man 'greedily' (*avec gourmandise*). As in both English and Czech, sex-food can be 'spicy' in French (*piquant*). A man can also be 'tasty' or, more literally translated, 'lickable' (*alléchant*). The appetite of desire can, however, at times mistake the food it requires. In one French horoscope, those of the Cancer star sign were warned against 'feeding upon phantoms'. Given the supposedly nostalgic, melodramatic nature of those belonging to the Cancer sign, it was to be gathered from the article that indulging in sweet and sour reminiscing on past lovers was a pastime to which Cancers were often prone.

Desire in French was conceived of in terms of thirst. Desiring someone was also described in terms of 'breaking up' or 'falling to pieces' (*craquer*) for the object of desire. In an apparently contradictory representation, desire in French could also be conceived of as a building, a construction to be built (*à construire*). This conception seems strange to the English and Czech imaginations. More familiar to them is the idea of desire as a spark (*étincelle* in French), a metaphor which has already been discussed in the representation of love.

If the metaphor of Desire-as-Construction seems curious, far more shocking is the conceptualisation of desire as an electrical appliance. True, in expressions like 'turn on' and 'turn off', something similar has become a routine representation in English. But the idea of phantasms functioning like an 'appliance for recharging one's libido' (*rechargeur du libido*) will probably appear somewhat grotesque when translated into English. Mechanistic metaphors seem to have entered all levels of love and sexuality in both English and French. In Czech they do not yet seem to have taken such a firm hold of the imagination.

In one French article, desire was defined as an unconscious process of scrutiny. The desiring eye was 'an X-ray eye' (*œil radiographique*). In a more traditional metaphor, the same process of scrutiny was described as 'sifting' (*passer à crible*). In a more contemporary metaphor (which betrays the way the professional woman's imagination is shaped by her everyday environment) scrutinising men, objects of desire, was described as 'ticking off a checklist' (*valider une checklist*). As is commonly the case, work metaphors for sex in French often take the form of borrowed terms, anglicisms (*sex warrior*, *hard*, from 'hard core' and hence *hardeur*, a porn star). This does not, however, necessarily imply that the metaphors themselves are derived from English. The rich network of work-related metaphors in French seems, on the whole, to be the work of the French imagination. Because of the association between sex and American films in the French imagination, and because of the association of work in French society with globalisation (and thus with English), it seems natural to the French to forge innovative metaphorical links between desire, sex or work based upon the English words they have come to learn from these fields of experience.

In a slightly more romantic vein, desire in the French texts was conceived of in terms of 'being on a cloud' (*être sur une nuage*). It was also described in terms of a fever (*fièvre*). The English song by the same name testifies to the presence of this metaphor in English. More common in French than in English is the idea of desire as drunkenness. In one article, a woman described herself as being 'drunk on carnal pleasure' (*enivrée de plaisir charnel*). Sharing desire was described in terms of a flower, in French. The word used (a key word in French) was *épanouissement* (blossoming).

The transformation of our conception of love and sexuality into an increasingly mechanistic, inhuman conception can be seen in the conception of the body as a machine with parts which 'work' or do not 'work'. 'Function' (*fonction, funkce*) is a word used in all three languages to discuss desire and the sexual act. This requires the reduction of love and desire to an unthinking, unfeeling process whose success should, if the metaphoric framework has any real expressive potential, resemble the smooth running of a well-oiled machine. Though this may seem like a shallow and unconvincing framework for understanding desire, it is, nevertheless, one which has taken hold of the French imagination. Failure to become aroused is referred to in French as 'having a break down' (*avoir une panne*). One woman described her desire and potential for lust and satisfaction in terms of a spare part which could be screwed on. Unfortunately, for her, she lamented, she was not 'equipped for the orgasm' (*équipée pour l'orgasme*).

Though commerce and money are associated with Anglo-American culture in the French imagination, commercial and money metaphors are not rare in the representation of love and desire in French. In one article, admiration for an object of desire was described in terms of 'investment'. Young women were warned not to 'over-invest' (*surinvestir*).

Touha

With the exception of a few remarkable metaphors, the Czech imagination appears to follow similar courses to those mapped out by desire metaphors in English and French in constructing its own concept of desire, *touha*. Desire can be hungry, and this entails a whole host of culinary metaphors employed to distinguish between the various tastes of desire. One would-be connoisseur, a 24-year-old by the name of Štěpán, described good sex as something like good food, all of which is good in the right proportion, whether it be 'refined', 'delicate' or 'piquant' (*ostrý*, *Katka*, 27 August–2 September 2003). Since desire is associated with heat in Czech, frigidity (*frigidita*) represents the absence of desire or the incapacity for it. This *dead metaphor* is activated or 'reanimated' in the more explicit expressions 'emotional coldness' and 'coldness of feeling' (*citový chlad*). Following the same logic, relationships themselves 'cool down' (*ochladnout*) once desire is lost. Interestingly, the dual parallelism between desire and heat, on the one hand, and frigidity and coldness, on the other, can be inverted. This was the case in one example in the Czech corpus: one woman, reminiscing upon an erotic adventure, was described as being 'aroused by the delightful chill of his fingers on her skin' (*Jeho dotky jí na kůži vykouzlí slastné mrazení*).

In Czech, desire was not so much expressed in terms of a drive (as in English) as in terms of a force. One Czech woman (using the Prague dialect, which lengthens the final 'ý' of adjectives to 'ej') described her desire for a man as 'irresistible' (*neodlatelnej*). Another woman found herself forced 'to fully surrender to her feelings' (*se uplně podát svým pocitům*). All of these metaphors participate in the same process of externalising the most intimate of emotions and transforming it into the master to a slavish self who must obey it. The 'I' of the will is drowned or overcome by an unquestionable (or at least unquestioned) force.

Because desire is difficult to control and tends to follow its own course irrespective of the will or self-control, society censures practices which excite desire inordinately. In the interests of decorum, forms of behaviour and dress which are considered provocative are often criticized. This was the case in one article concerning a controversy which had sprung up over the right of high-school girls to expose their midriffs and belly buttons at school. The girls predictably defended their right to self-expression. Those who wished to censure this practice argued that 'sexy clothes give another direction to the thoughts' of the girls' teachers. Desire, it would seem, is represented as moving (if not driving) the thoughts of the teachers in this example.

Desire can be measured in Czech on a vertical scale. For this reason, desire can be said 'to fall' or 'to decrease' (*poklesat*). Passion was also considered in terms of 'a possession'. Consequently, it could be 'lost' (*touha si vytrátí*).

The rhetoric of love and desire

Our study allows us to make a contribution to discourse analysis, in enumerating a number of curious discourse strategies, which can be defined as follows.

Reification

Reification was common throughout the three corpora. Men were frequently considered as objects. In the French corpus in particular, men were something 'you should try out' (*essayer*). In one English article, the author described a certain type of woman by saying she was a whole woman in her own right who did not need a man to complete her: the man was denigrated in this example and referred to (somewhat grotesquely) as 'a boyfriend bolt-on' accessory (*Cosmopolitan*, November 2007). Interestingly, it was men not women who condemned the objectification of women, as in the criticism of 'monkey-like love' which made some men search elsewhere for 'what' they do not get in one place. Women expressed ambivalence about objectification when it came to themselves. In one French article (*Glamour*, November 2005), a 30-year-old woman was described by the analyst Dr Sylvain Mimoun as undergoing a testing period in her relationship in which she was assuring herself that she was not being considered '(solely) as an object'. But in the same article, a 28-year-old woman described as 'orgasmic' the dirty talk and insults that she said could 'excite me by reducing me to the status of a woman-object' (*femme-objet*). Elsewhere implicit reification went largely uncensored: the body, desire, the sexual act and relationships can all be expressed in terms of machines which function and can break down. Sex (in French) can be compared to the 'fuel' (*carburant*) of a relationship.

Personification

Personification was as common as reification if not more so in the three corpora. As we have seen, in French, a love story can be kicked out of the door like an unwanted guest. DNA can take over and direct the course of behaviour.

Personified reification

Once people or relationships have been sufficiently reified by the imagination and reclassified as inhuman objects of experience (as, for example, when men are considered as experiences to be tried out), then discourse can personify its own objectifications. This seems complicated, and is indeed contradictory, but it is, nevertheless, a fairly commonplace procedure. We have already discussed one example in which one young French woman claimed 'Me and love stories were not made to get along'. Elsewhere, in the French corpus, women, apparently insensitive to the words and feelings of real living men, listened to their own desires who 'spoke' to them.

Regrounded metaphors

The metaphors used to express love and desire frequently made explicit the implicit symbolic frameworks of the concepts we think and feel with. The sensual nature of ego-stroking was exposed when juxtaposed with stroking the clitoris in the English corpus. Another English article (*Glamour*, June 2007), played with puns such as the 'ins and outs … of our latest encounters'. This process of revealing the concrete physical nature of abstract language can be termed 'regrounding'. In one French example, a man used a new fascination with fishing to hide an affair. The author concluded that in marriage 'a grouper can hide a cod'. Once translated, this phrase is, of course, meaningless. Only once it is explained that the word for 'cod' in French (*morue*) is used metaphorically to mean 'whore' does the meaning of the expression '*un mérou peut cacher une morue*' become clear (*Cosmopolitan*, September 2002). The metaphor brings us back with a bang to the fishmonger.

Blends

Blends were common in all three languages. These blends can be divided into three noteworthy forms.

1. Some blends take the form of logical extensions. In one French article, for example (*Cosmopolitan*, May 2007), 'to succeed in a love story' (*réussir une histoire*), a psychologist argued it is necessary 'to know your own worth' (*reconnaître sa propre valeur*). This is because, according to him, in love 'it is necessary to give yourself'. Self-esteem, symbolically represented as the evaluation of one's own 'worth' is here juxtaposed with another metaphor, *loving is giving yourself*. Self-esteem and self-offering combine in this narrative of love stories.
2. Other blends are somewhat more original. They juxtapose unrelated spheres of experience. In one French article, sex, alcoholic drinks and explosions were all linked up into one original metaphor. The metaphor in question, 'an explosive erotic cocktail', was used to describe the excitement of sexual intercourse in the bathroom during a party, which one woman was reported to have described as being particularly exciting due to the combination of 'the expression of his desire, the strangeness of the thing, and the fear of being caught' (*Cosmopolitan*, May 2007). The aptness of this metaphor hinges not only on comparing the combination of experiences to a cocktail but also on the association of sex with alcohol, and passion with an explosion. The fact that cocktails themselves are frequently described in terms of explosives, helps attenuate the incompatibility between drinking and combustion. In another original blend, promiscuous women who were 'up for it' were said to be 'hot to trot' (*Elle*, November 2005), a blend which transforms women into horses, sexual hunting into trotting (i.e. picking up the pace) and sexual readiness into heat.
3. Many blends do not bear close scrutiny.
   • Some might be described as mixed metaphors. Describing infidelity in French as a 'lightning quiver' (*vacillement éclair*), for example, seems

more like a slip of the pen than an intentional juxtaposition of different sensory spheres (sight and kinaesthetics).

- Other blends result simply from the fact that much of our language is already symbolic without our being conscious of it. Unless an intentional effort is made to draw our attention to the underlying symbolic nature of speech, we are not usually bothered by the juxtaposition of incompatible symbolic frameworks. For example, in criticising the obsession of young girls with their weight, one Czech psychologist claimed such girls did not know how to value the gift God had given them. The gift was their body. But the word used to mean 'to value' in colloquial Czech is 'to weigh' (*vážit*). Weighing the body, was, of course, literally speaking, what the author was criticising in obsessive dieters. Unless analysed, such juxtapositions are rarely noticed, and can in no way be considered to be bothersome. On the contrary, the rhetorical process of 'regrounding', by attracting our attention to the fundamental symbolism of language, highlights the fact that we are capable of awakening the attention to unconsciously integrated patterns of thought and feeling. What regrounding does as a conscious procedure, mixed metaphor does inadvertently. Both strategies introduce blends. The former awakens language with the work of the mind, the latter dulls the spirit with murky and muddled expressions.

Countering metaphors

Since Lakoff and Johnson published their *Metaphors We Live By*, there has been an ongoing trend to attribute to metaphors an influence upon thought and behaviour. Lakoff himself has always tried to make us more conscious of the metaphors we live by in order to help us avoid being manipulated by the conceptual frameworks with which everyday speech invites us to think. This implies a flexibility of thought. Nevertheless, there is an underlying supposition throughout the work of Lakoff and Johnson that we need those two thinkers to awaken us to our own metaphorical frameworks.

Philip Eubanks, in his book-length study of 'Trade-is-War' (2000), found that the reality of the way we deal with conceptual metaphors in everyday life is considerably more complicated. Though metaphors do tend to represent certain perspectives, Eubanks found that intelligent people tend to position themselves in relationship to metaphors as they would in terms of fixed positions. Some endorse them, others negate them. But we can also adopt metaphors ironically. We can ridicule them. Or we can modify them. All of these practices formed part of what Eubanks termed our 'discursive strategy', by which he meant the way we choose to use conceptual metaphors for our own ends. One noteworthy form of discursive strategy involved inventing what Eubanks called 'counter metaphors'.

In examining the material of our corpus of English, French and Czech articles, it is Eubanks' more refined position that turns out to be more useful in describing the host of manners by which rhetoric can be consciously and semi-consciously harnessed to advance one's arguments, defend one's own opinions and perspectives, and describe one's own experiences. This starting point allows us to propose the following classification of rhetorical strategies, some of the names of which have been coined to provide labels for the processes identified thanks to this corpus.

Irony

As the articles are, by definition, intended as light entertainment, humour was often central, and the metaphors that came up were often used ironically. Strangely, it was the traditional metaphors of eternal love, fairytale love full of princes and princesses and so on that were subject to the greatest ridicule. This was especially true of the French corpus which oscillated between romance and hard realism, investing equal energy in developing each of these metaphoric fields. There is nothing particularly surprising about this lack of constancy. Irony does not tend to provide alternatives, but rather undermines concepts without offering replacements.

Negated metaphors

In contrast to irony, negation involves taking a clearly defined position in relation to what is negated. Negated metaphors are parasitic, because they depend upon existing metaphors. The common targets for negation were romantic ideas about love, selfish expectations of relationships and traditional representations of women. One woman negated the traditional conceptual metaphor of love being the centre of a woman's life using the following terms: 'I *love* men. But I don't want men to be the centre of my life. I multidate and enjoy seeing how things develop' (*Elle*, November 2005). This woman belonged to a new breed of women we have already encountered, the DCDs (Don't Care Daters), who manage to slot numerous casual dates into their tight schedules but who prefer FWBs (Friends with Benefits) and quick-fix lovers who will compliantly provide the sexual services ('action') they require without making emotional demands. Throughout the rhetoric used, 'no', 'not' and 'don't' are crucial to the worldview of the DCD and the negatively defined philosophy her lifestyle implies. Her ideal is 'no-strings sex', the author of the article would have us believe. And she not infrequently takes up this form of promiscuity, we are told, after a failed or dissatisfying long-term relationship.

Counter metaphors

Counter metaphors can be original proposals intended to open up new modes of conception. Frequently, however, they take the form of reminders. Since metaphors (as Lakoff and Johnson insist) highlight and hide aspects of a concept, counter metaphors can serve to highlight exactly what one metaphor hides by contrasting it to another form of representation. The function of the counter metaphor is not necessarily to debunk the existing metaphor but simply to awaken us to other aspects of experience. To say that love is not about collecting love stories but about a girl offering herself as a precious gift aware of her own value, is to offer a counter metaphor. Often contradictory metaphors will be used by the same person in describing his or her love life. Rather than constituting a carefully composed coherent whole, these contradictions, though ultimately unresolved, allow us to glimpse multiple facets of one complex composite experience. The worldview represented constitutes a mass of fragmented perspectives, just as experience, for many of us, remains a complex and paradoxical series of ambivalent reactions to the world.

Mirror metaphors

Mirror metaphors work by setting in motion the logic of existing metaphoric frameworks, but by setting them in reverse. This forms part of a fundamental process in language. Heat and coldness are set up as opposites, as we saw, and we can exploit the explorative and innovative frameworks of the one, by setting up a contrasting network of frameworks in the other. Desire can heat up and cool down. There is nothing intrinsically perverse about the logic of mirror metaphors. However, perversion is particularly well served by mirror metaphors, because they allow us to twist and invert traditional forms of representation. In one English article (*Elle*, November 2005), Valérie Tasso, the French author of an autobiographical book about her own 'sexual marathon', a project to sleep with 10,000 men, makes much of her capacity to invert traditional roles. In order to denounce the idea of demure passive female sexuality, Tasso claims she is 'proud about her desires, and hers is a decidedly male take on sexuality. She is assertive, delighting in the thrill of the chase and the sheer physical pleasure of no-strings sex'. It will be clear that Tasso takes her erotic and emotional bearings from what she understands to be typical or traditional male stereotypes. But she takes inversion to extremes by metaphorically reinterpreting other fields of sexuality: prostitution, for example, becomes for Tasso, not the humiliating, debasing experience of 'sexual enslavement' but rather 'a way of liberating herself'. Her justification of her behaviour depends upon maintaining the archetypes of masculine sexual behaviour (predatory in nature) and usurping those archetypes for herself. As a consequence, it will be impossible to understand what Tasso claims is the 'logical step' of going into prostitution as a means of exploring her experiment by maintaining 'a perfect balance' (two clients in the morning, two in the afternoon), unless we bear in mind that Tasso gets a kick out of refuting and inverting stereotypes. Tasso's logic is always that of inversion. She discovered more dignity in prostitution than in an unhappy relationship: 'I felt more used and violated when I was in love with Jaime and he was treating me badly. Prostitution never made me feel like that', she tells readers. Though we might not all be convinced by Tasso's rhetoric, her improvisations are noteworthy, because they provide evidence that conventional conceptual metaphors set up, not mental and emotional constraints, but rather configurations, patterns which we can reshape to represent our own experiences and perspectives. Inversion is simply one such strategy.

Paradoxical metaphors

Tasso's story offered a further example of the way conceptual metaphors can be harnessed, namely in the form of what I will call the 'paradoxical metaphor'. In the paradoxical metaphor, two opposite terms are harnessed to describe the same idea. Though it may seem unlikely, at the end of Tasso's story, she claimed she had found true love (the happy end all books require). It was Giovanni, her new boyfriend, however, who claimed to have been celibate up to the time of his meeting with Tasso who drew the paradoxical parallel: 'I behaved the same way as you but in the opposite way: I stopped having sex to discover myself, whereas you used it to discover yourself, but the process was the same' (*ibid.*). Self-discovery is thus represented in the form of both the promiscuity of the sexual marathon and the celibacy of Giovanni. Indeed, these two extremes do meet in the shared logic that motivates the self-centred individual who seeks to realize his own personal destiny in his associations with others and who attributes to his concept of love the ultimate form of self-realisation.

Foregrounding

Throughout his work, the Czech poetician Jan Mukařovský considered the way certain aspects of the text draw attention to themselves, forcing themselves into the foreground while leaving other aspects in the background. What he called *aktualizace* in Czech has come to be known, since the seventies, among English-speaking linguists as 'foregrounding'. For Mukařovský, metaphors constitute foregrounded elements of the structural activity of the text, points of focus. But it becomes clear in our corpus that metaphors themselves are often foregrounded, highlighted to redouble the rhetorical effect. That is to say, different strategies are used to highlight the metaphors used. Rhyme was commonplace, especially in English. We have already noted one example above:

sexually aroused women were said to be '**hot** to **trot**'. In another example, the singer in a girl band scorned her colleague as 'a **chick** with a **dick**'. Insults – invariably of the most traditional kind – were used exclusively by women for women in our corpus. The men quoted in magazines in English, French and Czech were almost all polite, tender, sensitive and considerate in their dealings with and their descriptions of women.

Alliteration (such as '**m**attress **m**oves' for sexual techniques) was commonplace. We have already quoted one French example above (the grouper that hides the cod: *mérou/morue*). The repetition of the *m/r* is made all the more efficient since it links up two kinds of fish. The meaning of one folds into the other. The tension of one being used literally, and the other metaphorically, is further heightened by the sonorous equation. The Czech corpus also provided some examples of metaphors foregrounded by alliteration. One article which ironically provided the lessons of how to destroy a relationship, bore the title **D***struktivní* **D***esatero* (The Destructive Ten Commandments). A traditional metaphorical expression which was often ironized or negated was also foregrounded with alliteration *křehká květinka* (fragile little flower). Examples of alliteration were, however, rare in the Czech corpus. And though Czech as a language offers far greater potential for rhyming, rhymes also proved rare in the corpus.

Conclusions

This multilingual ethnolinguistic study has allowed us to break out of the limits of the mode of conceptualising love and desire that English opens up to the imagination. The advantage of using a corpus over studying isolated expressions as Kövëcses and Lakoff tend to do, is that it plunges us into a level of complexity which is scarcely possible to imagine. Our corpus has forced us to interpret complex rhetorical processes such as 'personified reification' and analyse ironic strategies used to debunk and redefine metaphors in relation to conventionally accepted paradigms. The advantage of a tripartite study is that it prevents us from opposing one language to another and thereby exaggerating the significance of contrasts. The corpus also reminds us that all conceptions are developing constructs, and that, as discourse strategies oppose one another and joust for dominance, the concepts of love and desire in English, French and Czech undergo change.

To a large extent, traditional metaphoric paradigms tend to overlap and, curiously enough, emerging trends tend to overlap also. The tendency to employ mechanistic metaphors for love and desire seems to be taking hold of the feminine imagination more and more (particularly in French and English). Czech seems to be resisting the reduction of men to objects to some extent, a conception increasingly prevalent and indeed almost inescapable in French and

English. Other contrasts were also observed: the down-to-earth vulgarity of English discourse on love (and sexual intercourse in particular) was unrivalled by the other languages. And this bears witness to the celebration of bestial sexuality (the necessary counterpart of English etiquette) which has been increasingly colonized by would-be feminists of the third generation who seek to outdo their drunken male counterparts by rejoicing in what they call 'ladette' culture. One aspect of this culture involves making use of men as sexual toys, sources of amusement for young women.

French texts tended to spend much more time exploring the experience of infidelity and the upsetting effects it has on the self-image and the structure of the personality. The contrast between the self-seeking woman who uses men and the woman who depends upon the love and fidelity of her lover for her own sense of well-being was often underlined in the French texts. In the English text, the French woman, Tasso, incarnates both sides of this complicated feminine psychology.

Only in Czech texts was the link between love and procreation preserved. Children and pregnancy were banished from the discussions of love and sex in the French and English texts, which tended to promote sexual activity not only as a carnal end in itself but also as a consumer item, a possession which was vital for the self-image of the desirable young woman. No self-respecting young woman could hope to become the envy of her friends and the ideal of such magazines without this new consumer item, the modern man.

In all three languages, the texts of our corpus tended to focus upon no other ideal feminine role model than the desirable and professionally successful young woman. Despite all the rhetoric that served to dress up this ideal, the paltriness and shoddiness of this ideal could not be hidden: the articles tended to focus upon the self-centred 'little me', the dissatisfied man-eater, the jilted lover, the sexually frustrated career woman or the confused woman torn between boyfriend and lover. For all the celebration of love, and all the pages of analysis and investigation, love, the encounter of two people, was rarely considered in any detail: and only when the self-seeking individual found herself abandoned or disappointed were the reasons for her failure to enter into and maintain a loving relationship discussed. Strangely, though love and sex were central to the magazines in the three languages, men themselves scarcely seemed to interest the authors and the women quoted. The articles studied tended to give quick formulas for success in given situations, notably in the art of seduction.

Predictably, the authors of articles flattered the egos of their readers without questioning the legitimacy of their desires. Rather, they encouraged their readers to seek their own satisfaction irrespective of the desires and feelings of their lovers. The title of one Czech article typified the pandering to the reader's daydreams and desires that has become the hallmark of specialized magazines:

Můžete mít vschechno! (You can have it all!). 'All' seemed to imply, love, passion and fidelity from your partner. The Client-is-King rhetoric is all too obvious here. Love has become something you can pick up from the supermarket shelf, these magazines would seem to imply.

The short-sighted advice these magazines gave, advice which inflates selfishness, and encourages the logic which harnesses drives and desires and sends the solitary individual spiralling into its own self-centred soul, will doubtless fail to help anyone naive enough to take it. Could such advice be expected to help people to find happiness? This seems unlikely.

Nonetheless, it is clear that the authors of the articles were, for the most part, indifferent to love and to happiness. As any capitalist form of propaganda, the sole aim of such articles (despite the paraphernalia of specialist terms and interviews with psychologists) is to provide consumers with products which satisfy their desires. These articles tell readers what they want to hear. They are ultimately products, and all of their complex metaphorical and rhetorical strategies serve ultimately only to transform love, desire and sex into a product which can be marketed … and consumed.

5   Hate

The two ethnolinguistic studies we have considered so far have taken a resolutely comparative approach. Truth and love were traced as organising paradigms, metaphorically constructed and elaborated within different languages. The study of truth took a language-based approach, while the study of love sought to draw conclusions from the discourse of a trilingual corpus. This study of hate aims to elucidate some of the fundamental influences which have gone to construct and maintain our concept of 'hate'. Why has 'hate' been found to be a useful concept for so many languages? How does 'hate' allow alliances to form in the face of opposition? By investigating biblical concepts of hate, we should be able to ascertain ways in which our concept of hate has evolved, and ways in which the central discourse of the Bible has conditioned our conception of hating.

But ethnolinguists must not fall into the trap of believing that hate is a universal concept which functions in the same way in all languages. In order to remind ourselves of the language-specific, culture-specific nature of 'hating', three short studies will investigate the way this activity manifests itself in French and English. In French, two curious forms of animosity will be investigated. These will be juxtaposed with the hatred of communism as it manifested itself in the 'Evil Empire' discourse of Reagan, a political discourse which has continued to condition our conception long after the close of the Cold War.

The ethnolinguistic approach to hate will not be moralistic as religious accounts of hate often are. On the other hand, it will demonstrate that moralising strategies are implicit within the language system, and that discourse often harnesses metaphoric paradigms in order to promote oppositions and antipathies. In this sense, the ethnolinguistic approach should go some way to 'cleansing the mind' of 'small-minded' antipathies which are motivated for political reasons, and which tend to encrust in the worldview of a language, often outliving the ideologies which generated them.

Do we need hate?

In 1967, Lennon and McCartney were preaching 'All you need is love!' The song was broadcast by satellite on *Our World*, the first global television link, and was watched by 400 million people in twenty-six countries. Those two great songwriters were neither philosophers nor men of action, but in as much as their lyrics reflected and reinforced an essential truism of the Zeitgeist of their times, they are worth taking seriously. Lennon and McCartney's catchy song consolidated the denunciation of aggression by a generation who had not known Hitler, Mussolini or Stalin, or the threats they posed for the West. Like their fans, the songwriters were eager to turn their backs upon fear and suspicion, on aggression, violence and war. (Something largely similar was motivating the 'Yes We Can' sentiment that launched the first mixed-race president into power in the USA in 2008.) Above all, what Lennon and McCartney's generation of Westerners espoused (and what many of the young people of Eastern Europe were seduced by) was a post-Christian revival of *agapē*, brotherly love. And embracing all of our brothers and sisters throughout the world meant denouncing hate.

Hate was seen as a destructive force which not only brings about anarchy in the world, but also gnaws away at the hater's very soul. From such a point of view, hate is soul-destroying as much as it is world-destroying. The 'free love' that accompanied the celebration of love and the hatred of hate was of a quintessentially modern, urban, individualist nature: but it did resemble, in certain important respects, many of the revolts against the sexual and marital constraints imposed by the Catholic Church throughout the Middle Ages. From the eleventh to the fourteenth century, the Cathars of South Western France[1] combined a critique of marriage with an unprecedented respect for women and sexual egalitarianism. Love and simplicity were their founding principles. They were, predictably, brutally suppressed by the Catholic Church. The Beghards of Cologne celebrated masses naked in the fourteenth century and the Brethren of the Free Spirit, to whom they were related, preached and practised free love. Inevitably, Pope Clement V condemned them as heretics in the Council of Vienne (1311).[2] The Church was faced with similar social and sexual revolts in Lombardy in the fourteenth century and in fifteenth-century Bohemia with the Hussite movement led by the great military commander Jan Žižka. The Catholic Church is founded upon love, but this entails organising it and monopolising it: legitimising and curtailing the forms of love allowed becomes a question of policy. In political terms, the Church's promotion of love involves hating heretical forms of unsanctioned love.

It is hard not to be moved by the wilful naivety which brings people together, generates trust and closeness, and rejects resentment, hatred, suspicion and prejudice. Religion, society, the class system, work and family life all set up and impose fairly rigid social and sexual divisions and categorisations. Such forms of organisation set people in opposition to one another. And our hierarchies often seem to have little to do with us or with providing us all with a comfortable place in our worlds and engendering harmonious relations between people. Can't such constraints be simply cast aside? Can't we simply turn our backs upon hate?

The great men of history would seem to be sceptical. Those that transform society and history would appear to have an entirely different relationship to hate. On 22 September 1797, in his proclamation at his General Headquarters, Passariano, Napoléon Bonaparte declared:

La haine des traîtres, des tyrans et des esclaves sera dans l'histoire notre plus beau titre à la gloire et à l'immortalité.

The hatred of traitors, tyrants and slaves will be our crowning glory in history and in immortality. (Oster 1993: 91)

Hate would define the revolution and transform society. The destruction of the Old Order (*l'ancien régime*) was a *sine qua non* condition for founding a new and better world. And a new and better 'world' was certainly on the agenda; Napoléon, the Corsican, saw beyond the frontiers of France and had set his sights on the domination of Europe and on spreading the founding principles of the revolution throughout the world. The French revolution was soon to be transformed into a 'universal' project.

Curiously, the French revolutionaries shared with the hippies a quasi-religious belief that we are all 'brothers'. But in Napoléon's version of that universal bond, there was, from the outset, a clear desire to divide men up and to assign them a rank. Military and nationalistic concerns were never deeply hidden below the discourse of *fraternité*. Subjugating foreign peoples to French rule, Napoléon was willing to welcome certain members into the select circle of what might be called, to use an oxymoron, the 'universal French brotherhood'. Indeed, in Milan on 24 May 1796, Napoléon told the astronomer Oriani: 'All men of genius, all those who have obtained a distinguished rank within the Republic of Letters, are French, no matter what country they are born in.' (*Tous les hommes de génie, tous ceux qui ont obtenu un rang distingué dans la république des lettres, sont Français, quel que soit le pays qui les a vu naître*) (Oster 1993: 91).

Napoléon was attributing an entirely new meaning to the idea of being 'French', but in one respect, his concept ties in with a long-standing French tradition of cultural absorption. The expansion of the Francs, as a people, had begun after the final great battle that opposed Attila the Hun and Flavius Aetius and his Gallo-Roman army in Gaul in 451.The battle which opposed Romans and 'barbarians' ended uncertainly. Interestingly, the Francs had been serving on both sides. Both armies were largely composed of various Germanic tribes. As both Rome and the Huns had been militarily, politically and economically weakened by the confrontation, the Germanic Francs began to take a firmer hold upon Gaul. The conquest of what is now northern France and of Marseilles to the south-east and Bordeaux and Gascogne to the south-west was to take almost a thousand years, but finally all of France was assimilated into the expansionist project, a project which had been orchestrated long before the revolution from the centralized power in Versailles and Paris. In this light, Napoléon's attempt to make the world 'French', although a great step, was, nonetheless, a logical step, a consequence of subjecting the world to the French (Frankish, *français*) worldview. For revolutionaries and for warrior-statesmen such as Napoléon, the world could and should become 'French'. France was the future. France would bring *les droits de l'Homme* to all men. France would be the liberator.

This revolutionary project did, of course, entail the destruction of ancient cultural institutions, the suppression of a class and, inevitably, the death of countless thousands of people. Victor Hugo, writing a couple of generations later, saw clearly that love and liberty had brought about suffering and hatred and had engendered oppression:

> *Flux et reflux. La souffrance et la haine sont sœurs,*
> *Les opprimés refont plus tard des oppresseurs.*

> Flux and reflux. Suffering and Hatred are sisters.
> The oppressed will later become the oppressors.
> > *À ceux qu'on foule aux pieds*
> > (Oster 1993: 263)

At any rate, Hugo clearly understood the nature of men like Napoléon. What the author said about some men in *Les Misérables* (I:iv:3, *ibid.*: 257) is certainly true in Napoléon's case: '*Certains natures ne peuvent aimer d'un côté sans hair de l'autre*' (Certain natures cannot love, on the one hand, without, on the other hand, hating). Hugo was interested in making a statement about a certain human type, a personality which had universal meaning. And his reflection of hate must be understood in this light.

It would, however, be a mistake to lift men out of their socio-historical contexts and to assume that Napoléon would have been the same man whatever era he inhabited. Such a naive account tends to people history with conquerors and kings, inventors and innovators, individuals who act as catalysts to change, without encouraging us to seek to understand the economic, social and religious forces driving change and cultivating the individuals who will contribute to bringing about change. Napoléon became Napoléon thanks to the French Revolution and thanks to the dynamic potential which *le peuple* gave rise to as an active force for social transformation. The great Prussian military philosopher Clausewitz (1780–1831) saw all too clearly that with the French Revolution, neither society nor warfare between nations would ever be the same again. The concept of a 'people's war', and of wars between peoples, radically changed the power struggle in Europe from a series of dynastic conflicts to the confrontation of ideologies and visions of the world. In such conflicts, labourers and artisans were no longer the hired hands used to impose the will of princes and kings. The soldiers of Napoléon believed they were fighting for themselves, fighting for French universal ideals, fighting for the future. Without wishing to overstate the idealism of the period, it must be admitted (as Clausewitz found himself forced to admit) that no nation could hope to compete against France unless it harnessed the people. France had introduced a universal element to warfare. Wars would henceforth be 'total wars', wars which would be represented, not as struggles over resources and territories, but as conflicts between Good and Evil. With the advent of the French Revolution, we move into the era of ideological warfare, wars which would be fought much in the same spirit as the wars of religion. Love and hate would structure and define those conflicts. And each individual, from the foot soldier of the First World War (Hitler, for example), to generals such as Napoléon, would define himself within that opposition between love and hate. Love and hate motivated the souls of the foot soldier and the general as they went into battle. Love and hate gave a vocation and a role to such men. They allowed men to act: and, in acting, those men defined themselves as social and historical actors.

Defining hate

Revolutionaries from Lenin to Castro, generals from Napoléon to Trotsky, and statesmen from Churchill to Charles de Gaulle have all defined themselves in terms of hate. Their hatred for the forces they opposed defined them and gave them the courage and conviction to struggle against opposition. It would be unfair to equate such men with Hitler. But Hitler too was defined by hate. From *Mein Kampf* onwards, all political struggle was conceived of by Hitler in terms of a violent struggle against what he hated. The desire to destroy is manifest in his speeches and his writings. His overflowing hatred envenomed the idealism of the Germanic people, however, because, though he did sincerely seek to transform the Germans into a noble race of warriors, the 'shining glory' of that ideal was never brandished without hatred. Hatred was the perverse counterpart of the love of the *Vaterland*. And indeed it was hatred more than love that defined the Germans in Hitler's cultural mindset. The Germans were always negatively defined, set up in contrast to what he perceived as the decadent Jews, the people who had corrupted society with their capitalism and weakened the purity of the Aryan race with their sickly blood and their insipid intellectual ideas, their communist philosophy and their soulless, 'nationless' wandering (see Klemperer's critique of *Hitlerdeutsch* in Klemperer 2000).

The Jews became the central concept of the Nazi *Weltanschauung*, Hitler's worldview. To put it in Hugo's terms, Hitler could not love without hating. And his hatred had two perverse effects. It emptied German idealism of all content.

And it transformed the object of his hate into precisely that, an 'object', a dehumanized entity which must be eradicated from the planet in order to preserve all that it corrupted. The Jews were a 'disease', the 'plague' come from the Middle Ages to menace Mittel-Europa. Himmler (Pois 1986) calmly preached to those who had qualms about the fate of their Jewish neighbours that, contrary to their pleas, there were no 'good Jews'. Such feelings of pity, he argued, showed a febrile moral failing, an incapacity to harden up to the facts of life. All Jews shared the same essential 'jewishness', an irretrievable decadence, and they must, like lice, be stamped out, he asserted.[3]

Despite the moral fervour of their ideals, the writings of Churchill, Lenin, Trotsky and de Gaulle show nothing of this all-perverting hate. Their hates did not swallow them up in a fantasy world of tormented visions, as the hatred of the Nazis transformed their vision of the world. The Nazis rejected the world, and then sought to draw all of the world within the scope of their perverted 'world'. They sought to dominate what they did not understand. And the fury of their hatred can, to some extent, be attributed to their failure to understand the world and all those who opposed them. Like all children who find themselves at odds with the world, they felt themselves to be the victims of great injustices, and their violence was the expression of a desire to right the wrongs which they perceived themselves to be suffering from. The invasion of Russia was represented as a 'defensive war' against the menace of communism, 'the Red Terror' (*der Rot Terror*). And, by pursuing this delirium, this skewed reasoning, to its logical end, the whole Second World War was conceived as a 'Jewish war', a war forced upon the German people.

There is something of the spirit of Hitler in the neoconservative crusade. There is a paradoxical desire to flee from the world and to dominate it at the same time. The neoconservatives did not simply enlist fear as a tool of propaganda: like all demagogues, they became caught up in their own manipulative strategies. Throughout the first decade of the twenty-first century, they threw themselves into a frenzy of fear which subsequently appeared in their own eyes to justify the cynical ruthlessness with which they strove to stamp out all that they saw as a menace to them and their interests. If we understand the psychology of hate-inspired bad faith, we will find it easier to perceive the motivations behind the pressure put on the CIA to extract 'confessions' from tortured detainees regarding alleged links between Hussein's regime and terrorist forces, for example.

The influence of America's means of persuading others to support its interests waned with the loss of the justification of the Cold War. Despite the honeymoon period of triumphant capitalism following the end of the Cold War, increasing doubts concerning the International Monetary Fund, and the emergence of new global market players such as China, India and Brazil, made American world power even more precarious. And it was at this stage that the military was increasingly enlisted as a means of maintaining control over strategic markets and regions throughout the world. This, at least, is the analysis of David Harvey in his *New Imperialism* (2005). How else are we to understand the re-emergence of a militaristic display of strength with the new wars and occupations, after half a century of minor conflicts and diplomatic stand-offs?

Complex geopolitical and economic tensions create contradictory and paradoxical consequences, however. In the context of recent conflicts, it seems strange that an almost messianic figure such as Obama should emerge, preaching brotherly love, understanding and peace. In contrast to the obtuse affirmation of Bush that love and God and America are all fighting on the same side, the words and tone of Obama's approach proclaim him to be a man of both astute political acumen and spiritual conviction. What has happened to the defining hate that gave a vibrant vocation to statesmen such as Churchill, Hitler and Napoléon? Can Obama truly preach 'All we need is love' like Lennon and McCartney? Can he inject a New-Age religious dimension into the contemporary American worldview? Certainly, despite opposition and amidst much criticism, this charismatic leader would seem to have a gift for putting into practice a social and spiritual project that seeks to bind Americans more closely together and to give community a common purpose. And in contrast to Bush, who blindly made enemies of allies, Obama's election was welcomed throughout the world. His efforts in world diplomacy were soon to be rewarded with the Nobel Peace Prize, a curious turn in events, considering that Obama is the Commander-in Chief engaged in two wars.

At home, in the USA, his promotion of love, at the cost of hate, has taken on a very concrete legislative turn. On 28 October 2009 CNN reported that Obama had signed the 'Hate Crimes Bill' into law, a ruling which made it a federal crime to assault an individual because of his or her sexual orientation or gender identity. Understandably, the expanded federal Hate Crimes Law was hailed by supporters as the first major federal gay-rights legislation. Those who have been so often 'excluded', saw this as a gesture to 'include' them within American society. In Obama's worldview, the question which had to be answered had become: 'Do they belong?' Obama's answer was: 'Yes they do'. Can we accept gays? Yes we can.

Obama was making a stand against segregation and against bigotry. These two are the partners of civil strife, the enemies of social harmony. The gesture was part of a movement of the soul. Americans, Obama was urging, had to open up their hearts. Earlier the same month, Obama had told the Human Rights Campaign, the country's largest gay-rights group, that the nation still needed to make significant changes to ensure equal rights for gays and lesbians.

'Despite the progress we've made, there are still laws to change and hearts to open,' he said in an address at the group's annual dinner. 'This fight continues now and I'm here with the simple message: I'm here with you in that fight'.[4]

Obama's fight was one with many fronts and could not be restricted to gay liberation. True, the hate-crimes measure was meant as a tribute to Matthew Shepard, a gay Wyoming teenager who had died after being kidnapped and severely beaten in October 1998. But it was equally dedicated to the memory of James Byrd Jr., an African-American man beaten to death in Texas the same year. Obama's worldview is an expansive worldview. Obama is essentially and instinctively 'inclusive', and he is best suited to all-embracing brotherly love.

The main exponent of the Frankfurt School, Theodor Adorno, would have scorned the scope of Obama's focus, because expansive love dilates to take in more and more until it loses focus. In this way, the crucial political and social dimension of individual problems is watered down and washed away. Adorno disparaged the decision of Anne Frank's father to dedicate the memorial to her suffering to all of the victims of oppression. The vitriolic attack was characteristic of Adorno's passionate mode of philosophising, but he had put his finger on one important point. The human attention can only truly comprehend fragments. We only feel the fragment. When we enter into contact with reality, it is always through the encounter of particular people in particular circumstances. We can neither love nor understand humanity as a whole. The suffering of Jews was bound to a particular people at a particular period of history and by forgetting that, Anne Frank's father was, unwittingly, inviting others to forget the reality of one individual's suffering. The meaningful encounter which we can have by reading Anne Frank's diaries was watered down and washed away in a wave of well-meaning but universal goodwill. The problem is twofold: we lose sight of what we should and can remember, and we lose sight of what that memory should remind us of in the future. We can all adhere to a universal goodwill easily enough without having to take a stand in terms of people, institutions and ideologies. Ironically, universal love brings with it surprisingly few pressing immediate moral obligations.

Obama's conception of man and politics is certainly closer to that of Anne Frank's father, but it would be unfair to criticize him for losing himself in an unfocused universal goodwill and for lacking in pragmatism. Obama is endeavouring to transform the reality of American society. After all, the former president, George W. Bush, had threatened to veto a similar measure concerning anti-gay acts. Obama's stand reversed White House policy. He was tackling a social phenomenon. His law would provide a legal framework within which to judge a rampant form of antisocial behaviour. The Senate Judiciary Committee was told in June 2009 that the FBI had reported more than 77,000 hate-crime incidents between 1998 and 2007, that is, 'nearly one hate crime for every hour of every day over the span of a decade'.[5] Where Bush had achieved consensus by playing on fear and by promising stern paternal care, Obama moved forward by moving others: he continues to strive towards a growing 'we', where Bush promoted an 'us-or-them' philosophy.

Despite the fact that the ongoing economic downturn has eroded *Obamania*, Obama remains charismatic. And the potent efficiency of Obama's charisma lies partly in his apparent humility. Obama publicly refuses to see himself as the origin of his acts and presents himself as the instrument of the will of well-meaning Americans. For this reason he argued concerning the anti-hate Bill: 'Because of the efforts of the folks in this room, particularly those family members standing behind me, the bell rings even louder now'.[6] Family, friends, party members and American citizens are all invited to the celebration of *agapē* which Obama cultivates and promotes. Characteristically, at the end of his speech, as weeping relatives applauded, he hugged them in a very physical expression of his engagement in the fight for love and understanding.

That fight is likely to be just that, though: a 'fight'. On 17 December 2009, the *New York Times* announced that federal hate-crime cases were at their highest level since 2001. The journalist Ian Urbina wrote that two days after the Justice Department announced federal indictments related to the fatal beating of, Ramirez, a Mexican immigrant in Shenandoah, federal authorities said the charges 'were part of a larger effort to step up civil rights enforcement after nearly eight years of decreased hate crime prosecutions'.[7] In the same article, Thomas E. Perez, head of the Justice Department's Civil Rights Division, was quoted as saying that the department dealt with more federal hate-crime cases in 2009 (i.e. Obama's first year in office) than in any other year since 2001. Mr Perez made no bones about condemning the laxity of the previous administration in handling such crimes. He said he was 'shocked to see the downtick in prosecutions of hate crimes' during Bush's two terms in office. For his own part, he proudly declared that 'The Civil Rights Division is again open for business'.

There is obviously a crusade for love in this policy and in its implementation, but in this fight, what hate defines the struggle? What does Obama hate? It would appear that Obama hates hatred. Whether that hatred is directed against colour or sexual orientation, Obama staunchly takes a stand against it and sets out to give state bodies the legislation and administrative power to attack it. That the Ramirez case has come to the attention of the American people proves that the hatred of hatred is moving beyond the scope of US civil society. In the new American worldview which Obama is promoting, not only citizens but immigrants should be included and protected. There is therefore something universal in this hatred of hating. But there is also something deeply Christian: Obama's faith is rising up against the spirit of websites such as the homophobic Westboro Baptist Church site and the more explicit www.godhatesfags. com, which promote hate and inevitably predispose supporters to intolerance if not violence. For this reason, the relationship between hatred and homeland deserves to be considered from the perspective of the religious rhetoric in which it often manifests itself.

Love, zeal, hate and God

The great Irish poet Yeats had an ambivalent relationship with his homeland, a relationship which contrasts starkly with the unquestioning patriotism of Napoléon and Churchill, Bush and Obama. Yeats found in his homeland a constant source of inspiration for his verse, yet he was constantly tormented by the struggles his country was embroiled in, and he was perturbed by the difficulty of its people to rise above those struggles. In a sense, it would be fair to say that he had a love–hate relationship with Ireland. As he put it, commenting on his generation:

> Out of Ireland we come,
> Great hatred, little room,
> Maimed us from the start,
> I carry from my mother's womb
> A frantic heart.
>
> Remorse for Intemperate
> Speech, 1933

Yeats saw all too clearly the dangers of being eaten up by hatred. The hatred of the British could fire the soul of the Irish, but could it forge a new identity? Could it do anything more than educate its generation in hate and lead them from resentment into violence? What does hatred engender? What does hate cultivate? For Yeats, his small country was the small stage to an overwhelming violence which washed over it like a flood. Even those who escaped the Emerald Isle could, he believed, never fully escape the resentment which it had instilled in them, even within their mothers' wombs. The Irish were saddled with a 'maiming' violent hatred which scarred the soul.

Yeats' reflection echoed the teachings of Saint Luke, who, in his famous advice, taught love for those who hate us:

But I say unto you which hear, Love your enemies, do good to them which hate you,
   Bless them that curse you, and pray for them which despitefully use you.
   And unto him that smiteth thee on the one cheek offer also the other; and him that taketh away thy cloak forbid not to take thy coat also. (*King James Bible*, Luke 6:27–28)

Of course, Luke's advice was intended to incite us to resist falling prey to the cycle of evil and aggressive behaviour. He was inviting good people to rise above violence, and to instruct evil-doers by their example as to the foolishness of evil behaviour. Luke was teaching 'as ye would that men should do to you, do ye also to them likewise' (*ibid.* 6:31). But he was also teaching that to repay offence by offence was to fall prey to a weakness which would partially destroy those who succumbed to hatred. In doing so, we fall victim to a greater outrage to ourselves than the one done to us by the evil-doer. Our hatred is unkind to ourselves. We lose ourselves in hatred.

In the restraint Luke preaches there is a very real passion: because for Christians, love of good, like love of God, is a passionate involvement. Christians love God 'zealously'. Isaiah taught that in time to come, to the 'increase of his government and peace, there shall be no end', because when the child was born, that 'Prince of Peace' would bear upon his shoulders God's government (Isaiah 9:7). 'The zeal of the Lord of hosts will perform this', Isaiah declared (Isaiah 9:7). And when Aaron saved 'the children of Israel' from the wrath of God, he did so because, as the Lord said, 'he was zealous for my sake' (Numbers 25:11). Aaron is only one of the figures in the Bible to recognize that God's love is a passionate, potentially destructive, love. God himself admits his desire to 'consume' the chosen people. But he relents. I will not destroy, he says 'the children of Israel in my jealousy' (*ibid.*).

Zeal is a form of love which appears to predispose the soul to hatred and destruction. Saul sought to slay the Gibeonites 'in his zeal to the children of Israel and Judah' (Samuel II 21:2). Zeal could also isolate. King David, a great 'hater' and warrior-king, lamented in the Psalms that his zealous love of the Lord had made him an orphan:

I am become a stranger unto my brethren, and an alien unto my mother's children.

For the zeal of thine house hath eaten me up; and the reproaches of them that reproached thee are fallen upon me. (Psalm 69: 8–9)

David's love was a violent love. And in this respect, his love was divine, since the Lord, too, loves zealously, jealously.

Curiously, it is exactly this consuming passion which tortures Yeats' soul. These were the passions that the poet was struggling to escape. What David took upon himself, Yeats yearned to shake off. He lamented that his Irish homeland had left him with a 'frantic heart', as he strove to find peace within himself. Yeats was not willing to subject himself to the consuming fire of passion, however lyrical and passionate his verse often sounds. Yeats was no zealot.

Zeal is a form of passionate love, what Aquinas would call an 'appetitive love', a consuming passion which tends towards the 'object' (or subject) of its love and wishes to unite with it. This love is a 'movement towards', in contrast to what Aquinas called 'apprehensive love', the love which is content simply to perceive the other, and to wish it well, without needing union with it.

In zealous love, union is conceived of in terms of appetite: it brings about a mutually consuming passion. David is both consumed by his passion, and he wishes to consume (that is to enter into contact with) the divine house of the Lord. This leads him to abandon all of his close relatives, an act which – it should be remembered – is hardly conceivable within the clan-like society in which he was raised. In separating himself from his kinsman, David is stepping towards the divine.

Words are not innocent. And neither are translations. Interestingly, where the *King James Bible* opts for 'For the **zeal** of thine house hath eaten me up' (Psalms, 69:9), and where Dhorme translates this love into French as *zèle*, the great contemporary translator Henri Meschonnic reaches beyond the Greek text which formed the basis of the *King James Bible* into Hebrew, and reclaims the word 'jealousy' (Meschonnic 2001: 69:10). How are we to understand his translation *la jalousie de ta maison m'a mangé* (the jealousy of your house has eaten me up)? *The Oxford Concise Dictionary of English Etymology* (1986) informs us that 'zeal', in biblical language, means fervour, ardent love, fervent longing. Zeal involves an ardour which sets us off in pursuit of the object of our passion. *Zele* enters Middle English, deriving from the Latin *zēlus*, which in turn derives from the Greek, *zēlos* (551). This is interesting, in itself, perhaps, but for our purposes the *Trésors des racines grecques*, by Jean Bouffartigue and Anne-Marie Delrieu (2008), is more helpful. As the authors point out, the term *jaloux* (jealous) derives from the Latin term *zelosus*, meaning emulation and jealousy, and that term itself had derived from *zêlos* in Greek, meaning ardour, emulation and envy. In this respect, the translation of Luther (who unlike Meschonnic had no access to the Hebrew original) was inspired. He translated David's words into German as *der **Eifer** um dein Haus hat mich gefressen* (jealousy for your house ate me up, *Die Bibel nach der übersetzung Martin Luthers*, 1999: 578).

There is nothing tepid or temperate in the love of the Lord in the Old Testament, and David partakes in his potentially destructive love, his jealous, zealous love. That love can inspire wrath, all-consuming anger, which destroys the object of its love if it is betrayed. Such love approaches hatred. And consequently, hatred is not infrequently celebrated throughout literature, especially from the Romantics onwards. The narrator of Balzac's *La peau de chagrin* is only one of those who praises the inspiring nature of hatred.

La haine est un tonique, elle fait vivre, elle inspire la vengeance; mais la pitié tue, elle affaiblit notre faiblesse.

Hatred is a tonic, it makes us live, it inspires vengeance; but pity kills, making our weakness all the weaker.

> Honoré de Balzac, 1831 (in Oster, 1993), *La peau de chagrin*

According to this view, hatred makes us strong. Balzac is celebrating a sentiment which resembles the defining hatred of Napoléon. And, to a certain extent, this was the kind of hatred that Bush appealed to with his zealous patriotism and his celebration of the just war against 'terror' and 'terrorists'. Would it be fair then to consider Bush a 'zealot', a man who defined himself in politics in terms of his ardent love of democracy and his hatred of all those who opposed the will of the USA to impose its model upon the world? If so, how are we to understand Obama's faith? Are we to see him as more moderate? A lover rather than a hater?

Biblical rhetoric

On Friday, 3 March 2006, the BBC informed the readers of its internet website that Blair 'prayed to God when deciding whether or not to send UK troops to Iraq'.[8] The admission had taken place during the shooting of a now famous ITV1 chat show hosted by Michael Parkinson, which was to be screened the following day. Questioned as to whether he had sought 'divine intervention', Blair replied, 'Of course, you struggle with your own conscience about it … and it's one of these situations that, I suppose, very few people ever find themselves in'. Blair went on to expound his soul-searching experience: 'In the end, there is a judgement that, I think if you have faith about these things, you realize that judgement is made by other people … and if you believe in God, it's made by God as well'. God was in part responsible for the invasion of Iraq, in Blair's opinion. Blair stressed that the choice to back invasion had not come easily. As he put it: 'When you're faced with a decision like that, some of those decisions have been very, very difficult, most of all because you know these are people's lives and, in some case, their deaths'.

Andy McSmith, writing in *The Independent* the next day, the day the interview was screened, quoted Blair as stating 'God will be my judge on Iraq'.[9] Whatever judgement we form of Blair's actions, and however much we might doubt his honesty, there was a certain staunchness in standing up for this position. After all, the British public and Blair's own party had already shown themselves highly sceptical about the rhetoric with which he had defended his conviction that invading Iraq was an essentially good act. No one can criticize a Christian for believing that God will be his ultimate judge, and the fact that a believer is willing to face the day of judgement is perfectly laudable. Nevertheless, the British had two objections to Blair's stance. He was seen to be 'echoing statements from his ally George Bush', as McSmith put it. And he was mixing politics and religion (thereby disregarding warnings from his advisers).

In a strange way, this latter objection shows to what degree the British (and indeed the French and German publics) failed to understand the significant shift in the Western worldview which was being driven by the neoconservatives but which would be taken up joyfully and fervently by all of America's enemies. Faced with the anti-American Islamic fundamentalism which had made the bombing of the twin towers possible, the neoconservatives were countering by embracing that fundamentalism. Ultimately, the introduction of religious rhetoric into politics was to enact a profound change in our conception of the state, and the rights of citizens and of those who infringe our laws.

Curiously, in accepting the religious worldview, the Americans were drawing nearer to the fundamentalist culture which inspired fear in them. Faith has always been important for Americans, but in many respects, religion had hitherto been cordoned off in public life and excluded from many domains of public space. Business does not have any place in religion, as far as most Americans are concerned. For this reason, American managers sent abroad to Muslim countries in the 1980s were instructed to be careful of putting business first and failing to take into account the religious dimension of society in their negotiations. Properly speaking, for Muslims, there is no 'religious dimension'. To the Muslim, all things belong in Allah. Americans, on the other hand, like to put business before pleasure. And in very practical terms, they prefer to do business before sitting down to eat. Muslims, on the other hand, find the hurried relations that American businessmen engage in, in order to make deals and make money, insulting and 'godless'. Only projects blessed by Allah will have any chance of coming to fruition in this world, they believe.

In the same way, the idea of separating the state from religion seems absurd and grotesque to the servant of Allah. And it must be remembered that any nineteenth-century Catholic or Protestant would have agreed wholeheartedly with the idea that only a holy state, blessed by God, could govern its citizens justly. The separation of the state and religion in modern capitalist democracies was a gradual transformation which took centuries, and only for the past hundred years has it come to seem normal and 'natural' that religion should not interfere with politics.

The neoconservatives, and above all the born-again Christian Bush were perversely inspired by the Islamic fundamentalists in that they were all too willing to reinstate concepts such as the 'holy war', the defence of Christendom (in the rhetoric of the 'clash of cultures'), the condemnation of opponents as 'evildoers', lost souls, incapable of finding 'the path' towards democracy. It would have seemed surreal if someone had suggested back in the middle of the Cold War, in the 1960s or '70s, that such rhetoric, smacking of the Middle Ages, would have gained currency by the beginning of the twenty-first century. And yet, there was the British Prime Minister in 2006, calmly insisting 'that his interest in politics sprang from his Christianity' and that its 'values and philosophy' had guided him in public life (Blair quoted by Andy McSmith in *The Independent*, 4 March 2006).

Bush was often disparaged and mocked for claiming to have a hotline to God, but the consequences of the President of the USA believing he was enacting the will of God is anything but a laughing matter. The *Guardian* journalist Ewen MacAskill, writing on Friday, 7 October 2005, was right to show concern when Bush declared 'God told me to end the tyranny in Iraq'. That journalist affirmed:

George Bush has claimed he was on a mission from God when he launched the invasions of Afghanistan and Iraq, according to a senior Palestinian politician in an interview to be broadcast by the BBC later this month.

Mr Bush revealed the extent of his religious fervour when he met a Palestinian delegation during the Israeli-Palestinian summit at the Egyptian resort of Sharm el-Sheikh, four months after the US-led invasion of Iraq in 2003.

One of the delegates, Nabil Shaath, who was Palestinian foreign minister at the time, said: 'President Bush said to all of us: "I am driven with a mission from God". God would tell me, "George go and fight these terrorists in Afghanistan". And I did. And then God would tell me "George, go and end the tyranny in Iraq". And I did.'

Mr Bush went on: 'And now, again, I feel God's words coming to me, "Go get the Palestinians their state and get the Israelis their security, and get peace in the Middle East". And, by God, I'm gonna do it.'[10]

As MacAskill pointed out, the fact that Bush was one of the most overtly religious leaders to occupy the White House, far from estranging him from his electorate, brought him much support in middle America.

Already on 16 September 2001, Bush had 'vowed' to 'rid the world of the evil-doers'. Many journalists had always found something laughable about Bush. Comics around the world had enjoyed the first year of his mandate because of his monumental slip-ups and his ridiculous turns of phrase. From the 11th of September onwards, irony and scorn were poured upon him. Comics had a field day. Anti-Americanism in Europe was festive. And truly there is something grotesque in the way this religious rhetoric is so easily and enthusiastically harnessed by commercial concerns. Marketing made much of the God-hype. Soon websites such as Zazzle were selling 'God Bless Iraq' t-shirts as part of a range of products including 'war and peace freedom coffee mugs'.

And yet, however much we despise and deride this perversion of religious rhetoric, it is important not to lose sight of the way religious convictions were transforming the exercise of power in liberal democracies, and it is equally important not to underestimate the influence of fervent believers in the 'war against terror'. Those believers had, for example, begun to justify torture associated with medieval, pre-industrial societies and banana republics, on the grounds of 'the ticking bomb' argument. According to this argument, it was urgent to ascertain the degree of danger posed by potential terrorist suspects. For this reason, torture was conceived as 'benevolent torture', 'well-intentioned torture' or even 'moral torture'. Such torture, it was argued, could not be compared to torture as it is employed by totalitarian regimes to terrorize the population. It was used to protect the population from terrorist attacks. Security was the goal in such torture, not suppression. The implications of this argument are terrifying. Torture was being rehabilitated: after war, and the promotion of hate, the neoconservatives had begun theorising the active physical suppression of the 'hated', those who allegedly opposed the American way.

Much to the world's relief, one of the first decisions Obama took was to set in progress the closure of the Guantanamo detention centre. Obama denounced torture and mocked the rhetoric used to defend the 'war against terror'. Most importantly, he mocked the incessant references to hellfire and the discourse of damnation which had become widespread in Republican discourse on the defence of the homeland, and which McCain, the presidential candidate of 2008, had in turn adopted.

Neoconservative discourse constantly invoked chaos and the threat of the abyss, in order to inspire fear and thereby justify the authoritarian and aggressive nature of its policies. But this was not simply a rhetorical ploy, it was a deeply religious reflex. In this respect, the neoconservative worldview shares something in common with the Wandering Kabbalists of the seventeenth century who were preoccupied by the *achra sitra*, the demonic darkness of the world. For the Wandering Kabbalists, the *achra sitra* was the abyss that lay on the 'other side', the dimension separated from God. If Americans love God, and God is on the side of the Americans, then all those who oppose America offend God and attack his work. McCain was simply joining in the Republican chorus in reassuring the American people that the USA could win the war against darkness.

What is essential here is that Obama's critique was very different from the irony of the British press who found Blair's faith absurd and misplaced. Obama was countering faith with faith. Obama was not mocking faith but 'blind' faith. Obama, too, derives his faith in the American people and his faith in its capacity to do good in the world from his Christian faith. For this reason, biblical rhetoric cannot simply be dismissed. It can no longer be considered an aberration: it has once more become a driving force in modern geopolitics. Biblical rhetoric is likely to have a direct impact upon Obama's attempt to change US society. And faith will shape his attempt to impose upon the world his conception of a just society. For this reason, but not for this reason alone, it is worth trying to understand more fully how the concept of hate and love are entwined with one another in the Bible and in Christian philosophy.

Old Testament hate

When investigating the origin of a concept, Wierzbicka shows only too clearly how misleading it is to focus upon individual words in isolation. Words compete with one another in taking their place in the language system. Words define themselves in opposition to one another. Opposites and synonyms serve to fix the meaning of concepts within the language system, just as the context of discourse situates them in speech and writing. And classical texts, civilisation-founding texts, like the Bible, allow words to take on specific connotations, when they take root within the imagination of a culture. For that reason, the Bible is the obvious place to look if we are trying to understand more fully what hate means to our culture.

Hate, as a word, is rather uncommon in the English translations of the early books of the Bible, though. This hardly means that violence and aggressive emotion is absent in these books, however. The God of the Old Testament is often described as a passionate angry God, a jealous God. The Creator threatens many times to destroy his Creation, and, as the great Flood shows, such threats are not empty.

However, it is 'wrath' and 'anger' which figure most prominently in the early books. In Genesis 39:1, Joseph, who throughout his story bears a grudge against no one, will suffer the wrath of his master. Joseph had been sold into slavery after his jealous brothers had decided to dispose of him. Initially, he was bought by the Egyptian, Potiphar, and because his master was impressed by his talents, he made him steward of his house. But 'his wrath was kindled' against Joseph when his wife (who was enamoured of Joseph's charms) tried to take him to bed, then falsely accused Joseph of trying to rape her.

Jacob is another famous biblical figure given to wrath, when he is provoked. When Jacob berated his sons for their waywardness, he cursed his first-born for being 'unstable as water', and for having lain with his wife (Genesis, 49:4). And he chastized Simeon and Levi for being 'instruments of cruelty' (49:5), since 'in their anger they slew a man, and in their selfwill they digged down a wall' (49:6). 'Cursed be their anger [Jacob declared], for *it was* fierce; and their wrath, for it was cruel' (49:7). Meschonnic, translating directly from Hebrew, opts for the word *colère*, where the *King James Version* (henceforth KJV) opts for 'anger'. Where the KJV uses 'wrath', he opts for *furie*, meaning 'fury', 'violence' or 'passion'.

> Maudite leur colère car elle est une puissance
> et leur furie car elle a été dure
>   Meschonnic 2002: 233

He translates the earlier phrase, 'in their anger they slew a man' as *dans leur colère ils ont tué de l'homme* (*ibid.*). What the *King James Bible* translators render as 'selfwill' (a word which has fallen into disuse, but which means 'obstinacy'), Meschonnic renders as *fureur*,[11] which can be translated as 'fury' or 'fit of rage'. The important point which the various translations of the Bible demonstrate, is that 'anger', 'fury' and 'fits of rage' are all expressions of violent emotion, and they constitute synonyms for one another to a large extent.

As we move into Exodus, the second book of the Bible, wrath belongs to God. The alliance between Yahveh and Abraham was of a personal nature. God negotiated with Abraham: he promised him a son, threatened to force Abraham to sacrifice him, then showed his mercy by indicating that the sacrifice of the first-born (a custom common throughout pagan societies and one which the followers of Baal practised) was not pleasing to Him. This seems to make Him a loving god. The God of the Old Testament appears to love His chosen people as a father loves his family. The fearsome God that Moses dares not look upon commands Moses to do His bidding and deliver the people of Israel from the slavery of Egypt. This love inevitably engenders violence against the oppressors of the chosen people. And when God sends a pillar of fire (Exodus 14:24) against the Egyptians pursuing Moses and has the sea open up to engulf the Egyptian army and their chariots (14:28), Moses literally sings His praises.

15:2 The LORD is my strength and song, and he is become my salvation: he is my God, and I will prepare him an habitation; my father's God, and I will exalt him. 15:3 The LORD is a man of war: the LORD is his name.

This Lord is a violent and victorious god, and Moses sings to Him in praise because He has bestowed upon him His divine anger as an instrument to crush the enemies of the people of Israel.

15:7 And in the greatness of thine excellency thou hast overthrown them that rose up against thee: thou sentest forth thy wrath, which consumed them as stubble.

This is the cult of power, something closer to Nietzsche than to Christ. Hate seems to be channelled into fury and wrath. Hate appears less frequently in the early books than these terms, but it does exist. When, in Genesis, Rebekah is blessed by a group of women, she is told by them that she will become 'the mother of thousands of millions, and [they say to her] let thy seed possess the gate of those which hate them' (Genesis 24:60). Rebekah's marriage to Abraham had been barren, but she is promised not only a prodigious posterity but also a victorious one, which will crush and subdue its enemies.

Fratricide is a recurring biblical theme, and hatred of one's brother begins with Cain and Abel. Indeed, a fundamental fraternal animosity perpetuates in many of the relations between brothers. Esau hates his brother Jacob because the latter tries to inherit in his stead. Though he had mockingly sold Jacob his right to inherit his father's goods in exchange for a bowl of lentils, Esau had no intention of honouring his promise. When Jacob manages, through the manoeuvres of his mother, to dupe his father into giving him his blessing in place of his brother, we are told 'Esau hated Jacob because of the blessing wherewith his father blessed him: and Esau said in his heart, The days of mourning for my father are at hand; then will I slay my brother Jacob' (27:41).

The difference between wrath and hatred are palpable in these examples. Anger and fury take possession of the soul and direct violent acts, which will in time be judged just or unjust. Hatred is seething. Hatred takes hold of the soul and will not let go. Hatred is a fixed disposition of the soul, a relationship. For this reason, in grammatical terms, the aspectual state of ongoing hating should be stressed. Where the *King James Bible* describes the enemies of Rebekah's future sons using the verb form (those which hate them), Meschonnic's French version aptly renders this animosity in the form of a noun 'their haters' (*haïsseurs*, Meschonnic 2002: 117). These opponents are defined by their hating. In the same way, Meschonnic stresses the longevity of hating, when he renders Esau's hate as *rancune*, 'resentment' (*Essav avait de la rancune envers Yaaqov, ibid.*: 133).

The animosity between Esau and Jacob echoes the primary struggle between brothers, the confrontation which set the first two brothers of the Bible against one another. As Cain killed Abel, so Esau plans to kill Jacob. But juxtaposing the two stories highlights an essential difference of disposition. Cain is overcome by anger. He is 'wroth' (KJV Genesis 4:5). This expression is rendered somewhat more banally by both the English Standard Version (3), and by the New International Version, as 'very angry'. Meschonnic's translation from the Hebrew is more poignant: in his version, God's choice to bless Abel's offering and to scorn Cain's is experienced as a 'burning' (*brûlure*, Meschonnic 2002: 38).

The stories of Esau and Jacob and of Cain and Abel awaken something very deep in our own subconscious, reminding us of essential primary rivalries and animosities. We don't need to be Freudians to admit that the passions which are born in the cradle and in the first years of sibling rivalry remain animating, defining forces which shape our personalities and which give us our bearings in the emotional landscapes of our inner worlds. Sibling struggles force us to question the legitimacy of that founding concept which is believed to be the basis of society, i.e. 'brotherly love', *agāpe*. In our most intimate relationships, animosity can spring up, as it does in the case of Cain and Abel, and when that animosity finds no vent or resolution, it can be transformed into a lasting violent disposition.

This is the lesson of the story of Esau. True, when Jacob returns decades later with his wives and his children, fearing to meet Esau, the latter does not lift his hand against him, but embraces him 'as a brother'. Nevertheless, the two quickly go their own ways, as if to indicate that their presence is insufferable to one another. Esau invites Jacob to stay with him as he must, being his host, but Jacob insists on declining his hospitality. Esau is no longer 'wrathful', faced with the brother who has unsuccessfully tried to trick him out of his inheritance. He masters himself and does not fly into a fit of rage, but he may well not have been able to eradicate from his heart his hate and his resentment, emotions which refuse to let go of the soul once they take hold. A similar unflinching hatred will take hold of Joseph's brothers, who resent his being his father's favourite and who decide to leave him in a pit to be devoured by wild animals, before finally relenting and selling him to slave traders.

Hate will become more important in the later books of the Bible, and it is not surprising that those who bless Rebekah mention the 'gates' of those who will hate her sons. Gates signify the existence of cities, walled cities. Though the people of Israel are given to wandering, the age of the later books of the Bible is no longer the age of nomads. The shepherds with their flocks moving across the land are still an important part of this age, and David will come from such a group. But from Exodus onwards, we see the emergence of the sedentary age, the age of cities. And cities mean wars. Wars mean the organisation of armies and the increasing militarisation of society. Battles will be celebrated, victors will be held up as lofty heroes. In order to face the inevitable menace of opposing armies, Samuel admits, reluctantly, that only a king will be able to protect the people. With the emergence of kings in the Bible we see the centralisation of 'resources' (flocks, gold and women, wives and concubines) and the incessant wars of succession, in which Saul and his successor and usurper will be involved. Saul and David define themselves in war. And as David outdoes his benefactor Saul, the latter comes to hate him as his rival.

David, the protagonist of both books of Samuel and the author to whom the Psalms are attributed, was a warrior-king: and his god was a warrior-god. 'The LORD is my rock, and my fortress, and my deliverer,' David proudly declares (KJV, Samuel II 22:2). For David, God was a 'shield': 'thou savest me from violence' (22:3). Consequently, David offered praise for the divine force which would save him from 'his enemies' (22:4) When the abyss threatened to engulf David, and adversity threatened to send him into despair, it was the divine anger of the Lord which would preserve him from his enemies:

22:5 When the waves of death compassed me, the floods of ungodly men made me afraid; 22:6 The sorrows of hell compassed me about; the snares of death prevented me; 22:7 In my distress I called upon the LORD, and cried to my God: and he did hear my voice out of his temple, and my cry did enter into his ears. 22:8 Then the earth shook and trembled; the foundations of heaven moved and shook, because he was wroth. 22:9 There went up a smoke out of his nostrils, and fire out of his mouth devoured: coals were kindled by it. 22:10 He bowed the heavens also, and came down; and darkness was under his feet. 22:11 And he rode upon a cherub, and did fly: and he was seen upon the wings of the wind. 22:12 And he made darkness pavilions round about him, dark waters, and thick clouds of the skies. 22:13 Through the brightness before him were coals of fire kindled. 22:14 The LORD thundered from heaven, and the most High uttered his voice. 22:15 And he sent out arrows, and scattered them; lightning, and discomfited them. 22:16 And the channels of the sea appeared, the foundations of the world were discovered, at the rebuking of the LORD, at the blast of the breath of his nostrils.

This magnificent display of wrath is made to what end? To demonstrate the solidarity that exists between God and his chosen servant, David. David must accomplish the will of the Lord of the Old Testament, and any enemy of David must consequently be smitten and destroyed. God saves David from hate which threatens to overcome him: 'He delivered me from my strong enemy, and from them that hated me: for they were too strong for me (*ibid.*, 22:18).

In many respects, the Psalms are a festival of hate and violence, despite the fact that it is the invitation to lie down in lush green pastures that is usually associated with these deeply personal reflections upon the relationship between man and God. David vows to love his God fervently and absolutely. In that identification, he feels protected, knowing that if he clings to his Lord, that Lord will protect him, by taking on his enemies as His own. All who offend David are, according to this logic, the enemies of God, evil-doers.

David promises to be the instrument of his Lord's wrath and to punish all who offend Him. And he does this in the name of hate. He declares: 'The foolish shall not stand in thy sight: thou hatest all workers of iniquity' (KJV, Psalms 5:5). God will assist him in this task. David trusts in the Lord and calls upon him: 'Have mercy upon me, O LORD; consider my trouble which I suffer of them that hate me, thou that liftest me up from the gates of death' (9:13). God will deliver David's enemies into his hands: 'Thou hast also given me the necks of mine enemies; that I might destroy them that hate me' (18:40). Hate will be destroyed by violence in a celebration of divine hatred of the Lord's enemies. The Lord will be tireless in this mercilessness. 'Thine hand shall find out all thine enemies: thy right hand shall find out those that hate thee' (21:8).

This fusion between the will of David and the will of God should form the legitimacy of the reign of the kings and the reign of the house of David. The significance of David's legitimacy can hardly be exaggerated: Christ's own claim to represent the Jews was based upon the fact that he belonged to the house of David. But though these examples all serve to show that God loves the righteous and despises those who go against His commandments and offend against His will, it is clear in the following quotation that David is not only concerned with legitimising his own divine right to destroy those he hates. He also wants to achieve a monopoly of violence. For this reason, he seems to contradict himself and to condemn himself when he claims: 'The LORD trieth the righteous: but the wicked and him that loveth violence his soul hateth' (11:5). If ever a man loved violence, it was David, who, from the moment he leaves his flocks to slay Goliath, seems to have hardly any respite from bloodshed and butchery. He will even, against his own will, find himself at war with his son Absolom who, like his father, is a warrior.

Indeed, with David, we enter into a whole new era of complexity when it comes to representing the bonds of love and hate which relate and oppose the characters who people the Old Testament. David declares himself to be the one who is capable of discerning the nature of evil and of dividing the good from the evil-doers, but like any general, he is in desperate need of violent men to support him. In this role, his behaviour resembles that of the governments who liberate criminals in times of war to supply soldiers for the front lines. In Chapter 5 of the Second Book of Samuel, David proclaims:

And David said on that day, Whosoever getteth up to the gutter, and smiteth the Jebusites, and the lame and the blind that are hated of David's soul, he shall be chief and captain. (KJV, Samuel II 5:8)

David surrounds himself with violent men and advances them in his court.

Fatally, it is in his own house that hate will bring havoc and disorder. And it will bring about this disorder through love. Amnon sins twice against his half-sister, Tamar. First he rapes her (KJV, Samuel II 13:14), then he spurns her:

'Then Amnon hated her exceedingly; so that the hatred wherewith he hated her was greater than the love wherewith he had loved her. And Amnon said unto her, Arise, be gone' (13:15). Tamar justly rebukes him: 'There is no cause: this evil in sending me away is greater than the other that thou didst unto me. But he would not hearken unto her' (13:16).

Amnon falls into the trap that Shakespeare so eloquently describes when he contrasts the lust for the object of affection prior to the satiation of desire with the disgust and frustration that the accomplishment of desire sometimes brings:

> Before, a joy proposed; behind a dream.
> All this the world well knows; yet none knows well
> To shun the heaven that leads men to this hell.
> *Sonnet 129*, 67

Amnon's 'lust in action' is like the one Shakespeare describes:

> [...]murderous, bloody, full of blame,
> Savage, extreme, rude, cruel, not to trust;
> Enjoy'd no sooner but despised straight;
> Past reason hunted; and no sooner had,
>   Past reason hated, as a swallowed bait,
>   On purpose laid to make the taker mad:
>   Mad in pursuit, and in possession so,
>   Had, having and in quest to have, extreme;
> (*ibid.*)

No one would contest that Amnon's act is outrageous, an expression of vice. But what is vice exactly? For Aquinas (1990: 479), 'vice is contrary to virtue. Now the virtue of a thing consists in its being well disposed in a manner befitting its nature'. The influence of Aristotle (who Aquinas referred to as 'The Philosopher') is obvious here. Each thing should act in accordance with its nature. If Amnon spurned Tamar, it was because he loathed to look upon the object of his lust, his misguided desire. Having satisfied his animal lust, he is confronted, not with an inspiration of desire but with his sister, desire for whom the laws of all societies forbid. Amnon has sinned not only against his sister (a fact which he is too ashamed to recognize as he has his servant throw her out and bolt his door), he sins against his father and his king. But most of all, Amnon has sinned against himself, in acting in direct opposition to the desires which should govern his lust. Amnon has done evil to himself in allowing his desire to become perverted and in succumbing to his perversion. Amnon allows himself to 'love' what he should not love. And once that 'love' vanishes, Amnon is faced only with the evidence of his sin and with his own self-loathing, which he displaces by pouring it upon the victim of his prior lust.

This story can hardly end well. Indeed, it seems almost like a further chapter in a conspiracy to discredit 'fraternal love', because not only has Amnon sinned against that love, he himself will be cut down by the hand of his half-brother Absalom, the full brother of Tamar. This action will not resemble the act of fury with which Cain struck down Abel. This hating is more akin to the seething loathing that Esau feels when faced with Jacob's trickery. Absalom will bide his time and, not until two years after the rape of his sister, when the time is ripe for vengeance, will Absalom command his men to slay Amnon at a feast when his 'heart is merry with wine' (Samuel II 13:28).

The incredible, almost magical, economy with which biblical stories fit fundamental human tensions and traumas into tight narratives is truly marvellous. In this story, we are introduced to that ambivalent blend of emotions which combines love and hate in the act of lust, we consider the ambivalent nature of brother–sister relations, we contemplate the emotional bond of dependency to which the act of sexual union disposes some women, we consider the sexual possessiveness of the natural brother and his outrage (certainly sexually charged) at the misuse of his sister, and finally we consider the rivalry of brothers who must both vie for the approval of the father and whose fates depend upon the blessing the father will bestow upon them. In one act of dysfunctional folly, Amnon separates himself from his sister and his brother, his father and himself, and thereby seals his fate.

The narrative continues, however, with plots of patricide. Like the father-hating sons of Dostoyevsky's *Brothers Karamazov* (which inspired Freud to write on patricide as a natural infantile fantasy) Absalom will plot to destroy his father, the king. Absalom can hardly hope to find approval in the eyes of his father after killing his brother. The stealth with which he restrains his revenge proves that he knows this all too well. In fact, David has nurtured Absalom and intends to make him (not Solomon) his successor. When he receives the news of Amnon's murder, he takes no action because Absalom has already fled. But when, after several years, he returns, King David refuses to allow him into his presence, a decision which is a source of torment to Absalom. Though the king finally forgives him publicly, Absalom seems not to be appeased after this treatment. Once more he bides his time. Biblical time is renowned for hyperbole, but we are told in the Second Book of Samuel (15:14) that forty years pass before the father–son tension erupts into confrontation. David receives word (15:12) that Absalom has raised an army and that 'the men of Israel are with Absalom'. Once more, from love, hate is born.

David is the great king of the Old Testament, but, in many respects, he is an unlucky father. Forced to do battle with his son, he can hardly hope to find contentment either in victory or in defeat. And indeed, once victorious, his reign as king is rendered precarious by the despair he displays when his servants bring him the news that after sacrificing many men, they have vanquished their king's enemy.

19:4 But the king covered his face, and the king cried with a loud voice, O my son Absalom, O Absalom, my son, my son! 19:5 And Joab came into the house to the king, and said, Thou hast shamed this day the faces of all thy servants, which this day have saved thy life, and the lives of thy sons and of thy daughters, and the lives of thy wives, and the lives of thy concubines; 19:6 In that thou lovest thine enemies, and hatest thy friends. For thou hast declared this day, that thou regardest neither princes nor servants: for this day I perceive, that if Absalom had lived, and all we had died this day, then it had pleased thee well.

Once more, hatred embroils us in paradoxical passions. The loyal servants of David, as soldiers, destroy the one who hates him. But they feel themselves slighted, disparaged and hated for having saved their king when he shows himself incapable of rejoicing in their victory. David is caught between opposing desires, the desire for self-preservation and the love of his most cherished son. In many ways, David suffers greatly throughout his life. Nonetheless, the series of tragedies to which he is subject is justified in biblical terms in the sense that David betrays God. And his children, in their turn, will break His commandments. Though David will leave Solomon as his heir, he sins in seducing his mother Bathsheba and in sending her legitimate husband off to war to be killed. Perversely, he employs those who hate him to do his will and misuses the loyalty of his servant (that is to say, his servant's love) to destroy him. In Aquinas' terms, David acts not only against the will of God but against his own well-being. No one sins willingly, knowingly, in Aquinas' opinion. No one can hate themselves: and sin can, after all, only bring evil to the soul, since it consists in allowing oneself to act in contradiction to the desires to which the soul should by nature and by divine law be disposed. For Aquinas, love is always a disposition to an object, a movement towards something. In David's case, his desire for Bathsheba, Solomon's mother, so often celebrated in the Bible, is an evil and unfitting desire which he should be able to master. A major source of perplexity for Bible scholars derives from the contradiction of good coming from evil. Solomon, the great king of wisdom, must become king, inheriting from his father, but he is born of sin.

Amnon must respect his sister, and does not. Absalom is left with the impossible but inescapable obligation of forgiving Amnon. The obligation to forgive one's brother and to love him is part of the Law of Moses, and Absalom cannot hope to be spared from that decree. In Leviticus, God instructs Moses to preach love of their fellow men to the people but above all brotherly love: 'Thou shalt not hate thy brother in thine heart: thou shalt in any wise rebuke thy neighbour nor suffer sin upon him' (KJV, Leviticus 19:17). Absalom cannot, however, listen to the God who warns that those who do not 'hearken' unto Him and observe His commandments will have reason to regret it: 'I will punish you seven times for your sins' (*ibid.*, 26:18) He warns. God takes pains to explain this in the words He speaks to Moses and which Moses preaches to his people:

for I the LORD thy God am a jealous God, visiting the iniquity of the fathers upon the children unto the third and fourth generation of them that hate me, and shewing mercy unto thousands of them that love me and keep my commandments. (KJV, Deuteronomy, 5:9–10)

This God demands adherence to His statutes, and in the event of disobedience or defiance He tells His people: 'I will break the pride of your power' (Leviticus 26:19). How does He propose to do this? This God no longer has recourse to pillars of fire and pestilence, to famines and floods: he will use the enemies of the children of Israel to destroy or enslave them. He will use their hate:

And I will set my face against you, and ye shall be slain before your enemies: they that hate you shall reign over you … (26:17)

In fact, much of Moses' teaching concerns explaining the nature of God's love (which can at any time erupt into 'just wrath', destructive fury). The children of Israel constantly forget, neglect and misjudge God. But are they being unfair in their evaluation of God's will towards them? Given the fact that natural disasters are commonly interpreted as expressions of the discontent of God, attributing their forty years of wandering throughout the wilderness after their liberation from Egypt as a punishment appears reasonable enough:

Because the LORD hated us, he hath brought us forth out of the land of Egypt, to deliver us into the hand of the Amorites, to destroy us. (KJV, Deuteronomy 1:27)

The potential victory of the Amorites was perceived as the Hand of God using the enemies of Israel to destroy them. Prophets are constantly required throughout the Old Testament to explain God's actions and His will. His ways are impenetrable, strange. But there is no question as to His relationship to hate. The Lord God does not hate hatred. He loves and hates with lust and passion. That is to say, His love and His hate are always the expressions of an engagement, an encounter, a relationship. The idea of loving universally, or loving without clearly defining the individual concrete object of love, is inconceivable in the first books of the Old Testament. God's love cradles and nurtures the children of Israel, but His wrath threatens to strike down upon the heads of particular men and women, and upon particular cities (such as Nineveh, the city He tells Jonah He will destroy). As soon as the people of Israel stray from His commandments or turn their backs on His will, the stage of the Old Testament seems set for fury and wrath.

Though certain of the quotes from the Old Testament coincide with the concept of a just war and the destruction of evil-doers as found in the rhetoric of Bush, and though Bush himself did at times quote some of the famous passages from the Psalms, this short study of biblical hate has allowed us to move far beyond the limited scope of Bush's concept of hate. The Bible offers multiple perspectives of various forms of love and hate, and if the stories it tells have found such great resonance for over three millennia, it is because it has something to tell us about the nature of love and hate and about the relationship between the two. So far, we have considered eight forms of animosity and hate.

1. God's hate of disobedience, infidelity to the binding contract made between Him and the 'chosen people'
2. Brothers' envy and rage and fury against brothers
3. Brothers' seething unappeasable hatred for brothers following slights or mortal insults
4. Men's disgust for women after possessing them
5. Women's resentment after being spurned by men (Joseph's Egyptian mistress)
6. Hatred of foreign peoples and their armies (city warfare)
7. Hatred of sin and evil-doing
8. The self-loathing of the sinner.

For obvious reasons, the early Christians were concerned with stressing that the New Testament brought believers the 'Good News' that God loves them. Consequently, they tend to stress that their God is a god of love, not of hate. It would, however, be a mistake to assume that hate is found more rarely in the New Testament than in the Old Testament. In fact, the concept of hate is omnipresent in the New Testament. The social and political context is one of conflict verging on the brink of chaos. And hatred for sinning, the final form in the list above, forms an essential dynamic principle in the discourse of the Gospels. As we shall see, other more perplexing forms of hatred also transpire to form part of the structuring framework of the Christian worldview.

New Testament hate

Matthew preaches love of those who hate us. Matthew sees beyond seething hate and confusion to a world in which love will beget love. He discerns the evil that hate engenders. Matthew is not simply reiterating the Law of Moses, the commandment to 'love thy neighbour as thyself' (KJV, Leviticus 19:18), a law which was so often forgotten by the children of Israel. Matthew is preaching a more extensive form of love:

Ye have heard that it hath been said, Thou shalt love thy neighbour, and hate thine enemy. But I say unto you, Love your enemies, bless them that curse you, do good to them that hate you, and pray for them which despitefully use you, and persecute you; (Matthew 5:43–4)

Matthew looks beyond the present, the here and now. When he looks forward to a world of love, that love has no place in the immediate present. Matthew's faith is strong, but his view of the present is pessimistic, to say the least. In the world he inhabits, he realizes there is little place for love, and he clearly perceives that even his love of his enemies will earn him hate. He recounts that Jesus taught his twelve disciples: 'ye shall be hated of all men for my name's sake: but he that endureth to the end shall be saved' (Matthew 10:22). Salvation comes as recompense for the capacity to bear enduring hate.

The choice Jesus offers his disciples, and the decision which Matthew lays before those who listen to him, is to choose between love and hate. The choice of love entails rejecting hate and hating, and embracing the true faith. Rejection and hate are inseparable. Hating and rejecting are part of the same movement of the soul. Hate is the logical consequence of love, for, Matthew, who argues:

6:24 No man can serve two masters: for either he will hate the one, and love the other; or else he will hold to the one, and despise the other. Ye cannot serve God and mammon.

The Gospel of St Matthew may be contrasted with *The Revelation of St John the Divine* for the sage calmness of the love he preaches, where John recounts a sublime allegory of fire, destruction and damnation. Nevertheless, Matthew does himself predict the coming of chaos:

24:7 For nation shall rise against nation, and kingdom against kingdom: and there shall be famines, and pestilences, and earthquakes, in divers places. 24:8 All these are the beginning of sorrows. 24:9 Then shall they deliver you up to be afflicted, and shall kill you: and ye shall be hated of all nations for my name's sake. 24:10 And then shall many be offended, and shall betray one another, and shall hate one another. 24:11 And many false prophets shall rise, and shall deceive many. 24:12 And because iniquity shall abound, the love of many shall wax cold. 24:13 But he that shall endure unto the end, the same shall be saved. 24:14 And this gospel of the kingdom shall be preached in all the world for a witness unto all nations; and then shall the end come.

The end of the world is coming, Matthew preaches: the era of the false prophets will come to stir confusions, deceiving the people who have grown cold to love. The hate of the loveless and the deceived is inevitable, Matthew believes, but those who anticipate the danger can arm themselves against this coming strife. And it is for this reason that he preaches we should choose the right master and hate all other gods, the gods that the false prophets will set up in the place of the true faith.

Like Matthew, Mark is preoccupied by the hate that will be his sole earthly reward for loving his enemies. He recounts Jesus' prediction and joins Matthew in believing that by facing hate, he will be saved: 'And ye shall be hated of all men for my name's sake: but he that shall endure unto the end, the same shall be saved' (Mark 13:13). Luke, for his part, extrapolates, arguing that the hate of the people is the very proof of sanctity:

Blessed are ye, when men shall hate you, and when they shall separate you from their company, and shall reproach you, and cast out your name as evil, for the Son of man's sake. Rejoice ye in that day, and leap for joy: for, behold, your reward is great in heaven: for in the like manner did their fathers unto the prophets (Luke 6:22–3).

This rejoicing in hatred may seem perverse. Indeed the whole principle of loving enemies is perplexing. In Aesop's fable, the man who takes pity on a wounded snake is bitten by the animal after having tended it. As he lies dying, he philosophically concludes that we should know better than to aid those who wish us evil. Aesop is offering a practical moral for the way things work in our world. Matthew, Mark and Luke are preaching an otherworldly worldview, though, a worldview in which this 'world' is not the real one but the transitory, imperfect world of men, which is of little consequence when set against the kingdom of God, the eternal world of the divine spiritual presence.

Luke is preaching that we must learn to cut ourselves off from this world. Paradoxically, this involves a double movement: the soul must focus all of its faith upon the divine world, but the heart must open up to those around us in the world of the here and now. This closing off to terrestrial comfort, the warmth of brotherly love, the community of those who love us, and this simultaneous opening up to hatred, is in itself a hard principle to observe. But even more confusing is the celebration of hate for those who begot us. Because in direct opposition to traditional teaching, in direct opposition to the Law of Moses, Jesus preaches that we must violently break away from our parents in order to join him. Love of him and his God entails not only a rejection but a hatred of our parents, our spouse, our children and our very lives:

If any man come to me, and hate not his father, and mother, and wife, and children, and brethren, and sisters, yea, and his own life also, he cannot be my disciple. And whosoever doth not bear his cross, and come after me, cannot be my disciple. (Luke 14:26–7)

This curious injunction from Jesus, recorded in the Book of Saint Luke, finds no echo within the other Gospels, though the idea of turning from one's clan, one's family and from life itself is essential, and will be the principle which inspires the monastic life for the next two thousand years.

Matthew, Mark and Luke are the great teachers of the New Testament. The Gospel According to St John lacks the prosaic charm of their teachings. Those three were reaching out to ordinary people with an extraordinary message. They are pedagogues. John introduces us to a more abstract kind of faith, a cult of the Light, and his explanations show a taste for paradox and enigma. But once more, John's teachings are framed in, and founded upon, hate as much as love: 'He that loveth his life shall lose it; and he that hateth his life in this world shall keep it unto life eternal' (KJV, John 12:25). Hating life becomes the condition *sine qua non* of entering into 'life eternal'. This obscure doctrine requires some interpretation. How are we to understand this concept of 'life', which not only implies a double meaning but which sets one of the meanings against the other?

A rigorous philologist must reach back into the Greek text to try to disentangle these two meanings. *The Kingdom Interlinear Translation of the Greek Scriptures* (1985: 472–3) should help us to clarify this paradox. The word-for-word translation of the Greek is, admittedly, incomprehensible, since it respects the syntax entirely. But the transcription of the literal wording renders the following translation into English: 'He that is fond of his soul destroys it, but he that hates his soul in this world will safeguard it for everlasting life'. This translation has the advantage of disentangling the 'everlasting life' from the life of the soul which must be either loved or shunned. 'Soul' in English derives from *sāwol* in Old English, a word which was used to designate 'the vital principle', 'the essential part'. 'Soul' has come to mean the spiritual or emotional part of man, the disembodied spirit of man. But the Hebrew word *nefesh* and the Greek word *psyche* both referred to life itself, the living body. Translating into *anima* in Latin, this word gave us such terms as 'animal' and 'animate'. The words the Hebrews, Greeks and Romans used to cover the meanings we render by 'soul' all designate life forms. This will become clearer if we consider the following English expressions: 'not a soul was there', or 'a village of fifty souls'. Though archaic, these expressions remind us that soul could, until modern times, mean simply 'living person'.

John was preaching an entirely different philosophy when he suggested we should shun our souls in order to reach into eternity. What he was advocating was that we turn our backs on earthly pleasures and all that binds us to this life and those who we love and who love us. This radical position involves not simply 'turning away' (the opposite movement to the act of loving in Aquinas' teaching), it involves actively hating all that hinders our movement towards the object of our desire, 'everlasting life'. If a father stands in our way, we must hate him. If a wife stands in our way, she must be cast aside. Such an act can hardly lead to spiritual and emotional calm. Indeed, destroying those who are close to us in our own hearts would inevitably destroy something in us. But this is exactly what John is advocating. We must hate our own souls in order to reach into the eternal life.

John's doctrines show the influence of the Manicheans. We must choose between extremes. We must choose between light and darkness. This is the organising principle around which John's teachings are structured:

1:2 The same was in the beginning with God. 1:3 All things were made by him; and without him was not any thing made that was made. 1:4 In him was life; and the life was the light of men. 1:5 And the light shineth in darkness; and the darkness comprehended it not. (KJV, John)

This is John's doctrine of Φως (light). Strangely obscure, at times John professes to know the light and to celebrate it. Condemning others to darkness and to the shadows of ignorance, John was affirming that the only true understanding was the revelation of light. He therefore divided the world into those who showed an inclination for light and those who preferred darkness. By darkness he meant all that could be perceived, enjoyed and loved in this world. To put this in Aquinas' terms (though Aquinas would hardly have approved of such a conclusion), John believed that love of this world was sinful: it was the inclination of the soul to that which was strange to it, unnatural to it. The true craving of the soul was for the otherworldly everlasting life, Φως.

John teaches that the world does not love light. Jesus had taught him that the world's hatred of him derived from the resentment people felt at being exposed for their sinfulness. About the world, Jesus reasoned, 'me it hateth, because I testify of it, that the works thereof are evil' (John, 7:7). Jesus reassures his followers that hatred for them derives logically from hatred for him. Ultimately what he is suggesting, though, is that it is their loathing for sin and for their own sinfulness which inspires this hatred among the people. They hate being exposed and having their sins brought to light. Jesus stands apart from the people. He leaves his family and his village. But more than this, he claims to have access to a spiritual kingdom from which he is derived. As John puts Jesus' explanation to his disciples:

15:19 If ye were of the world, the world would love his own: but because ye are not of the world, but I have chosen you out of the world, therefore the world hateth you.

Using the same logic David used in the Psalms, Jesus ascribes all antipathy for his person to sinfulness and infidelity to God: 'He that hateth me hateth my Father also' (John 15:23). Jesus preaches love, but that love involves a hatred of the hatred of God.

Paul is less perplexing than John. He brings us back to more familiar territory, and is a little more concerned with this world than John, who seems to live exclusively for the world to come, the world of everlasting life and light. Paul is concerned with sin and saving sinners. His love is defined in terms of hate and hating, nonetheless, because sinners are essentially 'haters of God' for Paul:

1:29 Being filled with all unrighteousness, fornication, wickedness, covetousness, maliciousness; full of envy, murder, debate, deceit, malignity; whisperers,
    1:30 Backbiters, haters of God, despiteful, proud, boasters, inventors of evil things, disobedient to parents,
    1:31 Without understanding, covenantbreakers, without natural affection, implacable, unmerciful:
    1:32 Who knowing the judgment of God, that they which commit such things are worthy of death, not only do the same, but have pleasure in them that do them. (KJV, Romans)

For Paul, haters condemn themselves. By hating God's commandments and by taking joy in breaking them, in taking pleasure in the company of those who join them in their sin, haters lose themselves in their folly and estrange themselves from their true nature. They are perverted from the path of righteousness.

This is a strong condemnation. But Paul does not spare himself or the virtuous. He reserves his sternest council for those who would condemn others: because, he argues, no one is a stranger to sin. If we want to find a sinner, therefore, we should simply look into our own souls, Paul advises.

2:1 Therefore thou art inexcusable, O man, whosoever thou art that judgest: for wherein thou judgest another, thou condemnest thyself; for thou that judgest doest the same things. (KJV, Romans)

Though Paul is down to earth in certain respects, and manages to bring a very abstract concept of truth to the everyday level of practical morality, the doctrine he preaches marks a new manner of turning from the world and from others. The preoccupation is no longer with our sins against others and theirs against us, the kind of deceit and evil that Cain and Joseph were guilty of. This new preoccupation is with the inescapable predilection of the soul towards sinning. As such, it focuses the attention of hate not so much on sins and sinning as upon the soul's propensity to sin. Paul takes sin out of the world and places it in the very nature of the soul. Sinning is no longer interactive in the social sense: it is implicit in men and women, a part of the make-up of mankind. This doctrine will expound a new concept of sin and entail giving a new sense to the history of sin, from the original sin of Adam's fall from grace to all other forms of sinning throughout the Old and New Testaments.

One of the essential tensions within Aquinas' philosophy is his attempt to introduce Aristotle's principle that all things must act in accordance with their nature to Christian philosophy. This principle stands at odds with the doctrine that Paul teaches because Paul sets the soul in opposition to the Law. He taught: 'the law is spiritual: but I am carnal, sold under sin' (Romans 7:14). Paul and Aquinas coincide in their belief that sin destroys the soul. Aristotle would have agreed with them, since he affirmed that vice involved acting in a way which was inappropriate to one's nature. Aristotle taught that all moral evil derived from ignorance, an incapacity to perceive what was good. And Aquinas followed him on this point. Paul, on the other hand, was arguing that the soul was naturally disposed towards evil. In this respect, evil-doers were not simply acting in contradiction to their ultimate interests in losing themselves in sin. They were not simply 'unenlightened', as Aristotle and Aquinas would have considered them to be. They were acting in accord with their nature. They were clinging to this world and to its pleasures. And it was precisely that world and those pleasures which the Christian teachers of the Gospels were advocating we should renounce.

Strangely, Paul does not seem to be able to abandon this world. And he is often quoted for reminding us of the tradition which goes back to the Song of Solomon in celebrating love of an erotic kind. This involved celebrating the Church as a 'body'. This is ultimately no more than a metaphor, but the Christians have a very passionate relationship with allegory. Paul reasoned in his Epistle to the Ephesians:

5:28 So ought men to love their wives as their own bodies. He that loveth his wife loveth himself.
5:29 For no man ever yet hated his own flesh; but nourisheth and cherisheth it, even as the Lord the church:
5:30 For we are members of his body, of his flesh, and of his bones.

This does not prevent Paul, in his Epistle to Titus, from warning against succumbing to 'divers lusts and pleasures, living in malice and envy, hateful, and hating one another', however (KJV, 3:3).

This summary should have gone some way to distinguishing various forms of hate. The teachings of the Gospels overlap and interweave with one another, of course, and their central messages bear much in common. But analysing their teachings from the point of view of hate, it would not be unfair to argue that while Paul's hate is directed against sinning and the sinful soul, John's hate is directed against darkness, the unenlightened state of Godlessness, on the other side, the abyss, what the Wandering Kabbalists called the *achra sitra*. Matthew, Mark and Luke, for their part, were more concerned with spreading love and with hating hate, although they embraced hate as repayment for their love, considering it as both a test of their faith and the guarantee of their holiness. In this, they bore their share of that sanctifying hate which had persecuted and crucified their leader, Jesus. They thereby partook in his sanctity.

Paul's love and hate remains terrestrial. In his Epistle to the Hebrews, Paul teaches: 'Thou hast loved righteousness, and hated iniquity' (KJV, Hebrews 1:9). He was to expound the difference between the two in terms that remind us of John's distinction, teaching: 'He that saith he is in the light, and hateth his brother, is in darkness even until now' (John I 2:9). But where John reaches into the other world and into abstractions, Paul hears his words and reaches back into this world. He will tolerate no declared affinity with light which is not backed up by a very real love of the living, breathing brothers around us. Otherworldly light should enlighten this world and touch men and women with its warmth. John's conception of love and hate, light and dark, is far more tortured. He expounds the same belief as Paul in his First Epistle:

4:19 We love him, because he first loved us. 4:20 If a man say, I love God, and hateth his brother, he is a liar: for he that loveth not his brother whom he hath seen, how can he love God whom he hath not seen? 4:21 And this commandment have we from him, That he who loveth God love his brother also. (KJV, John I)

But this love is conceived of as an arm against hostility and violence. The perfect love that John yearned for was a fearless love, a love which could bear suffering and the hatred of others. The love Christ gave his disciples made them fearless. Love gave them the courage to face the hatred of the world and to accept that they would be despised. He that feared could not be said to love in this perfect way, according to John. 'There is no fear in love; but perfect love casteth out fear: because fear hath torment. He that feareth is not made perfect in love' (*ibid.*, 4:18).

Is there not, however, a contradiction, or at least an incompatibility, between this declaration of a tranquil fearless faith and the anarchic hellish imaginings which animated John's teaching? The taste of the Armageddon is the taste of fear. And John does not seem possessed of peace of mind when he declaims:

And the ten horns which thou sawest upon the beast, these shall hate the whore, and shall make her desolate and naked, and shall eat her flesh, and burn her with fire. (KJV, Revelation, 17:16)

The hatred of whores is a long and complex theme in both the Old and New Testaments. Israel was considered the 'bride' of the Lord, and the waywardness of the children of Israel had always been referred to in terms of 'infidelity'. This underlying allegory often mingles with more concrete diatribes against prostitutes and promiscuous women. The Proverbs warn against women who make the most of their husbands' absence to seduce the just from the contemplation of the Law of Moses and the contemplation of the divine. The priestesses of Babylon and the celebration of Baal involved festivities with fornication in forms found in many pagan rites. All of these threads come together to weave a tapestry which is particularly hard to contemplate at a time in which feminist revisions of biblical scripture are trying to disentangle God from the representations of God which patriarchal societies were able to form based upon their own limited and prejudiced view of men and women, of society and of the world.

It has become commonplace to denounce the marginalisation of women in society, in religion and in mythology today. That gods were ripped from the thigh (the strongest muscle in the body and the pride of the warrior) in Greek mythology now seems a laughable attempt to deprive women of their gift to the world in giving birth and to attribute Creation to a universal masculine force. The fate of a woman's children was symbolically taken out of her hands, too. The sacrifice of the first-born becomes, in the Bible with the story of Abraham and Isaac, the negotiation over the life of the son between the father and a masculine god, the Spiritual Father, the King of the Kingdom of the Heavens.

This masculine conception of the divine is obviously problematic. The consequence that the laws of men and women which should conform to the will of a divine father figure is no less problematic. As soon as we accept that the body is a source of distraction from the contemplation of the true life, the light, the otherworldly realm, women inevitably become the agents of the Devil in perverting the will of the pure of heart. It goes without saying that from a traditional perspective, contemplation is the activity of the male soul, who must leave the body to unite with the divine. The Bible is famous for the celebration of women. But no amount of celebration of the women of the Bible can compensate for this. The heroines of the Bible are not negligible or marginal characters. Esther, the Jewish beauty who is married to Xerxes the Persian ruler uncovers the plot of the Vizir, Haman, to exterminate the Jews, and persuades her husband to punish him. Solomon's tribute to feminine charms is legendary. Self-sacrificing mothers such as Jesus' own mother, Mary, are found throughout both the New and Old Testaments. Samuel's mother, for example, in repayment to the Lord for 'opening up her womb', devotes her son to His worship. Wives often prove wiser than their husbands: Isaac's wife sees clearly that Jacob is a worthier heir than Esau. She does not dare to openly defy Isaac, however.

The celebration of women throughout the Bible remains, on the whole, the celebration of obedience. And the charms that Solomon sings in praise of are the charms of the seductive object which offers itself to man. When female figures fail to conform to the roles of objects of desire and exchange, or faithful servants, they are disparaged or demonized. The misogyny of Revelation is palpable. When evil takes a human form, in the form of Babylon, it takes the form of the whore: and it is this whore which animates the imagination of John with a great, frightening élan:

18:2 And he cried mightily with a strong voice, saying, Babylon the great is fallen, is fallen, and is become the habitation of devils, and the hold of every foul spirit, and a cage of every unclean and hateful bird. 18:3 For all nations have drunk of the wine of the wrath of her fornication, and the kings of the earth have committed fornication with her, and the merchants of the earth are waxed rich through the abundance of her delicacies. 18:4 And I heard another voice from heaven, saying, Come out of her, my people, that ye be not partakers of her sins, and that ye receive not of her plagues.

18:5 For her sins have reached unto heaven, and God hath remembered her iniquities. (KJV, Revelation)

This is a delirious diatribe. What Plato and Aristotle criticized in the sophists was their tendency to lose sight of truth and their tendency to confuse people, convincing others with the force of their rhetoric. In direct contrast to this, both Aristotle's *Ethics* and his *Rhetoric* aimed to make rhetoric the servant of truth. Rhetoric was part of politics and politics was ultimately dependent on ethics for Aristotle, who reasoned that those who seek to impose their arguments in society by the skill of their rhetoric should ultimately have knowledge of themselves and of reality. This would allow them to judge what course should be taken and to supply reasoned and reasonable arguments to convince others, not simply to persuade them.

Biblical scripture, on the other hand, is deeply allegorical. And it is not always clear whether what animates the spirit of the biblical writers and spell-binds our attention in reading them is the target or the vehicle of their alle-gories. The force of Revelation is of an obscure but a sublime nature. And it is uncertain to what extent the hatred of woman is animating the hatred of Babylon, and to what extent the hatred of Babylon is merely served by the image of the whore. At any rate, the anguish experienced at trying to cut our-selves off from our desires, and refusing the body, while striving towards the world beyond, and towards eternal life, seems to have generated a great tension and a great animosity against all that might distract the biblical writers from their quest. Woman would always be the primary temptress in this spiritual struggle for men, and the whore, the available woman, craving sexual union, would inevitably be held up as antithesis of holiness. This was the misogyny which was to stoke so many bonfires during the witch hunts of the Middle Ages and early modern period. Though the Christians priests were certainly more ascetic than the Hebrews in turning away from marriage and from woman, it would, however, be unfair to attribute the hatred of woman to the Christians. This is a recurring theme throughout both the Testaments.

The conclusion we are left to draw is perplexing. Love implies hating, this is the moral the Bible teaches us. And the further the Christians reached into the otherworldly realm, the more they hated all that prevented that flight into the divine. All that is around us, in society, in our intimate relations, and even within our very living, breathing, desiring souls, becomes subservient to that overriding desire to love. And that considerably widens the scope of hate, hat-ing and the hated.

A philology of hate

Studying biblical hate involved an exercise in discourse analysis. Told and retold over centuries, this largely oral set of texts evolving over time allows us to interpret the way the key concepts of love and hate condition one another in a dense but coherent narrative. On a more purely linguistic level, though: what can philology tell us about the nature of hate and the way it manifests itself in society?

Translation, which was always at the centre of philological study, is of immense importance for spreading the diverse concepts of hatred found in the Bible. The transmission of Christian and Jewish philosophy was dependent upon translators. And translators themselves have often had a profound impact upon the history of ideas and the course of history. If the English translation of Wycliffe (1384), the Czech translation of Hus (towards the end of the four-teenth century) and Luther's German translation (1534) were all to have revo-lutionary consequences, it was because translation entails interpretation. Those translators felt that in grappling with words and concepts, with metaphor and with grammar, they were coming closer to the truth of the text, the essential expression of men living thousands of years before them. Meschonnic and other translators working today continue working in the same spirit. For this reason, considering the way hate emerges throughout the text which has had more influence than any other on the Western world, and indeed on the world as a whole, has been meaningful and worthwhile. It has helped us understand the interdependence of love and hate, the diverse forms of hate that emerge in biblical thought, and it has helped us to move beyond a naive rejection of hate. Hate can no longer be simply denounced and stored away in a category for negative emotions. Hate must be engaged as a concept, as a defining force which must be faced up to.

In the same way, neither the hate that the neoconservatives have been promoting nor the biblical rhetoric which inspires their 'crusading capitalism' can simply be rejected. To dismiss them is to adopt the stance that the media have taken up in recent years, and indeed Obama is endeavouring to maintain the very same stance. But in taking up this stance, we act in a way similar to the cynics of communist countries in the seventies. Fidelius, in his stunning critique of Czechoslovak communism, took his friends to task for denouncing communism as nonsense. In contrast to them, he claimed that the worldview of the communists *did* make sense. Though he himself did not subscribe to it, he believed that there was a logic organising the concepts of the communist worldview and that it did hold together as a system. If we are to understand the worldview of the neoconservatives we must enter into their system of thought and the logic which organizes their concepts. This requires a leap of faith (or folly!). Without that leap, though, we can neither understand how they think and feel, nor can we resist the impact of their ideas: because if we do not understand that worldview we are all too easily seduced by the central concepts which operate within its workings. We fall, all too easily, into rejecting their strategies for 'winning the war against terror' without questioning whether that 'war' exists or not, or whether the idea of a 'war' on 'terror' itself makes any sense. We start attributing the concept of 'rogue state' to the USA, without questioning whether the concept itself is coherent.

The analysis of the Bible takes us deeper into ourselves, since our fundamentally Judeo-Christian tradition has contributed to shaping the concepts with which we think and the principles by which we live. We cannot simply break away from that tradition. Any radicalism, be it communist, fascist or, in recent years, neoconservative and neoliberal, will take position to some extent in relation to the founding principles of love and hate as defined within the Bible. This will involve rejecting certain principles and concepts and embracing others, but even those rejected will lead us to define ourselves in opposing what we reject, and what we modify.

Our study of the Bible and of the discourse of Bush and Obama was already philological in nature. Just as we considered in the opening chapters the use of personification to diabolize a nation, transforming Iraq step by step into a regime and then into a man, a criminal, an 'outlaw' offending against the world community and against human rights, we considered the metaphors which link and support the logic of Saint John's concepts of 'light', enlightenment, life and eternal life. In the same way, we considered the relationship between zeal and jealousy, and the crucial roles these terms play in constructing the discourse of love and hate. In many respects, Obama espouses the 'love thy neighbour–love thy brother' philosophy which germinates in the Law of Moses, but which is affirmed by the punishment of Cain at the very beginning of Genesis and which will animate the major Gospels of the New Testament.

Democrats and more moderate Americans will find this reassuring. But this account in itself constitutes an attempt to harness certain elements of biblical philosophy and exclude others. It is a not altogether informed (or honest) attempt to stigmatize Bush. With a sovereign condescension, Obama is seeking to take Bush's Bible from him. For though many people mock and disparage his use of biblical rhetoric, close reading of both the New and Old Testaments leads us to a perplexing conclusion: the 'Book of Love' is also a 'Book of Hate'. And this takes us dangerously close to the stance Bush adopts and the worldview he promulgated. Is Bush's persecution of his enemies in his detention centres any more unreasonable than David's divine lust to crush all who oppose him? Is the logic which he uses to define all his enemies as evil-doers, infidels, enemies of God essentially different from the one Bush uses to denounce all the enemies of democracy and the enemies of the USA?

An argument can be made against Bush, and a biblical argument too, but the fact is that this debate is not taking place. Bush's ideals and the logic of his worldview have been disparaged but not critiqued in terms of the emotive biblical rhetoric which rendered his arguments so seductive to vast segments of US society. Nor would it be fair to send Bush off into quarantine, attributing his faith to the outdated barbarism of the Old Testament. Jesus, too, says he who is not with me is against me. Jesus hates evil and evil-doing. Bush may fail to perceive the nature, the origin and the manifestation of vice and sin, but the logic of his arguments reposes upon the logic of faith. For all these reasons, it was necessary to enter into the spirit of the Old and New Testaments in order to see how the logic of their arguments is continuing to sway statesmen and direct the course of their actions today.

But a philology of hate cannot content itself with simply analysing discourse, redefining central concepts, and tracing their origins and historical developments. Philology in the form espoused by Humboldt and Wierzbicka encourages us to compare languages and to try to determine to what extent different language cultures develop distinct untranslatable concepts. It will be impossible in the space that remains to do justice to the approach Wierzbicka adopts. Even if we restricted ourselves to Czech, German, French and English, such a study of hate would require a case study in itself, if not a volume. Nevertheless, it is important to extend the scope of the present reflection to include the consideration of foreign concepts usually translated by our term 'hate'. Those concepts should be studied not simply as equivalents but as concepts in their own rights, acting within their own language systems. Opening up to different concepts of 'hate' in French and German will also allow us to trace curious mutations in the development of animosity of a social, political and national kind.

The etymology of hate

One of the most curious things about this concept is that two terms exist in English, closely related morphologically speaking; two terms which appear to cover exactly the same field of meanings, hate and hatred. Both appear as entries in *The Collins Robert French–English, English–French Dictionary* (1993), but certain dictionaries do not have an entry for 'hatred'. *The Chambers Twentieth Century Dictionary* (edited by William Geddie, first published in 1901 and re-edited in 1964), for example, includes it only as a subsection under 'hate'. In my own research, based upon a corpus of 732,411 words put together from English texts from the early modern era to the contemporary period, both terms figured.

Hatred was, for example, used by Bacon in his discussion of 'friendship' in his essay with that title. Quoting Aristotle's *Politics*, Francis Bacon argued that ' "Whosoever is delighted in solitude, is either a wild beast or a god." For it is most true, that a natural and secret hatred, and aversation (*sic*) towards society, in any man, hath somewhat of the savage beast' (Bacon undated: 77). Scottish biographers of Byron might be tempted to attribute the term 'hatred' to Scots dialect (Byron being half-Scottish) when he uses it in *Don Juan* (www.gutenberg.org), but such a claim would prove unfounded. Jane Austen uses the word, too, in *Pride and Prejudice* (www.gutenberg.org), and so do Charles Dickens and Oscar Wilde.

Shakespeare, on the other hand, would appear to prefer 'hate', and uses the word three times in *Macbeth* and four times in *Twelfth Night*, while he uses 'hatred' in neither play. Bacon, for his part, uses 'hate' and 'hatred' as synonyms. 'Hate' is used as both a noun and a verb with an alarming frequency in Byron. Satire is by nature 'biting', but Byron outdoes other authors in his propensity to hate and in his observations concerning the aversions of others, often to the most peculiar list of objects (pedants, red cloaks, herds of cattle and innumerable other things). Hatred, on the other hand, is rarely used by Byron. Is this a question of poetic technique? The potential for rhyming 'hatred' is limited. The monosyllable 'hate' is far more convenient for the poet's purposes, as we can see in the following example:

With Raucocanti lucklessly was chain'd
The tenor; these two hated with a hate
Found only on the stage, and each more pain'd
With this his tuneful neighbour than his fate;

Byron was a master-rhymer, and much of his wit comes from his ability to interject an unexpected rhyme, often with the effect of bathos.

Rough Johnson, the great moralist, profess'd
Right honestly, 'he liked an honest hater!'-
The only truth that yet has been confest
Within these latest thousand years or later.

Curiously, Dickens does not use 'hate' as a noun in *Great Expectations*, though he does use the verb. Austen uses both. Lewis Carroll in *Alice in Wonderland*, and Joyce in *The Portrait of an Artist* follow suit.

What are we to conclude? 'Hate' seems to be dominating today in everyday English just as it seems to have been the predominant term in Shakespeare's time. The Old Testament uses the words interchangeably. Admittedly, though, the translations of certain books do show a preference for one term over the other. Only one occurrence of 'hatred' can be found, in The Epistle of Paul the Apostle to the Galatians:

5:19 Now the works of the flesh are manifest, which are these; Adultery, fornication, uncleanness, lasciviousness, 5:20 Idolatry, witchcraft, **hatred**, variance, emulations, wrath, strife, seditions, heresies, 5:21 Envyings, murders, drunkenness, revellings, and such like: of the which I tell you before, as I have also told you in time past, that they which do such things shall not inherit the kingdom of God.

What can more extensive corpus research tell us? The search engine Google offers just over 17 million web links to 'hatred', but 185 million links to 'hate'. Even taking into consideration that some of these examples will apply to the verb form (I hate, you hate, we hate, they hate), the evidence seems fairly conclusive that hate predominates in comparisons of the terms in contemporary English. We speak of 'a love–hate relationship' not 'a love–hatred relationship', the British Nationalist Party is accused of 'race hate', and defends itself against such claims. There is even a rock group called 'Hate' with its official website. 'Love and hate' provided 336,000 web links, 'love and hatred' only 24,000. COCA, the Corpus of Contemporary American English, provided 181,100 uses of hate as opposed to 4,132 examples of hatred.

Where does the word hate derive from? The verb derives from *hatian* in Old English, according to *The Oxford Concise Dictionary of English Etymology* (1986). In Modern Dutch, the verb *haten* is clearly closely related to our own. Old Norse had *hatr*, which mutated into our 'hate' under the influence of 'hatred'. In the thirteenth century, speakers of Middle English were using *haterede* as the noun form. But in Old English the form *hete* (in which the accented vowel was pronounced in much the same way as the vowel in its contemporary equivalent 'hate') was already used. This form was closely related to *heti* in Old Saxon and *haz* in Old High German, from which *Hass* derives.

What can be said of words which derive from hate? 'Hater' is now relatively rare, though it appears to be making a comeback in slang according to the *Urban Dictionary* (2005), whose website can be consulted online (www. urbandictionary.com). 'Hateful' is still used, though the adverb 'hatefully' is rare, and 'hateless' had become sufficiently rare that it is now rejected by automatic spelling correctors, though it still remains in dictionary entries, of course. 'Hate-free' seems to be replacing it, but remains fairly rare.

Synonyms and antonyms

The noun 'hate' has numerous synonyms: disaffection, enmity, animosity, antipathy, acrimony, repugnance, loathing, detestation, execration and odium (which is rare but which is still active in the adjective 'odious'). When referring to a feeling of hate, regarded as the source of negative feeling, or the explanation of unpleasant conduct, we might use the words umbrage, or grudge. And when expressing hate as a state we are subjected to, we might speak of alienation, estrangement or disfavour. The verb also has numerous synonyms: to detest, to abominate, to abhor, to loathe, to recoil from, to shudder at, to shrink from, to view with horror. The adjective 'hateful' has similar synonyms: abhorrent, obnoxious, odious, abominable, repulsive, offensive, shocking, disgusting and so on. And when this adjective refers literally to a person 'full of hate', we can say that person is invidious, spiteful or malicious. Although using words such as 'abominable' and 'detestable' can have a certain impact since they are *expressive* terms which can be hyperbolic, the monosyllable 'hate' has a simple primal force which implies an irrevocable gut reaction: indeed the monosyllable 'guts' is often linked to 'hate' in the common expression 'to hate someone's guts'.

The opposite of hate is 'love', of course, but multiple antonyms for love exist which are formed using the negative prefix (dis-like, dis-taste, dis-affection etc.). Love has already been subjected to analysis in its own case study. It should therefore suffice here to remind ourselves that our concept of love covers at least the four definitions of love which can be translated into English as 'erotic love' (desire), 'brotherly love', 'friendship' (filia), love in the active sense, entailing carrying out shared projects, and *storge*, goodwill for those who are close to us (family and friends). Animosity does not seem to break down so clearly. We seem far less lucid about our hating. Hate has not inspired contemplation and reflection to the degree to which love has, and no philosophers appear to have differentiated the various forms of hating. Linguistics may go some way to rectifying this if it manages to distinguish between the objects of hate.

Collocations and associations

What do we associate hate with? What do we hate? COCA proves revealing as a linguistic tool in answering these questions. Of the first 100 examples of 'hatred', racial and religious hatred provided 15 per cent of the themes for entries. Hatred for Jews and for Israel took up seven of the examples, though those who spoke of anti-Semitism invariably denounced it. Hate for Israel turned out to be ninety-ninth in the list of associated words, hatred for Muslims came out as thirty-sixth and hatred for Arabs was forty-third. Given that anti-Arab sentiment was evoked in both of these categories and that it was also covered in other discussions of racial hatred, it can be concluded that hate for people of Arabo-Muslim cultures is a major preoccupation in the contemporary American worldview.

The word searches made possible by COCA offer access to the context of these quotes, and thereby allow us to form a fair idea about the collocations associated with hate. Hate remains a sentiment directed against persons. This explains why 'hate' was coupled with 'guts' more frequently than with any other word. The 'top ten' of word couples gives a fair idea about the preoccupations of Americans at the present time: 1. Guts, 2. Legislation, 3. Crimes, 4. Interrupt, 5. Disappoint, 6. Reported, 7. Federal, 8. Bigotry, 9. Discrimination, 10, Despise. Given that the couplings of 'hate' with 'interrupt' and with 'disappoint' are clearly derived from standard polite expressions, and that 'despise' merely serves to redouble the effect of its synonym 'hate', we are left with at least four of the ten major categories being potentially related to race and religion ('legislation', 'crime', 'bigotry' and 'discrimination'). The division of anti-religious sentiment into anti-Semitism, anti-Arab and anti-Muslim feeling also inevitably downplays religious and cultural animosity in this 'top ten of hates'. Considered together, the statistics would present a much more startling picture.

Other themes upon which hatred focused in the first 100 examples (all taken from 2009 COCA sources) were America (6%) and politicians (3%). Bush, Obama and Sarah Palin were all the focus of hatred in one example. Women were also the subject of hate (3%, though some of the examples were directed at persons rather than the sex in general, and examples of ex-girlfriends hating men were also found). Socialism was the focus of hate in one single example, suggesting that in the contemporary American worldview, the Cold War is dead and buried.

Metaphoric construction of the concept of hate

Metaphors can be considered as those frameworks or paradigms which permit the construction of concepts. In literary criticism, on the other hand, they can also be considered as those expressive personal touches which characterize the style of individuals capable of original metaphoric invention. Hate does attract a certain amount of innovation, but several underlying themes organize many of the metaphoric constructions which our concept of hatred adopts in everyday discourse. COCA provided the following examples which are fairly representative. Four primary paradigms emerged. Hate takes the form of:

1. an organism (perhaps a person)
2. an attack or weapon
3. a natural force
4. water or liquid.

Organism

Hate can be 'undying'. A situation, a problem or events can 'breed' hatred. Hatred can be 'fed'. Hatred can 'take root' and it can 'take years to ripen'. Hatred can be 'raw'. It is noteworthy that the organism can be active or passive: hate can 'feed on something' just as it can 'be fed' by something or someone.

Attack or weapon

Hatred can 'strike' us. We speak of 'the bite of hatred'. Claiming that something 'triggers' hatred may not necessarily imply a gun, since it could refer to any mechanism which provokes a mechanical reflex, but there can be little doubt that we are talking about 'whips' when we speak of 'the whiplash of hatred'. Interestingly, hatred itself can be 'whipped up', proving once more the ambivalent passive–active nature of metaphoric representation.

Natural force

Hatred, associated with violence, tends to attract violent metaphors related to natural forces which threaten us or overcome us. Hatred is often conceived in terms of fire: hatred can be 'stoked up', or we can 'feed the flames of hatred'. We can be 'consumed by hatred'.

Water or liquid

Certain liquid-related metaphors can be accounted for by the natural force paradigm. To say we are 'engulfed' by hatred or 'drowned' by hatred, to speak of a 'wave' of hatred, all imply the idea of a great natural force, perhaps not a tsunami but something equivalent to the waves caused by a storm or hurricane. 'Hate is rising' also presupposes the idea of hatred as a water level.

In one COCA quote 'a sea of tedium, hatred and rage' was mentioned. We speak of the 'depth' of hatred too. This mirrors the metaphoric paradigm used to represent love. Indeed, at times, opposites appear to be conditioned metaphorically by each other. The paradigms of one concept are transposed to its opposite. In the case study of love, we have already considered the way heat metaphors are mirrored inversely in representations of coldness and frigidity.

Other

These four paradigms cover many but by no means all of the forms used to represent hate. Hate can be said to be 'oozing from one's pores'. It is therefore a bodily secretion. It can be 'smelled'. It can 'boil up inside' someone, a metaphor which consolidates the idea that we can be 'hateful', i.e. 'full of hate'. Hate can also be radiation. The Chicago Police Department were said (in one COCA quote) 'to radiate hate'. Hate could 'circulate', and in contradistinction to the secretion metaphor, it could 'be absorbed'. Curiously, hatred could be represented as a treasure: one COCA quote described a man who felt 'the small cold emerald of the hatred in her heart'. And the protagonists of a Bergman film induced a film critic to ponder upon 'unfathomed hatred and boundless egocentricity as the pillars of existence'.

Translating hate

At first sight, the concept of hate does not seem to be particularly difficult to translate into other languages. Hate appears to cause less difficulty than 'freedom' or 'angst', for example. 'Freedom' will take on a dramatic, new, politically defining significance for the Americans when they break free from the 'yoke' of empire, and *liberté* in French follows a similar course with the abolition of the *ancient régime*. The idea of a universal concept of 'freedom' is, therefore, questionable. Wierzbicka (1997:125–55), for example, in considering the different concepts of 'freedom' which are found in Latin, English, Russian and Polish, discerns a considerable amount of difference, concluding that each tradition cultivates a culturally specific ideal of 'freedom'. 'Angst' will undergo a transformation in moving from German, in which it covers a vast variety of meanings, to English, in which it will be restricted to intense emotional, psychological and spiritual distress and anguish. But 'hate' seems to be more deeply enrooted (at least in the European imagination), and can be translated into French (*la haine*), German (*der Haß*), Czech (*nenávist*) and Spanish (*el odio*).

The ease with which we can translate 'hate' can be seen if we compare the French and English translations of Matthew's words when he preaches the need to modify the ancient Law of Moses: 'Ye have heard that it hath been said, Thou shalt love thy neighbour, and **hate** thine enemy' (KJV, Matthew 5:43). The *Bible de Jérusalem* (BJ) translates the latter part as '*Tu aimeras ton prochain et tu haïras ton ennemi*' (2001). Similarly, Luther's *Matthäus* quotes the Law of Moses as *Du sollst deinen Nächsten lieben und deinen Feind **hassen*** (Das Neue Testament, *Die Bibel nach der übersetzung Martin Luthers*, 1999: 5:43).

Spanish *odio* renders 'hate' in a great number of instances with no apparent problem. Debate on the Internet concerning tensions between ex-colonial nations and the ex-colonized lands was expressed in Spanish using much the same discourse as the press of Britain, as the titles of articles published clearly show: ¿*A que se debe el **odio** de latinoamerica a españa*? (What is the cause of Latin-America's hate for Spain? 1 February 2007). South Americans, highly sensitive to what they considered to be a display of contempt for them in Spain asked: 'Why does Spain have so much hate?' (¿*Porque tanto **odio** hacia España?*, 2 June 2007).

Enrique Oliva, writing in an article published on the website www.iarnoticias.com on 11 May 2005, 'Racism in Today's Colonial Europe' (*Racismo en la Europa colonialista actual*) drew parallels between the growing mistrust of Muslims in the USA and racism in Europe. He spoke of three magazines which he considered to constitute 'the media of hate' ('medios del *odio*'), magazines which had been condemned in December 2003 to maximum sentences by *del Tribunal Penal Internacional de Arusha*. He blamed such magazines for fuelling racism and quoted examples of the insulting chanting of football supporters directed at players from Africa, Arab countries and South America. He also highlighted the irrational nature of such racism by stressing that though poor immigrants invariably bear the brunt of such racism in the States, Islamic fundamentalist attacks are often carried out by individuals of wealthy or well-to-do backgrounds (a fact which the attempted terrorist attack of the 23-year-old Nigerian, Umar Farouk Abdul Mutallab, 26 December 2009, tends to confirm). These examples tend to indicate that *odio* in Spanish functions in very much the same way as 'hate' does in English.

Like Spanish, French and German, Czech translates our concept of hate with no apparent difficulty. Indeed, the most common expressions found in Czech follow patterns curiously similar to those found in English. For example, where we speak of 'undying hatred', the Czechs speak of a hate that will endure 'to death' (*na smrt*) or 'until the grave' (*až za hrob*). In the same way, a Czech can hate 'wholeheartedly', or rather, 'with his/her whole soul' (*z celé duše*).

Shared origin: shared tradition?

It would be tempting to attribute the fact that five European languages appear to share the same fundamental concept of 'hate' to the fact that they share the same Judeo-Christian tradition. The New and Old Testaments of the Bible have no doubt contributed through their translations to the consolidation of this shared concept. But is there a more fundamental origin to this shared concept? A linguistic derivation? The answer to this question remains ambiguous. Listening to the words in French and English, there is no apparent similarity. Since the *h* is silent in *haine*, from the phonetic and the morphological point of view, there is no correspondence between *haine* and hate. A much more solid link can be forged between *odio* in Spanish and the adjectives 'odious' in English and *odieux* in French. And we have no difficulty in understanding the nature of the aversion that the French writer Guilleragues (1628–85) expresses when his love turns sour and he claims the object of his love, a Portuguese nun, has 'become odious to him':

J'ai éprouvé que vous m'étiez moins cher que ma passion et j'ai eu d'étranges peines à la combattre, après que vos procédés injurieux m'ont rendu votre personne odieuse.

I felt that you were less dear to me than my own passion, and I experienced strange pains in fighting it, after your insulting behaviour made you odious to me. (Guilleragues, in Oster 1990: 348)

The silent 'h' in *haine* tells another story, however. Present in English, French and German, that 'h' correctly indicates a shared origin to the concept. According to *The American Heritage Dictionary of Indo-European Roots*, all three words derive from the Indo-European stem *kād*. This involves the mutation of *ka* into *ha*. Nevertheless, Watkins, who revised the dictionary, follows the great Indo-European scholar Pokorny in affirming the link *kād-*, designating sorrow and hatred, generated both 'hatred' and 'hate' in English, via *hete* in Old English. And the verb form *hatian* in Old English mirrors the development into *hassen* in Modern German. But *kād-* also generated heinous from the Old French *hair*, which carried the same meaning as its contemporary equivalent in Modern French and which was itself derived from the Germanic form *hartjan*. Contemporary etymology in French (Picoche 1994: 282) confirms Pokorny's account.

The importance of the Gallo-Roman roots of French has long been stressed.[12] However, if we are to understand the origins of 'hate' in French, we must look beyond the Gallo-Roman account and go back to the Germanic origins of the language of the Franks. Many words like *hair* are derived from words of Germanic origin. The influence of Celtic languages, though found in everyday words such as *chêne* (oak), is somewhat less widespread than words of Germanic origin (for example, *trop*, *(re-)garder*, *gars* and *garcon*, *riche* and *allemande*, Mitterand 1981: 17). Modern French linguists such as Henri Mitterand tend to speak of the 'gallo-latino-germanic primitive reserves' of French (*ibid.*: 23), and *haïr* certainly belongs to these reserves.

Curiously, this shared origin does not seem to have influenced the gender of the concept of 'hate'. Many concepts preserve their gender during the transition into another language system. De Beauvoir even contends that certain concepts are deeply associated with a specific gender in the imagination. As she argues, truth and wisdom are feminine in many languages (a fact which German, Czech and French bear out). She attributes this to man's tendency to erect his ideals in terms of a transcendental 'alterity': and the feminine, the ultimate Other, incarnates this otherness. Hate, on the other hand, does not seem to be restricted to either the masculine or the feminine form. In Spanish and in German it is masculine, while in French and in Czech (which does not share the etymology of the other languages based upon *kād-*) 'hate' is feminine.

What writers do with hate

We moved from political discourse into the language of the Bible in order to understand the ways cultural concepts shape the possible paths of thinking and feeling. If we discussed the etymological roots of hate, and discussed philological questions of synonyms, antonyms, associations, translation and metaphor, it was to investigate the way the concept of hate reaches out through the language system. This has allowed us to perceive something of the way hate fits into the English speaker's worldview and language system.

But when considering worldview more deeply, we must distinguish between the language system, which engenders a specific world-perceiving and world-conceiving, and the cultural mindset that animates a people at any given time. In the same way, it is essential to consider what each speaker, each writer, does with the cultural mindset which he inherits and which, to a certain extent, he cannot escape. Viewed from this angle, each individual's worldview must take its stance in relation to the relatively fixed concepts which the language system provides him or her with, and which are coloured by the societal and cultural influences of the discourses which are dominating discussion. Linguistically speaking, we can only discuss the relationship between love and hate if we have concepts for love and hate. As our comparison of the five languages has shown, English, French, German, Czech and Spanish all possess a concept of 'hate' which will make such discussion possible. As our examples from Spanish show, the contemporary discussion in both Spanish and English tends to focus upon racial tensions, terrorism and the cultural heritage of colonialism, in both its historic and its modern forms.

An ethnolinguistics of hate would go much further, however. Asking questions such as the following: what do French writers do with hate? How does it structure their conception of relationships? How do they reformulate the concept *haine* with which their language system has provided them? And how do they react against the cultural constraints of the mindset of their era? We have already considered the quotations from Napoléon and Balzac who see in *haine* (hate) an essential elemental force which invigorates the soul and which helps define the man who nurtures it. This idea has its roots in David's conception of divine hatred, the hatred he celebrates in the Psalms, when he sings his love to his jealous destructive God. This is the hatred of the zealot, the hatred which animated many of Bush's more 'successful' speeches.

An exhaustive study is not possible here. Emotions are so fundamental that they have attracted commentary and analysis from almost all of the academic disciplines. A full account of love and hate would therefore necessitate a critique of philosophical accounts of hate, taking on board not only Aristotle, Aquinas and Nietzsche but also Spinoza's *Ethics* (1677), Adam Smith's *Theory of Moral Sentiments* (1759), contemporary accounts of the philosophy of emotions (for example Martha Nussbaum's *Therapy of Desire*, 1994) and emerging neuropsychological approaches (Damasio 2003). An account of sociological or political literature on hate would by itself fill a small library. An enormous amount of vigorous comparative linguistic literature (see Catena and Lamprou 2009, for example) has been sprouting up over the last two decades. Because of the languages involved and because of the very diversity of the approaches, it would only have been possible to give an unsatisfying and unenlightening overview in an ethnolinguistic account of this nature.

I have preferred in this book to proceed by focusing upon only a few languages and by trying to get a grip on individual discourse. In this endeavour, it will, I believe, be instructive to consider as a whole the quotations found in two of the most reliable volumes of quotations, *Le Robert: Dictionnaire de citations françaises*, volumes I and II (Oster 1990 and 1993, hereafter RCI and RCII). Because of their length (818 pages for the first volume and 1,003 pages for the second), these two volumes offer a fairly representative selection of the ideals, ideas, reflections and witticisms which the French have found worthy of being preserved for future generations. Without being a fully satisfying account of French hatred, this corpus should at least have the advantage of forcing us, as English speakers, to break out of our own conceptual ruts and force us to accept that French *haine* cannot be fitted into any selected slot, as an exotic alternative form of emotion. *Haine* proves to be complex.

Baudelaire exemplifies the romantic tradition's celebration of hate we have already seen:

Le haine est une liqueur précieuse, un poison plus cher que celui des Borgia, – car il est fait avec notre sang, notre santé, notre sommeil et les deux tiers de notre amour! Il faut en être avare!

Hate is a precious liquor, a poison more expensive than those of the Borgias, because it is made of our own blood, our health, our sleep and two thirds of our love! We must be misers with it! (1997: 389)

Though Baudelaire is in fact advising moderation in hatred, and arguing that we should not waste our animosity on petty affairs, his celebration of a purified hatred distilled by the soul is all too clear here. Balzac, who belonged to an earlier age and would have shared few of Baudelaire's aesthetic or political convictions, nevertheless agrees with the spirit of this celebration of hate. Hugo, on the other hand, who lived through both the ages of Balzac and Baudelaire, was too concerned for the social injustices of his times to celebrate hate and, in his poetry and his novels, he was deeply concerned with understanding the forms of love celebrated in the Bible and how they might apply to the society of his time. Perhaps this explains why he was not tempted by Romantic celebrations of hatred.

Molière is often quoted for his expression 'those vigorous hates', *ces haines vigoureuses* (RCI: 292). The problem is, though, that in French society Molière is quoted as Shakespeare is quoted in English. English speakers are fond of affirming: as Shakespeare says, 'All the world's a stage'. It should be remembered that in Shakespeare's work, the playwright does not utter a word. Shakespeare leaves each of his characters to speak their 'truths': and it is invariably the evil (such as Macbeth) or the cynical (such as Jacques in *As You Like It*) who make such an affirmation as to the 'unreality' of existence. The plots of Shakespeare's plays lead us to the opposite conclusion: i.e. that life must be lived as life, and that sham and pretence will only lead us to destruction and despair. In the example of hate, Molière is suffering from a similar mistrial. Molière is concerned with denouncing hatred: for this reason he puts the words in the mouth of his anti-hero, in *Le Misanthrope* (Act I:i Alceste). Molière should by rights, therefore, be positioned at the antipodes of the Romantic tradition, whose philosophy of hate he anticipates and mocks in advance.

La Bruyère (1645–96), the famous *hommes de lettres* whose *Caractères* was inspired by the treatise of Aristotle's pupil, Theophrastus, seems to have shared the same vision of hate as the one identified by the Bergman film critic quoted above: enduring hatreds allow men to define themselves and position themselves in relation to one another. For this reason, La Bruyère observed:

Les haines sont si longues et si opiniâtrées, que le plus grand signe de mort dans un homme malade, c'est la réconciliation.

Hates are so enduring and stubborn that the surest sign of approaching death in a sick man is the act of reconciliation. (*Les Caractères: De l'homme*, RCI: 346)

La Bruyère's observation was ironic. He understood that strong men cling to strong hatreds, and only when enfeebled and frightened by the thought of judgement in the next world would they relinquish their hatred and forgive their enemies. This was no celebration of hatred in itself. Voltaire's character in *Candide* adopted the same sardonic tone when he observed:

Je n'ai guère vu de ville qui ne désirât la ruine de la ville voisine, point de famille qui ne voulût exterminer quelque autre famille. Partout les faibles ont en exécration les puissants devant lesquels ils rampent, et les puissants les traitent comme des troupeaux dont on vend la laine et la chair.

I have seen hardly a town which does not desire the ruin of its neighbouring town, or a family who does not wish to exterminate some other family. Everywhere, the weak loathe the strong at whose feet they crawl, while the strong treat them as they treat their flocks whose fleece and flesh they sell. (*Candide ou L'Optimiste*, Chapter 20, RCI: 546)

There is often only a fine line between literature and religion. A strong Christian tradition is at work in the French *vision du monde* of the early modern period. But it is the spirit of Matthew, not that of David, which is at work, the spirit of mercy. Descartes may have transformed philosophy and mathematics, but his views on hate are those of tradition, received wisdom of Church teaching. He argued that:

L'amour est incomparablement meilleure que la haine; elle ne saurait être trop grande ... joignant à nous de vrais biens, elle nous perfectionne ...

Love is incomparably better than hate; it cannot be great enough ... providing us with real goods, it perfects us ... (*Les Passions de l'âme*, Art.139, RCI:171)

Descartes, for his part, believed that however small it was, no hate could be small enough to make it harmless (*ibid.*, Art. 140). Considering love in conjunction with hate, Descartes concluded that jealousy, though it was a passion, was not in fact the expression of 'love'. Such possessiveness, on the contrary, only bore witness to the lowly opinion the jealous man had of his wife. For this reason, Descartes concluded that he and his jealousy were worthy of hate:

On méprise un homme qui est jaloux de sa femme, parce que c'est un témoignage qu'il ne l'aime pas de la bonne sorte, et qu'il a mauvaise opinion de soi et d'elle.

We despise a man who is jealous of his wife, because it bears witness to the fact that he does not love her in the proper manner, and that he holds a poor opinion of both himself and her. (*ibid.*, Art. 169)

La Rochefoucauld, who was Descartes' contemporary, was the great aphorist who pondered self-love and pretence. His maxims on love and hate often concerned those strategies we adopt when we seek to deceive others and, more secretly, to deceive ourselves. Always attentive to the pettiness of the soul and our tendency to accord great importance to our own hopes and desires, he liked to remind us that an excess of passion hid a certain pettiness. *Le grand amour*, which is so often praised, derives from inordinate self-love, the celebration of one's own passion. In parallel to this, he felt excessive hate also derived from a petty self-importance, and he concluded: *Lorsque notre haine et trop vive, elle nous met en-dessous de ceux que nous haïssons.* (When our hate is too lively, it puts us below those we hate. *Maximes*: 338, RCI: 217).

Reflecting upon the expression of love in words and acts, La Rochefoucauld concluded: *Si l'on juge de l'amour par la plupart de ses effets, il ressemble plus à la haine qu'à l'amitié.* (If we judge love according to its effects, it resembles hate more than friendship. *Maximes*: 72, RCI: 211) How are we to understand this? La Rochefoucauld was fond of paradox and this conversion of love into hate is certainly a perplexing one. La Rochefoucauld was thinking within the constraints of his language system, however. French does not provide the means to explicate this conundrum, and La Rochefoucauld could only point out the seeming contradiction in the nature of love. Comparative philology, on the other hand, should allow us to reach beyond the world-conceiving of any given language system. If we compare French to ancient Greek, we will see that the Greeks had the means to think through this seeming contradiction. Erotic love is a passion. But it is only one of the four forms of love defined in the Greek language. *Filia*, friendship is not a passionate form of love. *Filia*, as defined by Aristotle in the *Ethics*, consists in considering the friend as 'one's second self', i.e. considering what is best for him in his own right. This is the form of 'apprehensive love' which Aquinas spoke of in the distinction he drew between 'apprehensive love' and 'appetitive love'. Appetitive love is drawn to the object of love: it craves to penetrate its object and possess it. This is the passionate love with which La Rochefoucauld is concerned, and indeed, this has little to do with friendship. By comparing the attributes of love and hate, La Rochefoucauld finds himself forced to conclude that both express themselves after the same fashion, i.e. passionately.

Destructive love is well known, and Shakespeare, in *Romeo and Juliet*, for example, explores destructive love at various levels: that of fidelity to the family and the clan, for instance. But ultimately, if we integrate the conceptual distinctions drawn by the Greeks, we can resolve the paradox which dogs the concept of 'love' in English and *amour* in French in the following way: erotic love and hate both express themselves violently as passions, but neither can be considered to be either friendship or that benevolent goodwill which spouses express when they agree to act in accord with each other's welfare (*storge* in Greek). Philological research and ethnolinguistic inquiry thus allow us to escape from the knots in which the linguistic patterning of our language entangles us. Pole-vaulting over the confines of the world-conceiving engendered by French and English, reaching into other traditions we can, both in English and in French, conceptualize alternative forms of emotional categories.

This explains something of the French worldview. But we should be wary of quoting all the famous French quotations as 'French'. After all, was the Corsican, Napoléon Bonaparte, French? Did he inhabit the French worldview? To a large extent, he transformed the French worldview, and even his defeat could not reverse the ideals and ideas which he had helped to enroot in the French imagination. His critics, from Balzac to Hugo, all took up position in relation to the crusading élan of his individual soul. Byron celebrated him as a hero, and Goethe and Hegel couldn't help admiring him. As far as hate is concerned, Napoléon was embracing a Romantic version of hate as a violent invigorating passion.[13] His own concept of hate was innovative, and even epoch-making, but it relied, nevertheless, on the rejuvenation of an existing aristocratic concept of rivalry. That concept of rivalry is still alive today in American capitalism. It consists in the idea that a man will perfect himself through struggling against adversity.[14]

Enmity and hate were fundamental for forging the manhood of the medieval knight, the ideal of those times. The rival, the enemy, was essential to the process of testing one's mettle, spirit and courage. For this reason, warfare was made a prerequisite of society: it became an obligation to seek out enemies. Many primitive societies (and even some relatively sophisticated societies such as that of the Spartans) believed that a man could only become a man by taking the life of another man. Something of this spirit is present in the words of one of Racine's characters in *La Thébaïde*, when he regrets that with the departure of his enemy his own hate is halved:

> *Quelque haine qu'on ait contre un fier ennemi,*
> *Quand il est loin de nous, on la perd à demi.*
>
> That hatred we feel for a proud enemy is halved
>   when he is far from us.
>   (Act 2:2, RCI: 387)

In contrast to this, the same character reflects that because of its proximity, fraternal hate is by nature excessive (*ibid.*).

A similar regret is expressed later in the play, when one of the characters declares he would not like to be temperate in his hate for his enemy. He therefore fears his friendship more than his wrath. He desires his fury as a justification for giving free rein to his hatred.

> *Je ne veux point, Créon, le haïr à moitié;*
> *Et je crains son courroux moins que son amitié.*
> *Je veux, pour donner cours à mon ardente haine,*
> *Que sa fureur au moins autorise la mienne.*
>
> I do not wish to hate him by halves, Créon; / and I fear his
>   wrath less than his friendship. / I want, in order to give freedom
>   to my ardent hate, / his fury to authorize at least my own.
>   (Act 4:1, RCI : 387)

The hatred of which Racine's characters speak is the aristocratic equivalent of the hatred David felt for his enemies. It was a character-defining hatred. Nobles respected their rivals, and regularly exchanged captives in exchange for ransoms after having treated their 'well-born' prisoners with all the respect commonly accorded to someone of their rank. Racine was simply maintaining a tradition of noble hatred which was part of the ideals of his society and which Corneille had been famous for celebrating before him.

Hate is often celebrated. Pierre Corneille used the story of Pompée to celebrate hate, and in Act One, scene 4, of *La Mort de Pompée*, a character exclaims:

> *La source de ma haine est trop inépuisable;*
> *A l'égal de mes jours je la ferai durer;*
> *Je veux vivre avec elle, avec elle expirer.*

> The source of my hate is too inexhaustible; / Equal to my days,
>   I will preserve it/her; / I wish to live with it/her, and die with it/her.

> (RCI: 192)

The personification of hatred here makes ample use of the feminine gender of hate in French. *Haine* becomes a companion, almost a wife, one without whom a man can no longer live.

Corneille was once the quintessence of French culture, or at least one of its great symbols. More than Racine, it was Corneille who celebrated the culture of kingship and the ideals which the aristocracy had espoused: those ideals which served to maintain the warrior class in power as armed riders, experts in war who were (in theory at least) supposed to protect the peasants from persecution and invasion. The Revolution would not put an end to Corneille's fame. Though his celebration of the Francs and the aristocracy became cumbersome and outdated, the celebration of the defence of the French nation was assured a good hearing throughout the nineteenth century. And it would be reactivated with the two World Wars. In post-war years, however, the concept of rivalry and the celebration of 'noble' belligerence as an ideal has come to seem inappropriate, even ridiculous to French people. In days of post-modern scepticism, in an era in which the French people must face up to the European Union and globalisation, the hatred that inspired Corneille is hardly conceivable. Molière's mixture of scathing satire, fine wit and earthy vulgarity guarantees him a place in the hearts of French people today, and Racine remains popular for his poetry and the sublime beauty of his verse. Corneille, in contrast, rarely meets with success on stage in France today. Once the protector of French idealism, he has become the hero of a few nostalgic reactionaries.

This is only a short overview of *haine*. Nevertheless, it should at least alert us to the fact that the word does not have exactly the same place within the French lexicon and within the French worldview as 'hate' does in ours. In the following sections, we will investigate other more peculiar forms of *haine* and hate. Investigating these should enable us to understand more fully how certain structures of feeling are developed and sustained under specific social conditions at certain moments in history.

Avoir la haine: having hate

In 2000, Gad Elmaleh, the Morocco-born French comedian wrote and performed a parody rap song with Dieudonné, a comedian who, a few years later, would be denounced and prosecuted for the anti-Semitic nature of his sketches. At the time, though, the Gad and Dieudonné duo was promoting love (brotherly love, that is) and denouncing hate. They were joyfully denouncing the kind of community-based hatred which had so often led to violence and segregation in contemporary French society: and Gad, who is of Jewish origin, was widely known for promoting mutual understanding between Muslim and Jewish communities in both France and North Africa. The lyrics of their song are untranslatable. The refrain goes:

> *J'ai la haine haine comme Tarzan accroché fi l'hyenne,*
> *j'ai la haine haine comme un lapin careme,*
> *et j'ai la haine haine comme la menthe cityzen*
> *et cityzem zoum zem, alor ta pa la haine!*

> I have hate, hate, like Tarzan clinging to the hyena, /
>   I have hate, hate like the Easter bunny …

The invented words are employed to mock the wilful obscurantism of rappers who promote clan-like slang for the initiated, often involving the inversion of words, already an ancient slang tradition in French known as *Verlan*. Those lines which remain comprehensible parody the aggression, violence and resentment of rap lyrics in French. And the tone with which they are chanted – hammered out – exaggerates, in a ridiculous burlesque fashion, that forced malice, which has become the stereotypical stance of modern rappers. The whole parody serves to expose the absurd nature of this celebration of hatred, which expresses itself in a routine-like resentment that is endorsed and promoted by the culture industry.

That parody had great success, but it was too subtle to put an end to the posture *J'ai la haine*. Mister Moha, a contemporary French singer continues to sing 'They have hate' (*Ils ont la haine*), and *la haine* continues to be a theme which is raised by both the left and the right when riots or social unrest threaten the calm of the cities of France as it did in Grenoble in 2010. The term *la haine* had already been integrated into the 2000 re-edition of Jean-Paul Colin's *Dictionary of French Slang* (Colin 1990). As Colin pointed out, the expression *avoir la haine* involves an emphatic use of a commonplace term. Colin rightly quoted the 1995 film by Mathieu Kassovitz as the main vector by which the expression had passed into everyday French speech. However, the expression, like Kassovitz's film, gave form to a sentiment which was manifest in certain sectors of contemporary France, and the expression had a resonance for a certain generation of what would be called the 'underclass' in English, *les exclus* (the 'excluded'), those poorly educated, invariably unemployed groups of young people who live on the margins of French society in small towns in decline and in the ghetto-like suburbs of French cities.

Entering into the sentiment of *la haine* involves two steps: we must enter into the worldview of the underclass, but first we must enter into the world-perceiving and the world-conceiving of the French language itself. How should we translate the expression? The use of the article is problematic. *La* refers to nothing in the expression *la haine*: *la* is not a definite article. It does not refer to a specific form of hatred or a hatred of something in particular. To say *J'ai la haine* means 'I have hate in me', 'I'm full of hate'. Though hate must, we suppose, be motivated by something, this hate does not seem to have any specific object. Even prejudice involves a perverted obsessive fixation upon an object. Not so *la haine*: it implies a burning anger and frustration, the kind of frustration which finds no relevant target. This hate does not usually find a vent.

Gad and Dieudonné were satirising the way in which this resentment had been revivified by the culture industry. Amusingly, Gad and Dieudonné set their parody rap song in the studio of a music producer of the French establishment who was seeking to profit from rap-resentment and sell it as a commercial commodity. In doing so, they were exposing the reality of the culture industry that Adorno denounced. The culture industry turns everything into a commodity. Protest songs are quickly absorbed and refashioned into sellable goods. The adopted aggression of rap singers, both mainstream and marginal, only serves to underline this truth.

YouTube has in so many ways become an authentic means of communication for people of all horizons who are no longer constrained by established promoters concerned with a return on investment. As such, it tends to expose the way in which many young people have integrated the models of successful artists in recycling *la haine*. This constitutes a very creative and highly influential form of critique of the consumption of culture and especially of music. Satire acts as a means of breaking out of the ongoing circulation of symbolic representations, the circuit used by the culture industry to adopt, pervert and disseminate stances and 'attitudes'. Again and again, we are invited to live within the frames and references of the culture industry's representations of what are supposed to be authentic forms of expression and dissent. Even Kassovitz's film, figuring two of France's most talented actors, Vincent Kassel and Saïd Taghmaoui, could not escape the grips of the culture industry. Despite the evident sincerity of its director and actors, it became 'a success', and in 2006 the French media were already promoting a tenth anniversary DVD edition.

La haine is no doubt a fantasy, a fiction. But it is also a reality in the sense that it has become a fixed concept in the French cultural mindset of our times. If an act of outrageous violence is committed tomorrow, if a school is burned down in an upmarket district of Toulon or a policeman is stabbed to death in a poor neighbourhood on the outskirts of Lille, we can be sure that *la haine* will become the paradigm through which such events are interpreted. Inevitably, at least four perspectives will be represented. The right wing will denounce the acts, call for more security, promise greater resources for policing and demand a greater sense of responsibility from citizens. The left wing will point to the acts of violence as the expression of social unease and the rising resentment of members of excluded segments of society. Resenters and haters themselves will be invited to TV studios in order to vent their anger and explain their hatred. Members of the same excluded communities will laugh at and disparage what they consider to be the unconvincing claims of petty criminals and hooligans to justify acts of wanton destruction by entering into and reinforcing established modes of expression which the media encourages them to adopt. Gad and Dieudonné's contribution belongs to this fourth stance. Kassovitz's film owes its success partly to the fact that, like most moving films of a post-modernist, post-moral, realism, it appeals to three distinct groups of viewers: those on the left who denounce exclusion and the anger and violence which exclusion engenders, those hooligans who love violence and the cult and power, and those voyeurs who enjoy taking part in the celebration of violence by proxy.

Is it possible that harnessing hatred is also a political strategy? For many critics, the French Government has envenomed the problem of resentment and exclusion. Emmanuel Todd, the historian and specialist of demography, who had helped formulate the debate on the 'social fracture' in the 1990s during Jacques Chirac's term in office, argued, in an article in *Le Monde* on 26 December 2009, that the Government's decision to launch a debate on French identity served only to stigmatize excluded citizens whose parents were often of North African origin. Todd, who works at the National Institute for Demographic Studies, claimed that the Government's debate formed part of an attempt to promote the opposition Nation-versus-Islam. As a historian, Todd considered it to be a cynical and perverse strategy designed to court the electors of the National Front as part of a warm-up to the presidential elections in 2012. The title of the article was 'What Sarkozy is proposing, is hate for the other' (*Ce que Sarkozy propose, c'est la haine de l'autre*). Todd concluded:

Si vous êtes au pouvoir et que vous n'arrivez à rien sur le plan économique, la recherche de boucs émissaires à tout prix devient comme une seconde nature.

If you are in power and you can't manage to get anything done in economic terms, looking for scapegoats at any cost comes as second nature.

Laurent Mucchielli and Abderrahim Aït-Omar, writing in an article published in the anti-capitalist review *Socialisme International* on the 2005 riots in Seine-Saint-Denis, in the northern suburbs of Paris, denounced the tendency of the Government to argue that the violence was orchestrated by organized bands of hooligans, a fact which, they argued, the court rulings and most serious sociological investigation had disproved. They considered this strategy to be a pretext used to justify further oppressive measures. Whatever the truth may be, from the point of view of discourse analysis, it is interesting that Mucchielli and Aït-Omar offer rioters the chance to express themselves. From the socialist perspective, it is, of course, convenient to interpret all rioting as an expression of social revolt and 'class warfare'. It is not altogether clear, however, whether the arguments of the rioters coincide with this analysis. Let's consider a few examples quoted by Mucchielli and Aït-Omar:

Tous les mecs qui avaient une rage contre quelque chose: ils ont profité des émeutes pour tout niquer. (All the guys that had *a rage* against something: they made the most of the riots to fuck everything.) (T., 18, unemployed)

   Moi, ce que je voulais pendant les émeutes, c'était brûler le lycée parce que c'est eux qui ont baisé mon avenir. Avec du recul, j'ai la haine contre ces chiens du système. (What I wanted during the riots was to burn the high school because they fucked my future. Looking back, I *have the hate against* all of the system's guard dogs.) (S., 19, unemployed, small-time cannabis dealer)

   Donc, je te dis la vérité, j'ai brûlé des voitures près du lycée pour leur montrer qu'on existe et qu'on ne va pas se laisser niquer comme des p... On va leur faire peur, comme ça ils vont changer leur comportement et vont nous respecter ... On a rien à perdre vu qu'ils ont baisé nos vies. Tu vois, je suis obligé de vendre du shit pour aider mes parents, sinon qui va m'embaucher sans diplômes ? ... C'est foutu d'avance. (So, I'll tell you the truth, I fire bombed the cars next to the High School just to show them that we exist and that we are not going to let ourselves get fucked like w[hores]. We're gonna scare them, then they will change the way they treat us and treat us with some respect ... We've got nothing to lose, since they've fucked our lives. Look, I have to sell shit to help my parents out, after all who's gonna give me a job when I've got no degree or diploma ... It's fucked from the start.) (S., 20, unemployed, small-time cannabis dealer)[15]

Throughout the twelve interviews carried out by Mucchielli and Aït-Omar, the young rioters spoke most of all of their hatred for the police. They also expressed hatred for their school teachers, who they accused of racism, of putting them down, and who they resented for not encouraging them. A hatred for Sarkozy was expressed, though all politicians were blamed for hypocrisy, for promoting a discourse of integration and success while (so the rioters felt) refusing to allow them the opportunity to succeed in life. What is characteristic of such discourse is the absolute incapacity of reflecting upon personal responsibility. The way hatred tends to attach itself arbitrarily to objects is also interesting. Individual people are pretexts. People and situations 'trigger' a much more implicit hatred against 'the system' (*l'étabissement*).

But even a hatred for the establishment implies a relationship. A subject hates an object. Something becomes the object of a person's hatred. In such hatred, we remain within the dominion of personal relationships. An encounter is possible. This encounter might be violent. But it does involve a form of 'meeting'. The Jewish philosopher Martin Buber believed that hatred was closer to love than indifference, because it implied an engagement in reality and an affective relationship with the other. Buber believed that hatred remained within the dominion of *I–You* (what he called the *Duwelt*). Indifference and apathy belonged to what he called the 'world of It' (*Eswelt*). In that world nobody exists, not even the 'I', because, Buber believed, the individual 'I' only ever comes into existence in his encounters with others. Those who are capable of 'meeting' others recognize them as individuals in their own right, respect them as such and respond to them. This conception of meeting is radically different from the form of civic respect promoted by society's institutions. It bears little in common with the spirit of those militating against 'hate crimes', or with Obama's concern for the underclass crushed by the crisis. This is not the charity of *agapē* which Christians preach. The encounter with the other brings the 'I' back into contact with reality. In recognising the other as 'you', we refuse to use them as an 'it', a mere instrument to satisfy our wishes and desires. We do not treat the other as a servant or an employee. The 'I' him- or herself exists for and in the other. This is a religious or spiritual conception of being and meeting. It has the obvious advantage of situating emotions within relations, between people, rather than confining them within the individual subject. The reality of shared emotion, hate or love, contrasts starkly with the form of dislocated resentment present in *la haine*.

What is remarkable in *la haine* is the vacuity of all thought and feeling. Though rage is often expressed and affirmed, rage seems to play a relatively minor role in this form of hatred. This hatred seems closer to indifference and apathy. In *la haine* both subject and object are annulled. For this reason, those who say, *J'ai la haine* often express the words with a flat, emotionless voice. The eyes seem empty.

Though rare, in recent years, the same sentiment has been expressed in German in literally the same words.[16] There is even a rap song which (at least in December 2009) could be listened to on the Internet entitled *Ich habe haß* (I have hate). The voice of the song is monotone. The singer doesn't even seem to be able to find the energy even for suicide, though life (the tone of the voice encourages us to believe) is pointless and not worth living. This is the voice of the *Eswelt*, the world in which the encounter between living, breathing people, between 'I' and 'you', has become impossible. This is not the defining hatred of Napoléon, nor even the less expansive hatred of the Romantics, which was at least vigorous and passionate, even if it had begun to turn inwards. This is the hatred of despair and existential absence, the hatred of those incapable of breaking out of themselves in order to engage with others either in love or in hate. Pushed to its logical conclusion, this 'objectless', 'subjectless' hatred would inevitably lead to total passivity. Apathy, after all, implies the negation of all engagement.

Does such a hatred exist in our English-speaking societies? Certainly apathy and social discontent, resentment and hostility are present, and the present economic crisis encourages crime and rioting (see the summer riots, London 2011). Nevertheless, at least in linguistic terms, the dislocation of hate from social relations, the annulling of the object in the declaration *J'ai la haine* has no equivalent in English. Hatred in English is always the hatred of or for something or someone. In that sense, it always defines the hater. It shapes identity in opposition and struggle, and even in resentment and rejection. The hatred the French are speaking of deprives haters of all existence. In linguistic and conceptual terms, that hatred, cut off from social relations, encompasses haters and confines them to their ghetto. The haters of *la haine* spiral inwards into the solitary self. *La haine* excludes them from society and from contact with others.

Entering into *la haine* involves entering into the French language and into one specific cultural mindset as it is expressed in the various perspectives of individuals suffering from social exclusion and complacently ruminating over the reasons which provoke their *haine*, without having the political and philosophical distance, or the intellectual honesty, to allow them to question or understand the forces which create their destinies. This should help us to understand that worldviews mean one thing at the level of individuals, another at the level of cultural concepts belonging to a social class, and yet another thing at the level of the linguistic system. The ethnolinguistics that Humboldt envisioned and which is espoused by contemporary scholars such as Wierzbicka involves investigating concepts at all three levels. While refusing to confuse these different layers or dimensions of worldview, it would, however, be a mistake to perceive them as separate: in fact, these different dimensions constantly permeate and reshape one another. In discussion and in criticism, in jokes and in satire, we constantly argue over definitions and reshape concepts. The satirical rap song of Gad and Dieudonné shows the way individuals take a stance in relation to changing expressions of hatred.

The worldview of the language is negotiated and argued over. Strife, opposition, innovation and irony are all inseparable from communication, and only through communication can a language's worldview be sustained. In this sense, sustaining a worldview means questioning it and reaffirming it. Whether French speakers accept, denounce or ironize *la haine*, each time they mention it they reaffirm its place in the conceptual cosmos of the language system in which all French people orbit. The essential 'point' about 'positions' is that, like the planets, those who take up positions are continually both moving on within language and moving language itself forward. Worldviews are constantly being modified by the expression of individual perspectives

Ethnolinguistics should serve to make us more lucid about the ways we negotiate concepts in our own language. The fact that we, in English, do not tend to conceive of an objectless hate which the speaking subject 'has' hardly prevents us from inventing our own pernicious forms of unhealthy hatred. *The Urban Dictionary* (2005) testified to the creation of neologisms used to define new conceptions of hatred, such as 'hateration' (the act or process of hating, 171). And the second volume, the *Mo' Urban Dictionary*, published in 2007, added four more neologisms:

haterade: A figurative drink representing a mode of thought; those who drink it are themselves consumed by the negativity with which they speak.

hater blockers: A very large pair of dark sunglasses to block out the hate from any people who are jealous of you in this world.

hater tots: Like haterade, the figurative snack you consume when you're hating on someone.

Hatriotism: Proving your patriotism by hating the people your government tells you to hate. (134–5)

Hate was there in the beginning. In the first books of Genesis, the hatred of sibling rivalry that psychologists analyse and interpret today was there. And hate grows and develops into new and varied forms. Hate crosses cultural boundaries and takes root in the worldviews of all languages, so it would seem. The racism of Gobineau and the philosopher Chamberlain fuelled the German fascists, and they in turn 'inspired' those who collaborated with them in conquered nations.

But let us leave the question of the dissemination across languages of hate and hating, to proceed to investigate two more unhealthy forms of hatred which have emerged. The second form emerged in French society just as it has emerged in many other societies: anti-Americanism. But French anti-Americanism has a special flavour all of its own. Though the British, as ex-colonial masters, often express a condescension regarding present-day Americans, the prejudice the French express regarding the Americans is of an entirely different order. It is, however, difficult to understand modern forms of French anti-Americanism without taking into account the form of hatred that the United States began exporting at the beginning of the Cold War, and which reached its climax in the discourse of the Reagan administration: this was the hatred which fuelled the battle between 'Good' and 'Evil'. For this reason, we will begin with the hatred of our Soviet adversaries.

The crusade against the Empire of Evil

Love of America and hatred of its enemies involves the careful cultivation of a tradition which plays out scenarios in which Good conquers over Evil. The Second World War is the obvious focal point of such scenarios, but our Cold War enemies, Russia and the Soviet satellite states, played a great part in the celebration of America's cultural supremacy and its war against Evil. For this reason, the right-wing press is sensitive to any negligence on the part of the government or the media in upholding the tradition and in celebrating the crushing of America's enemies past and present. Those on the right in Western democracies tend to buy into this worldview and accept the USA as the world's legitimate superpower: and this entails adopting its enemies as their own.

On 10 November 2009, Nile Gardiner, a right-wing English journalist working for *The Telegraph*, took Barack Obama and Hillary Clinton to task over their handling of the celebrations of the twentieth anniversary of the demolition of the Berlin Wall. European politicians were inevitably irritated by the message that Obama was sending them. In a world plunged into economic crisis, facing social deprivation at home and war abroad, Obama couldn't find the time to join with his allies nostalgically looking back on the end of the Cold War. The marginalisation of European delegates during the Copenhagen Summit on Climate Policy a few months later was to send a similar message. The centre of political debate is no longer in Europe. The 'emerging' economic powerhouses of China, India and Brazil have 'emerged', and it is with them that negotiations must be initiated and bargains must be made on the world's stage in the twenty-first century.

For a British Conservative, looking to the future after fifteen years of their party's failure to hold office, the slight to Europe was an insult to Britain. The fact that Obama's first trip abroad after his election was not (as tradition demanded) to Britain, a symbolic act designed to consolidate the 'special alliance', but to the Chinese to whom the American economy had indebted itself, had not gone unnoticed. Searching for inspiration, Nile Gardiner sought comfort in nostalgia, looking back at the remarkable intimacy of Anglo-American relations and the special relationship that had existed between Reagan and Thatcher. Hillary Clinton, as a major figure in US politics and an expert on foreign relations, was well equipped to stress the importance for America, for Europe and for the world of the end of communism. She understood the crucial political significance of the reunification of Germany, but Gardiner found it intolerable that she should not do proper homage to Reagan in her speech in Berlin. Forgetting Reagan, effacing him, meant effacing Thatcher, the only surviving mentor of Tory ideals for someone of Gardiner's generation. Forgetting Reagan was an affront to Britain. For this reason he condemned the Obama administration for its skewered representation of history and argued:

Hillary Clinton would do well to learn from Margaret Thatcher, a great friend of the United States, whom I had the privilege of working for in her private office. Like Ronald Reagan she is a statesman who understands that evil must be confronted and defeated, and a true leader who believes in the greatness of America as a force for good on the world stage.

As Lady Thatcher observed in her eulogy to Reagan at his funeral service at the National Cathedral in Washington in June 2004:

'*We live today in the world that Ronald Reagan began to reshape ... It is a very different world, with different challenges and new dangers. All in all, however, it is one of greater freedom and prosperity, one more hopeful than the world he inherited on becoming president ... With the lever of American patriotism, he lifted up the world. And so today, the world – in Prague, in Budapest, in Warsaw and Sofia, in Bucharest, in Kiev, and in Moscow itself, the world mourns the passing of the great liberator and echoes his prayer: God bless America.'* [17]

Gardiner's discourse is interesting in two respects: it shows to what extent both he and Thatcher have entered into the religious-ideological worldview which would level the land of the American civilisation and pave the way for the neoconservative worldview which Bush would inherit and make his own. For Thatcher, Reagan had not only protected the world, he had 'lifted it up'. His message was evangelical. It was a prayer. That prayer was heard by the American people, and when he died, Reagan, his prayer and God-fearing America had to be remembered. 'God bless America' was not simply the token of respect that this particular foreign speaker was paying to her hosts in adopting their expressions and rhetoric. It was a fond evocation of a character-forming friendship which had transformed Thatcher. Reagan's mixture of Hollywood charm and unquestioning, uncompromising self-assurance had seduced Thatcher. She was a convert to the American worldview. Gardiner was simply following his mistress's master in reaffirming that America was 'a force for good on the world stage'. His use of pro-American rhetoric and sentiment to condemn the American Government, however, opened a curious new chapter in anti-Americanism (of which contemporary British Conservatives have often been accused). And it is instructive in revealing that the hatred of nations invariably involves setting up ideals and the enemies of those ideals.

The ideal America Gardiner was looking back upon was the America which had opposed Evil with Good. Though this attitude is omnipresent in American speeches, the tendency to represent US politics in sound bites and in snippets of speeches makes it difficult to plumb the depths of this religious rhetoric. We in Europe tend to view the conviction that the USA is battling at the side of God Himself with scepticism. Indeed, it takes an effort of the imagination to begin to understand to what extent this vision of American foreign policy is enrooted in the religious concept of a special God-given vocation.

Within this religious worldview, the idea of America's vocation is not a radical claim, but a fact of reality. And one doesn't have to be a zealot to espouse this concept. George W. Bush was regularly considered to be acting as his father's son in completing 'unfinished business in Iraq'. But his father neither proved to be a zealot nor an inspired or inspiring force when it came to rhetoric. He had played the faithful administrator to Reagan, and his term in office was very much a continuation of Reagan's ideology. George W. Bush, on the other hand, was very much the spiritual son of Reagan when it came to ideology and rhetoric. Throughout his two terms in office, George W. Bush saw himself as being engaged in a combat against evil and evil-doers. Like Reagan, his mission was a deeply evangelical one. And it is by no means an accident that Reagan's administration-defining speech on America's crusade against the

Evil Empire on 8 March 1983 was addressed to the National Association of
Evangelicals of Orlando, Florida.[18] The following extracts are unusually long,
but they should, for that very reason, allow the reader to enter fully into the
seductive logic which had converted Thatcher and which continues to fill nostalgic Conservatives like Gardiner with enthusiasm.

Reagan began by making a moving speech to urge Americans to finance
spending on the arms race; this involved frightening American citizens into
paying for security:

I urge you to beware the temptation of pride – the temptation of blithely declaring
yourselves above it all and label both sides equally at fault, to ignore the facts of history and the aggressive impulses of an evil empire, to simply call the arms race a giant
misunderstanding and thereby remove yourself from the struggle between right and
wrong and good and evil.

But as a showman, Reagan modulated the threat of fire and brimstone with an
affable show of fireside intimacy. He introduced a joke:

An evangelical minister and a politician arrived at Heaven's gate one day together. And
St. Peter, after doing all the necessary formalities, took them in hand to show them
where their quarters would be. And he took them to a small, single room with a bed,
a chair, and a table and said this was for the clergyman. And the politician was a little
worried about what might be in store for him. And he couldn't believe it then when
St. Peter stopped in front of a beautiful mansion with lovely grounds, many servants,
and told him that these would be his quarters.
     And he couldn't help but ask, he said, 'But wait, how – there's something wrong –
how do I get this mansion while that good and holy man only gets a single room?' And
St. Peter said, 'You have to understand how things are up here. We've got thousands and
thousands of clergy. You're the first politician who ever made it.'

Reagan was relying upon a commonly shared prejudice, a hatred of government and of politicians. By evoking the corruption of politicians in the form of
a joke, he neutralized it, and prepared his listeners for his main objective, a religious revolution in politics. In this revolution, politicians of Reagan's colours
would stand on the side of Good.

But I don't want to contribute to a stereotype. So I tell you there are a great many God-
fearing, dedicated, noble men and women in public life, present company included.
And yes, we need your help to keep us ever mindful of the ideas and the principles
that brought us into the public arena in the first place. The basis of those ideals and
principles is a commitment to freedom and personal liberty that, itself, is grounded in
the much deeper realisation that freedom prospers only where the blessings of God are
avidly sought and humbly accepted.
     The American experiment in democracy rests on this insight. Its discovery was the
great triumph of our Founding Fathers, voiced by William Penn when he said: 'If we
will not be governed by God, we must be governed by tyrants.' Explaining the inalienable rights of men, Jefferson said, 'The God who gave us life, gave us liberty at the same

time.' And it was George Washington who said that 'of all the dispositions and habits which lead to political prosperity, religion and morality are indispensable supporters'.

And finally, that shrewdest of all observers of American democracy, Alexis de Tocqueville, put it eloquently after he had gone on a search for the secret of America's greatness and genius – and he said: 'Not until I went into the churches of America and heard her pulpits aflame with righteousness did I understand the greatness and the genius of America … America is good. And if America ever ceases to be good, America will cease to be great.'

The time was ripe, Reagan believed, for a new spiritual era of politics.

America is in the midst of a spiritual awakening and a moral renewal. And with your biblical keynote, I say today, 'Yes, let justice roll on like a river, righteousness like a never-failing stream.'

Now, obviously, much of this new political and social consensus I've talked about is based on a positive view of American history, one that takes pride in our country's accomplishments and record. But we must never forget that no government schemes are going to perfect man. We know that living in this world means dealing with what philosophers would call the phenomenology of evil or, as theologians would put it, the doctrine of sin.

There is sin and evil in the world, and we're enjoined by Scripture and the Lord Jesus to oppose it with all our might.

Like Saint Paul, Reagan argued that Evil was everywhere: it was in the soul of each one of us. But he forgot the second part of Paul's teaching, namely that our own sin prevents us from judging others. Reagan evoked hatred and Evil in the history of the USA and denounced the manifestations of civil hatred of his times, but he in no way considered that this prevented Americans from judging the world. The world was essentially Evil, the USA was essentially Good. To an 'objective' observer, this 'truth' was irrefutable, Reagan believed.

I know that you've been horrified, as have I, by the resurgence of some hate groups preaching bigotry and prejudice. Use the mighty voice of your pulpits and the powerful standing of your churches to denounce and isolate these hate groups in our midst. The commandment given us is clear and simple: 'Thou shalt love thy neighbor as thyself.'

But whatever sad episodes exist in our past, any objective observer must hold a positive view of American history, a history that has been the story of hopes fulfilled and dreams made into reality. Especially in this century, America has kept alight the torch of freedom, but not just for ourselves but for millions of others around the world.

This led Reagan to the crux of his argument. Communism was by nature Evil, because it refused the Christian faith and subordinated all morality to communist ideology and the class war.

Morality is entirely subordinate to the interests of class war. And everything is moral that is necessary for the annihilation of the old, exploiting social order and for uniting the proletariat.

Intervention in the 'evil world' was not conceived of by Reagan as imposing US ideology and pursuing economic interests. It meant reaching out to the world.

This doesn't mean we should isolate ourselves and refuse to seek an understanding with them. I intend to do everything I can to persuade them of our peaceful intent,
...
Yes, let us pray for the salvation of all of those who live in that totalitarian darkness – pray they will discover the joy of knowing God. But until they do, let us be aware that while they preach the supremacy of the state, declare its omnipotence over individual man, and predict its eventual domination of all peoples on the earth, they are the focus of evil in the modern world.

This prayer for the salvation of the damned who walked in 'totalitarian darkness', and who did not know the joy of discovering God, was coupled with a threat to US citizens. It would be 'folly' to underestimate the capacity of the 'godless' to do evil to the American people. Reagan was preaching *realpolitik* in the same breath as he was spreading the word.

[I]f history teaches anything, it teaches that simpleminded appeasement or wishful thinking about our adversaries is folly. It means the betrayal of our past, the squandering of our freedom.

He reassured Americans that they were strong. But although their strength was inseparable from their military might, it lay primarily in the faith that animated American hearts and minds. This was the faith of the just.

While America's military strength is important, let me add here that I've always maintained that the struggle now going on for the world will never be decided by bombs or rockets, by armies or military might. The real crisis we face today is a spiritual one; at root, it is a test of moral will and faith.

The USA would overcome Evil, Reagan affirmed:

I believe we shall rise to the challenge. I believe that communism is another sad, bizarre chapter in human history whose last pages even now are being written. I believe this because the source of our strength in the quest for human freedom is not material, but spiritual. And because it knows no limitation, it must terrify and ultimately triumph over those who would enslave their fellow man. For in the words of Isaiah: 'He giveth power to the faint; and to them that have no might He increased strength ... But they that wait upon the Lord shall renew their strength; they shall mount up with wings as eagles; they shall run, and not be weary...'
...
Yes, change your world. One of our Founding Fathers, Thomas Paine, said, 'We have it within our power to begin the world over again.' We can do it, doing together what no one church could do by itself.

The Cold War came to a close, communism was defeated and the fall of the Berlin Wall was celebrated. Evil had been overcome, Reagan and Thatcher believed. But to a worldview so deeply entrenched in the spiritual awakening which Reagan preached, and to which George W. Bush was converted, the new challenges to America would inevitably be conceived of as new manifestations of Evil come to counter the fight of Light against Darkness. Though the neoconservatives wavered as to where to direct their denunciation, the emergence of new enemies in the form of terrorists would provide an ideal focal point for this pent-up religious fervour and would trigger the crescendo of a rhetoric which fired and animated the 1980s.

In many respects, the hatred of the USA for Evil and for its enemies can be understood in what Nietzsche called 'the morality of the masters'. Nietzsche argued, in the *Genealogy of Morals*, that 'every noble morality develops from a triumphant affirmation of itself' (1989: 36). Nietzsche would have found Reagan's religious rhetoric tiresome (though he himself often wrote in a similar prophetic style). Nevertheless, he would have found Reagan's affirmation of US strength and goodness to be the expression of a healthy society. Master morality 'acts and grows spontaneously, it seeks its opposite only so as to affirm itself more gratefully and triumphantly – its negative concept "low," "common," "bad" is only a subsequently invented pale, contrasting image in relation to its positive basic concept – filled with life and passion through and through' (*ibid.*).[19]

Nietzsche believed that the masters expressed themselves in their acts, in the expression of their will. The weak could not do this. They are 'denied true reaction, that of deeds, and compensate themselves with imaginary revenge' (36). This involves a perverse turning in on oneself. The weak man withdraws into his own fantasy world, a world in which the strong is perverted. Slave morality '*falsifies* the image of that which it despises' (37). This is the revenge of frustrated hatred, impotent revenge. The contempt of unvented hatred compensates for its impotency by ridiculing what it fears. Because it cannot make its enemy the object of its will, slave morality transforms it in its imagination into 'a real caricature and monster'.

If Reagan's affirmation of master morality has been quoted in so much detail, it is because by entering into his worldview we are able to understand two crucial points about the worldviews which will espouse anti-Americanism. From the point of view of the most powerful nation on earth, expressions of anti-American sentiment can only appear as perverted expressions of evil or absurd expressions of petty-minded resentment. And once we enter into the logic of many of the forms of anti-Americanism, we will be forced to concede that they are indeed deeply perverted. Those who hate the USA are always eager to misinterpret and misrepresent its intentions. A caricature is held up and burned. The reality, the USA as a living culture, looks on horrified or bemused.

Anti-Americanism *à la française*

When a gigantic anti-American demonstration is held in Kabul, Afghanistan, in October 2009, we may find it difficult to understand which parts of Afghan society are sympathetic to such a sentiment, but the existence of hostility does not surprise us. But how are we to understand a Swiss daily paper (*Le Temps*) when it gives an ironic account of the Cannes–Hollywood rivalry which had enraged American journalists, who felt that their cinema had not been fairly represented? The French-speaking Swiss were simply siding with the French against Hollywood in a defiant act of disapproval of American culture after the invasion of Iraq and a decade of bloody expansionism.

At the 2003 Cannes Film Festival, the American documentary film-maker Michael Moore was awarded the *Palme d'or*. This was a curious condemnation of America. Moore's documentary, *Fahrenheit 9/11*, a critique of Bush's warmongering foreign policy, would, of course, be considered by the neoconservatives as 'anti-American'. But the malicious anti-Americanism expressed by the French was of a specific nature. The French had been brushed aside throughout the build-up to war. Their contracts in Iraq had been annulled and their attempts to avert war by joining with Russia and Germany had been disparaged and condemned. While French politicians worried about veiled threats of making France pay for its betrayal of the country which had liberated it, and accusations that it had 'stabbed America in the back', the media joyfully used Michael Moore, an American, as the battering ram to pound at the doors of American imperialism.

The resentment is understandable. This is the impotent rage of slave morality which seeks to pull down the oppressor: fantasy combats for the feeble. What was more difficult to understand in this period, however, was the joyful party-like spirit which animated the Festival and which had been manifest throughout the street demonstrations in France's capital and in the country's provincial cities such as Grenoble since the previous autumn. Throughout those demonstrations, French people chanted *Halte à la Busherie* (Stop the Bushcry), using Bush's name to form a satirical version of *boucherie* (butchery). The expression had already been used in an article published on 23 October 2001 to refer to airstrikes by British and American forces in Afghanistan. The article would be added to the website of the *Nouveau Parti Anti-Capitaliste* in March 2009, a fact which testifies to the resilience of slogans and their capacity to migrate from conflict to conflict. *Halte à la Busherie* has outlived Bush's term in office, a fact which tends to indicate that resentment outlives the forces which cause it.

The joy of the demonstrators resembled the joy of medieval Christians stamping on their effigies of the devil. The same joy inspired the burning of effigies of Guy Fawkes while a Catholic revolution in England still seemed to be a real possibility. But what is the origin of this seemingly fundamental resentment against America, this self-righteous hatred which is ready to spark into flames at each conflict? Culturally speaking, what is curious is that concrete conflicts tend to trigger a routine reaction, a process of familiar behavioural patterns which demonstrators comfortably slip into and which express something that runs far deeper in French society. Specialists of anti-Americanism point to a long and extremely complicated tradition of resentment which has accumulated amazingly diverse and complex forms of condemnations of the United States and what it is held to stand for in the eyes of the French.

Philippe Roger gives a lucid and penetrating account of this complex and contradictory tradition which has remained unbroken for centuries. Asked what his book *L'Ennemi américain* (2002) had to say about America, Roger, a member of the elite research institute, the *CNRS*, and lecturer at the *École des Hautes Études en Sciences Sociales*, replied, 'Nothing'. What he meant was that his book, and anti-Americanism itself, had very little to do with America. His book concerned those fantasy caricatures that anti-Americans invented as objects of ridicule. And if those fantasies had something to reveal, he believed, it was something about the nature of the French society of the time in which they were invented. Each era, Roger argued, would invent a new adversary, and the role of each adversary was to enable France to play a glorious, noble role in contrast to the invented Other. It will not be possible to do justice to Roger's account in the following pages, of course, but some idea of the diversity of the caricatures to which Americans have been reduced should at least be attempted. This will give us an overview of diverse forms of petty hatred.

The sickly animals of a sick country

The French of the mid eighteenth century saw their country as a beacon of culture. This was the era in which Rivarol would declare in his *Discours sur l'universalité de la langue française*, that the French language was destined to spread throughout the world. Witnessing the prestige of his language among the ruling classes of the aristocratic regimes of what was soon after to become known as the *ancien régime* of pre-revolutionary Europe, Rivarol concluded that French deserved its success because of some implicit superiority. Many linguists celebrated not only the *beauté* but also the *clarté* of French. Dauzat (see Meschonnic 1997: 134–5) argued, for example, that French was superior to the ancient languages from which it had sprung in that it was 'analytic', (by which he meant that its grammar depends more upon prepositions than on inflexion (i.e. suffixes defining the relationships between words). French was *raisonneuse* (rational by nature and organisation). French classed ideas logically. The implicit value judgement of such an idea is self-evident. French was on the side of Reason. French partook in the Enlightenment: other languages tarried in the shadows of more primitive eras.

In this context, the superiority of enlightened France was taken for granted. This had not always been the case. The New World had been celebrated throughout the sixteenth and seventeenth centuries by French thinkers such as Montaigne as the birthplace and experimental field of alternative cultures. It would, however, be increasingly denigrated in the eighteenth and nineteenth centuries, the colonial age. In Paris and Versailles the caricatures of America took on the rigid simplicity of pedantic scholarly dogma. The enchantment of earlier centuries gave way to disenchantment. In the second phase, Roger argues (2002: 31–4), America becomes a swamp-like mass of decaying vegetation which is inhospitable to life and hardly conducive to agriculture. It is a land of flies. The 'celebrated zoologist' Buffon (and it is Jefferson himself who, daunted by Buffon's prestige, names him thus) devotes a series of treatises to the degeneration of animal life in America. His works, *Variétés dans l'espèce humaine* (1749), *Animaux de l'ancien continent, Animaux du nouveau monde, Animaux communs aux deux continents* (1761), *De la dégénération des animaux* (1766) hammer out the same litany: the animals of the New World were stunted and pitifully small in comparison to those nurtured in the healthy climate of enlightened France and in Europe in general. This is pure prejudice, of course. But Buffon combined the prejudice of the suave cosmopolitan who would shine in society with the typology of the scientist. Drawing up a list of correspondences, he proposed to prove the truth of his conviction by comparing the American tapir with the elephant, the rhinoceros and the hippopotamus. He compared the peccary to the pig. The llama he considered to be a stunted camel. Beware, beware, insists Buffon, we must study these animals carefully, since often the climate has transformed them to such a degree that they have become unrecognisable (Roger 2002: 35). Indeed, Buffon is so convinced that it is the climate which dictates the nature of all animals' development that he assumes the colour of the skin of humans to be subject to the same law. For this reason, he wonders how long it would take 'these blacks' (*ces Noirs*) to 'reintegrate' their human form were they to be 'transplanted' to Denmark (35).

De Pauw, Buffon's contemporary, follows the same line of reasoning in his *Recherches philosophiques sur les Américains* (1768, Roger 2004: 39). De Pauw concludes that the native Americans are of an 'abominable nature', 'debilitated in both body and mind' (*ibid.*). Their imbecile-like stupidity is incurable, he contends. Their principal characteristic is their 'insensibility', which De Pauw attributes to 'the bad circulation of the blood which leads to "weakness of feeling"' (*ibid.*: 45). These men are, he feels, of use neither to themselves nor to society. They lack all nobility of spirit and are given to an 'unpardonable laziness'. Because he believes they 'vegetate' more than they can be said to 'live', De Pauw declares he is 'tempted to consider them not having a soul' (*ibid.*). Going to live in America cannot be expected to do one any good, of course, and integration and *créolisation* will inevitably result in the contamination and degeneration of the mind and the spirit.

The decadence of the lost savage of the Revolution

During the revolutionary period, the French (led by La Fayette) became the brothers in arms of their American allies. The alliances did not hold, however: as soon as the Napoleonic wars broke out, the fight over the colonies became acute. Paradoxically, one of the dominant discourses of the revolutionary period was promoted by reactionary anti-revolutionaries who denounced America as an abomination, the logical consequence of revolution and democratic rule. In an inverted form, reactionaries celebrated their hostility for revolutionary France. Roger cites the haughty Savoyard, Joseph de Maistre, who refused to call himself an *émigré* when he left *la Savoie gagnée à la Revolution* (the Savoie region overrun by revolution). Forced to flee to Berne in Switzerland before settling in Saint Petersburg in the court of the King of Sardinia, he condescendingly remarked that the American Republic was 'a regrettable aberration, but was, fortunately, only temporary' (Roger 2002: 75). Radically anti-democratic by conviction, de Maistre felt that the *homo americanus* was a bizarre mixture of two types, the lost European and the savage. His only solace lay in his conviction that such a form of society was unsustainable.

In this he was following a tradition to which the great German thinkers Herder and Hegel belonged. For Herder, America was an 'unfortunate continent'. Hegel, for his part, believed that since America was purely natural and physical, and therefore deprived of 'Spirit' (*Geist*), it could play no part in History's march forward with the realisation of *Geist*, the spiritual project and destiny of Man.[20] A strong anti-Rousseau sentiment was emerging, a sentiment which attributed to America something very different from the noble savage of Rousseau's idealism. America was not home to the healthy natural man yet to be perverted by social constraints (that concept of man which would inspire thinkers from Nietzsche to Freud and Jung). De Maistre, for his part, disparages the savage and considers him to be ignorant of religion and incapable of political life. In his *Considérations sur la France* (1797), de Maistre asks of the French Republic '*peut-elle durer?*' (can it last?) (Roger 2002: 76). Waterloo will not contradict de Maistre's scepticism, in the short term at least. But what does he say of America? Nothing. He takes pains merely to stress he has no time to treat the question of the longevity of the American experiment. The United States do not exist for de Maistre. As to its constitution, he declares everything new in it to be essentially feeble and fragile: such things he says, 'inspire in him no confidence' (*ibid.*: 77).

The Yankee

The mutations of the American in the French imagination continue with a bewildering dynamism. By 1900, the American is no longer the caricature who peopled the stages of France in the mid nineteenth century, that rough, vulgar simulacrum of the Englishman (Roger 2002: 213). The new vision of the American is the Yankee, a brutal, cold-eyed, rapacious merchant, an inhuman industrialist. He loves only one thing, money. He is worldly and educated but incapable of 'elevation in his ideas' (214). His entire intelligence is put in the service of money making. Incapable of looking beyond practical questions, his pursuit of profit and his desire for enterprise are 'pathological'. He is nationalistic and arrogant: he is a barbarian, untouched by culture. He is an insatiable predator, a tireless expansionist. Now a potential rival to France's colonial interests, the American is refashioned as an 'imperialist'. He expresses himself exclusively in 'jingoism'.[21]

Two aspects of French anti-Americanism are noteworthy regarding the fantasy of the 'Yankee' seen through the eyes of the French. Initially, the term was not meant as an insult and it was only during the second half of the nineteenth century that the term took on its pejorative connotations. It was the complicated reaction of the French to the Civil War that transformed the associations the term held for them. During the war, only the enemies of Lincoln's northern armies spoke of the 'Yankees', and in France the term inevitably took on the prejudices attached to it by the Southerners. With the war, all Northerners were lumped together with the Yankees, and with Lincoln's victory, all of America appeared to fall under the dominion of the Yankees. In this way, the reactionary fairy-tale celebration of a cultured and civilized South, raped by grasping Yankee greed, made its way across the Atlantic and started to germinate in a specifically European anti-Yankee dogma which would consolidate clichés concerning the barbarism of the Americans and crystallize them in the light of ensuing economic rivalry between the States and Europe.[22]

No thanks for the liberators

De Villepin, the French Foreign Secretary in 2002, knew very well that the Americans would not forgive the French for not supporting their imminent invasion of Iraq. They would, as he is alleged to have put it, consider themselves to have been stabbed in the back. But the 'betrayal' of the Americans had taken place long before. Initially the GIs' brothers in arms, the communists, who formed the ranks of most of the Resistance, which would be integrated into de Gaulle's liberating army, would be the ones to lead the *mobilization antiaméricaine* of the 1950s (Roger 2002: 423). Roger sees in this a French denial of responsibility for the war and the occupation: that is why he entitles his chapter *Non coupables!* (Not guilty! Roger 2002: 423). The slogan that would prove most effective in this new bout of anti-American propaganda was the 'Defence of Freedom' slogan, however.

While Khrushchev was preparing to denounce Stalin's excesses, the French communists stressed the peaceful nature of their Russian brothers. In contrast to Russia, America was set up as a warmonger. Two themes merged in this new discourse, the reactivation of interwar pacifism and the fear of a new nuclear threat. It was argued that a nuclear society was incompatible with a democratic society (*ibid.*). The threat of nuclear warfare won allies to anti-Americanism throughout French society. *Le Monde*, *Esprit*, *Temps modernes* and *France Observateur* are all unashamedly anti-American. Their anti-Americanism is not necessarily that of the communists. But it is anti-colonial. America is considered to be setting up an *Empire-atlantique*. Between this empire and Soviet Russia, Maurice Duverger, writing in *Le Monde*, opts to support the former. But this choice forms part of a new *neutraliste* policy. The term *neutraliste* does not imply neutrality, it implies playing off both sides against the middle. Many French intellectuals of the time saw the Cold War as a period in which the two superpowers cancelled each other out (Roger 2002: 424). Already in 1948, Étienne Gilson had been advocating the *ni-ni* policy: support for neither Washington nor Moscow.

Writing on 2 March 1949, Gilson accused the Americans of wanting to buy the blood of the French with their dollars. Unashamedly reactivating the pre-war anti-Semitic rhetoric which had prepared the French for Vichy and collaboration with Hitler's Final solution, Gilson denounced Uncle Sam as Uncle Shylock. This was part of his attempt to prove the innocence of the French (*travail de déculpabilisation des Français*, Roger 2002: 425). A hatred of the Americans showed a love of the French, and Gilson somehow seems to have felt that anti-Americanism would help efface the French defeat and the shame of collaboration. The arguments are tortured and laborious: 'We bore the weight of the First World War for which the United States took all the glory' he argued (426). And 'with Poland practically alone, we bore the weight of the new world war' (*ibid.*). Britain's contribution to the liberation of France and the defeat of communism was brushed aside. America was represented as coming in at the end to steal the glory once more. Furthermore, Gilson argued provocatively, those looking for who was to blame for preparing the rise to power of the Nazis should look across the Atlantic. The Hoover Plan was thereby denounced. Gilson's rhetoric met with wide success, and the Communist Party was soon denouncing American culture with slogans such as 'Hitler made in USA'. The tactical use of English to satirize the Americans would be the hallmark of the ambivalent French attitude to the influence of American cultural models throughout the second half of the twentieth century. This discourse would not wary of coupling together Nuremberg and 'the civilisation of machines'. And far from denouncing the tacit collaboration of Vichy as one of the shameful periods of French history, Emmanuel Mounier went as far as to consider it one of the dreams of the Americans who would seek to re-enact the scenario the Germans had been forced to renounce. The Communist Youth movement in France satirically fuelled this satire by singing to the tune of 'Jingle Bells':

> *Mais le peuple a dit: 'Non, il n'y a rien à faire!*
> *À l'Union soviétique, on n'fera pas la guerre.*
> *Nous serrons pas les biffins des gros milliardaires.*
> *Finalement ces requins mordront la poussière'.*

> But the people said: 'No, there's nothing to do about it! /
> We'll not go to war with the Soviet Union. / We won't
> be the foot soldiers of fat billionaires. / In the end, those
> sharks will bite the dust'.

> (Roger 2002: 427)

In coming decades, America was time and time again to be recast in the grotesque form of some strange nightmare. The fantasy forms it took on have little or no bearing on what was actually going on in the States. Those fantasy forms were dressed up, tailor-made by French prejudice. They primarily served to flatter the French and pander to their desire to portray France in a noble role. The great French aphorist La Rochefoucauld would have perceived this as the workings of self-love (*amour-propre*), that tireless force which works to deceive us and to pervert our perception of others. Self-love invents hatreds to reassure us that we are essentially lovable. America would be the soulless teenager chewing bubble gum. It would be the nest of jungle-cities. It would be the exporter of toxic post-modern food products. The beef wars concerning hormones would spark off a chain reaction of trade wars in Europe (with Britain) and with America, and would lead José Bové to attack a McDonald's in protest (though McDonald's makes it a marketing strategy to insist they use only local beef).

All of these were minor conflicts, however, antagonisms which flared up and died down. With the twenty-first century we enter into the era of Bush's Middle East wars. And with the invasion of Iraq the fears of the 'Atlantic Empire' would soon be shaking the French into new jingoistic denunciations of the Americans. French politicians invariably find themselves in a strangely difficult position. They must contend with the realities of negotiating with their American allies, but at the same time they must satisfy public opinion upon which anti-Americanism preys. And that festering hatred of 'America', though it has little to do with the largely positive impression the French have of Americans as individuals, is always ready to break out in a new epidemic. *Halte à la Busherie* was in many ways the sincere expression of engaged movements denouncing warmongering, but in the joyful cries of hate and disgust there was something ringing in the background. That was the eruption of a gangrenous sickness, the joy-in-hate of latent anti-Americanism unleashed.

Conclusion

It seems likely that love and hate are here to stay. If we are to understand them and their relationship, it is perhaps true that religious philosophers such as Aquinas and Buber will help us to recognize the diverse forms that hate takes as it manifests itself or hides behind covert forms of love and affiliation. Certainly, in a world in which Blair asks his God if he can justify siding with the Americans' invasion of Iraq, and Thatcher asks God to bless America, a religious perspective of love and hate cannot simply be dismissed: it must be rationally, analytically and critically engaged. Bush and Obama do not stand outside of religion when they speak of love and hate, and their policies are conceived of and promoted to a large extent in religious rhetoric.

From an ethnolinguistic perspective, this state of affairs makes it necessary to take up a series of positions as we try to gain greater understanding of the diverse forms that love and hate take in various languages at different times. Circumnavigating hate involves trying to penetrate it at various points, as though we were reaching beneath the earth's crust to unearth something which is at one and the same time part-universal, part-unique. Our various mini-studies of hate: the hate that emerges in the Old and the New Testaments, the hate that becomes a key concept of individual writers, the objectless French hate (*la haine*), Reagan's hatred of the Evil Empire, and the grotesque and volatile forms of French anti-Americanism, are only fragments of a greater form of hate, something which might be considered a universal sentiment which manifests itself in culture-specific forms. If the analysis of symbolic representation and discourse have enabled us to fathom these specific manifestations of hate, then they will rightfully be regarded as useful conceptual tools of ethnolinguistic research. Our study will at any rate have taken us beyond two stumbling blocks. The first is the naive belief that hate is an unproblematic universal sentiment. The second is the idea that languages imprison their speakers within the walls of their worldviews, and that hate in English must take one specific form, in contrast to *la haine* in French. As the changing forms of hate show, nothing in speech is static. And as satire and critique show, individuals act upon the language, just as language acts upon the consciousness of individuals.

What political consequences does this ethnolinguistic approach to hate entail? Perhaps most of all, that language should be observed with great vigilance. Foreign political strategies seek to impose themselves upon us as we adopt the words and phrases of our allies and as we translate them from one language to another. Simple resistance is no guarantee of intellectual freedom, since opposition necessarily enslaves us to the cardinal concepts and frameworks of thought which we seek to escape. Only by thinking-in-language, and thinking-with-language, only by questioning both the origin of concepts and their place within the language system, the roles they play within ideological discourse, can we hope to move on and beyond the discourse which appears to be perverting our manner of perceiving and conceiving of the world. There is a hatred of obscurity in this effort, and a love of understanding.

This is the core and the heart of the ethnolinguistic endeavour. Ethnolinguistic research serves the work of the mind. Humboldt knew as a linguist, and Locke knew as a philosopher, that close analysis of speech reinvigorates language and rejuvenates understanding. The final case study will bring us back to our own language, English. In a call for vigilance, it will discern the way new forces are seeking to pervert one of our key concepts, 'war'. As ethnolinguists, our task will be to track the ways in which 'war' is being perverted. In its own small way, this should help us to take up a stance concerning the transformation of frames of thought in contemporary politics.

6 War

Why war?

The blurring of the term 'war', its proliferation as an organising concept of political rhetoric and the culture of fear nurtured by the Bush administration of the first decade of the twenty-first century can be considered as a defining moment in the transformation of the American worldview by neo-conservative thinkers and politicians. The present American wars, what have come to be known as 'Obama's wars', were provoked and justified within the paradigms of a radically new conception of war, a worldview-transforming conception of political struggle between powers. The transformation of the term 'war' was to deeply affect the conception of the nation, the homeland, the structure of society and civil rights. And inevitably, Obama now finds himself playing out a role assigned to him by a scenario which neither he nor his party scripted.

This short case study aims to do four things. Firstly, to demonstrate, in the same way as our other cases studies, that concepts are couched in metaphors: metaphoric paths open up and limit the concept we think with and colour the way we experience war and our role in it. Secondly, to demonstrate that the use of both traditional and novel metaphors must be considered within the scope of what Philip Eubanks has termed a 'discursive strategy'. We select and manipulate metaphoric representations in order to enable us to present our ideas in a certain way, a way that promotes and consolidates our point of view. Both consciously and intuitively we are thereby striving to achieve our ends. Thirdly, to show that the relationships between figurative uses of wars, 'metaphoric wars', are, at times, intimately linked with the process of representing real wars. And fourthly, to demonstrate that there exists a curious rhetorical trope which (at least to my knowledge) appears to have escaped classification. In the second part of the chapter the term *switch* will be introduced and defined as a rhetorical strategy using metaphor to enact a simultaneous two-way semantic shift. While one thing (war, in this case) is transformed into another, other things are transformed into the former element (war). The *switch* and the four aims presented above will be discussed by referring to a corpus-based study of the

English press coverage of the build-up to the war in Iraq. The corpus comprizes 150 articles from *The Economist*.

What does 'war' mean for ethnolinguistics?

The meaning of 'war' for ethnolinguistics is not the focus of this study. This is a study which brings to bear discourse analysis and metaphor theory in order to disentangle war propaganda and to help us understand struggles which are presenting themselves to English speakers as 'wars'. But before returning to the complexities of the Anglo worldview and trying to come to grips with the way in which neoconservative discourse has sought to harness and reconfigure that worldview, it is worth stopping to pause upon what we are passing over in the ethnolinguistic project. While I certainly hope that this study will be of ethnolinguistic interest in that it should enable readers to see to what extent discourse analysis and metaphor theory are useful for exploring the English speaker's worldview, a number of equally interesting ethnolinguistic projects could make a valid contribution to our understanding of the concept of 'war' and the cultural and linguistic dimensions of that concept in other languages.

What courses would such ethnolinguistic research take? Comparing 'war' as it is conceived of in English with comparable concepts in other languages brings to the forefront the following questions, which might stimulate fertile speculation and rigorous empirical research:

- Is there one key concept which coincides perfectly, or to a large degree, with the English concept of 'war'?
- Is there a clearly defined antonym, a counterpart, to our own term 'peace' in the war-and-peace opposition?
- To what degree do synonyms overlap (see 'struggle', 'fight', 'combat', 'attack')?
- Do Indo-European languages show converging or diverging patterns of conceptualisation in the terms they use to translate the English concept of 'war'?
- Do non-Indo-European languages show forms of linguistic patterning which differ radically from those used by Indo-European languages to construct the concepts used to translate the English concept of 'war'?
- What does etymology have to teach us about the various terms used to translate the concept of 'war'?
- Is this key concept gendered?
- Does gender affect the symbolism of the concept?
- How do men and women participate in 'war'? And to what extent does this participation colour the way men and women speak about this key cultural concept?

- How is this key cultural concept constructed in metaphors?
- What metaphoric wars are generated using the conceptual framework of war and warriors? For example, does it make sense to speak of 'trade wars' in Chinese? Would Hindi speakers know what is meant by the 'war on want'?
- To what degree has the 'war on terror' penetrated the cultural mindsets of other languages?
- How have other languages and cultures resisted the concept of a 'war on terror'?

Answering these questions would of course involve writing volumes on the subject of 'war'. But a few brief reflections might suffice to open up the debate and to demonstrate the ethnolinguistic interest of such questions. Before returning to the Anglo-American worldview, it is important, after all, to recognize the limits of the English speaker's culturally situated and linguistically framed conceptualisation of the term 'war'.

As regards the last two questions, Russian politicians, for example, immediately seemed eager to make use of the 'war-on-terror' discourse in order to justify the state's intervention in satellite states and its treatment of ethnic minorities seeking independence. Speakers of other Slavic languages, such as Polish and Czech, seemed far more sceptical about this discourse. This might be explained in part in terms of the historical relationship a culture has with war. The Czechs and the Poles have very much borne the brunt of invasions and occupations over the past few centuries. Unlike the Russians and the Americans, they are far less enthusiastic about the idea of war, and this inevitably makes warfare metaphors less attractive.

Gender poses two separate but linked questions. Is the concept itself gendered? And how do the two sexes feel about 'war'? Only thirty years back, the British and American feminists were declaring that women were more peaceful by nature than men and that empowering women would engender a more peaceful world. Two facts make such an argument seem somewhat naive today. Societies of women warriors have often existed. The Amazons is the obvious example, but the Spartan women were equally trained in arms, as were certain women in Japanese society. Besides, technology has transformed the art of war, and the Iraq invasion gave ample examples of the ways in which women embraced the 'termination' of enemy combatants.

As to the term itself, 'war' would not appear to be gendered in the English imagination, and the war poets of neither the First nor the Second World Wars tended to personify war as either a man or a woman, as, for example, death is personified as the Grim Reaper in English, and as *La Mort* is personified as a seductive woman in French Romantic and post-Romantic poetry. Nevertheless, we should not close off this path of investigation. Curiously, the terms usually used to translate 'war' in French, Spanish, Czech and Russian are all feminine (*la guerre, la guerra, valka* and *войны*, respectively). It would be premature to draw any conclusion from this fact, but corpus analysis and textual analysis would certainly seem to be justified in investigating this question further. It would seem that Slavic and Romance languages favour a feminine conception of war, or at least make one possible, while Germanic languages associate war with masculinity. But this immediately begs the question of how Mars, the god of war in Roman mythology is conceived of as a masculine force, while Athena, in Greek mythology, is the daughter of the great patriarch-god, Zeus. As soon as we reach into language and into culture, we find ourselves caught up in complexity. And this will only appear to us as a setback if we are seeking simple portable truths which can be brought back from one worldview to another, as we bring bottles of alcohol and trinkets back from the airports on our foreign travels. As we begin to enter into any worldview, a language reveals itself to be a complex and flexible means of expression. Mythology and symbolism will set themselves up in opposition to contemporary usage, and individuals will find ample freedom for exploring innovative strategies designed to surmount or to overturn existing symbolic paradigms. A 'feminine' war can be made 'virile'. Mars can be castrated. And contemporary icons such as Angelina Jolie incarnate the contradictory clash of traditionally masculine and feminine traits in one highly desirable, seductively violent ideal.

Etymology teaches us that, surprising as it might seem given their pronunciation, the Spanish, French and English forms all derive from the same Indo-European root *wers-*, meaning 'to mix up', 'to confuse'. Curiously, though 'war' derives from Old Germanic (*werra*), it comes to us through the Old North French term, *werre*, meaning, like its Old Germanic root, 'war'. Our term 'guerrilla' derives from the Spanish term *guerra*. But both derived from the same Old Germanic root (Watkins 2000: 100).

Reading the classical treatises on war in each of the languages we study will, of course, open up new facets of the concept. And indeed, if Sun Tzu's ancient treatise *Art of War* and Carl von Clausewitz' *vom Krieg* (1832; see Clausewitz 1997) continue to be translated and read today in English, it is because their authors and the Chinese and the German cultures have something to teach us about war. It is, however, important to bear in mind that the reception of these works is often incomplete at best, and often perverse. Sun Tzu's work is, in my experience, more often quoted than read. Among the most regular authors to quote it are the journalists of the English weekly magazine *The Economist*, but they invariably invoke the work in order to extrapolate arguments about trade wars. This comes from the fact that it has become fashionable to use Sun Tzu's text as a framework for thinking about management strategies taught on MBA courses in Western universities.

The absurd consequences of such a fad are perplexing. It has become customary to represent the Chinese (and Asians as a whole) as being sly and devious in their negotiating strategies.[1] Ironically, it is precisely these strategies which Western managers are invited to adopt and imitate. The place Sun Tzu has taken up in the Anglo imagination helps explain the argument which rose up about the decision of the Chinese at the Beijing Olympics in 2008 to impose gender testing (a controversial means of verifying the sex of competitors involving not only the examination of genitalia but also of the genetic make-up of individual contestants). The author of one blog (outsports.com) made explicit reference to Sun Tzu in both the title and the argument of his text, *Gender Testing as 'Art of War'*, posted 6 August 2008.

The Chinese are applying 'The Art of War' to international sports in a classic way. They want to win piles of medals and prove their superiority as an emerging world power. As the host country that sets policy for these Games, they have surely scoured their own team, to make sure all karyotypes conform to XX and XY. However, their late announcement that they intend to test will place other countries at a psychological disadvantage ... So it will constitute a pre-competition strategy for Chinese authorities to summon any athlete they choose for testing. Even if that individual passes the test, her psyche may be jarred and she may not perform as well. Imagine the anxiety of waiting for test results, when you know that loss of your career, your previous medals, might result. Either way, a medal prospect who can be knocked out by the gender test, or rattled enough to miss making the podium, will ensure more medals for the Chinese. 'The Art of War' was written 2500 years ago by a great Chinese general named Sun Tzu, who probably lived during the Warring States period (403–221 BCE). It's a brilliant study of military strategy and realpolitik whose principles can be applied to any non-military situation as well.[2]

Whether Sun Tzu enjoys the same status as the author of this text and the journalists of *The Economist* allow him in their conception of war and power struggles remains to be seen. Whether 'Trade-is-War' or 'Sport-is-War' are metaphorical frameworks which have any meaning for the Chinese is something which must first be established by ethnolinguistic research. Nonetheless, it seems fairly clear from the above example that Western critics are seeking to understand an official decision concerning a legitimate international question through the prisms of stereotypes projected upon the Chinese. Just as Eubanks suggests most companies and nations invoke the idea that trade is war only in order to ascribe it to their 'opponents' and to justify their own (often preemptive) retaliation, it seems that Sun Tzu is being brought in here in order to attack his compatriots on an entirely different terrain. It is in fact the metaphorical framework of 'war' which is being used as a battering ram to demolish a non-military decision.

A similar ethnocentric reflex can be observed in the way *jihad* spread throughout English during the Bush administration. This term is popularly understood to mean 'holy war'. And internet search engines offer ample evidence that the Anglo-American worldview (or at least the neoconservative worldview) has disseminated this conception throughout the world. French, German and Czech all certainly offer examples of such a usage.

In fact, though, the word *jihad* does not mean 'sacred war', but 'struggle' or 'effort'. The two words used for 'war' in the Koran are *Harb* and *Qitâl*. *Jihad* is used to mean the sincere and serious struggle made by both individuals and societies to draw closer to a world created in the image of God. Interestingly, the most popular source of encyclopaedic information, Wikipedia, while often criticized for errors, does do its best to counteract this misunderstanding. And this proves true of its entries for the term not only in English but also in French, German and Czech. In English, websites such as *Jihad Watch* (www. jihadwatch.org) insist upon the importance of distinguishing between 'the rise of a group of extremists who seek religion as a path to power and a means of domination' and the majority of Muslims by whom such a conception is 'repudiated'. But the very existence of *Jihad Watch* testifies to the perverse success of anti-Muslim propaganda which maintains the use of the Arabic term in order to give a foreign taste to all that the neoconservatives would dub as 'terrorism'.[3]

Repeated attempts have been made to clear up this semantic confusion. But as we shall see in the study of English propaganda, ideologies thrive on confusion, and destabilising coherent meanings forms part of an implicit strategy of denunciation and vilification. For our purposes, however, it is worth quoting one of those who strove to set things right by giving a 'fair trial' to the Islamic conception of *jihad* and its relationship to war. Dr Muzammil Siddîqî was quoted on the trilingual (Arabic, French and English) *Islamophile* website on 9 December 2002, clarifying the fundamental concepts of Muslim theology in relation to struggle and warfare. Muzammil Siddîqî clearly intended to warn Muslims away from being seduced into terrorist justifications based upon a misreading of the Koran. He stressed that *jihad* means 'struggling for God with all the effort that He deserves'.[4] This form of struggle could, Muzammil Siddîqî, admitted, take the form of warfare, but this was only one of the forms of expression of the will to serve God. He stressed that as a 'religion of peace', the Muslim faith teaches us that we must 'strive to eliminate evil on earth by peaceable means and without having recourse to force wherever possible'. In other words, 'Islam teaches an ethics which applies to war, [but] war is permitted for the Muslim faith, only when all other forms of peaceful means such as dialogue and negotiation have broken down'. Muzammil Siddîqî listed five rules governing the ethics of warfare for Muslims.

1. You must be sufficiently strong for your enemy to fear you, so that he dare not attack you.
2. You must not open hostilities. And you must work towards peace as much as possible.

3. You must fight only those who fight. No collective punishment is allowed. No harm should be done to non-combatants. Arms of mass destruction must not be employed.
4. Hostilities must be ceased as soon as the adversary turns towards peace.
5. Treaties and accords must be observed as long as the enemy honours them.

To what extent this account faithfully represents the will of Allah as it is inscribed in the Koran must be left to specialists of Arabic. But Dawood's translation of the Koran (1956/1999) would seem to support this account. References to 'war' in the index indicate passages in which war is represented as something which should be avoided if possible but accepted when necessary. Muslims are encouraged to be steadfast in defending the will of God and discouraged from shirking their duty. Muzammil Siddîqî ended his text with the following words:

Our modern societies form part of the global village, in which Muslims and non-Muslims live together in Muslim countries, and in which Muslims live in countries which are made up of a majority of non-Muslims. It is therefore our duty to bring about a greater mutual understanding: it is our duty to work for peace and justice for all peoples: it is our duty to cooperate with each other in order to attain the good, and this should be done in order to cease all terrorism, attacks and violence perpetrated against innocent victims. This is our *Jihad* today.

If ethnolinguists were politicians, or politicians were ethnolinguists, perhaps these words, and countless other speeches, would have had more impact on the course of events. But the Bush administration was set on promoting a very different scenario. The following study of the metaphoric reconstruction of 'war' in English might go some way to explaining why this was so.

What do *we* mean by 'war'?

As readers of the press or TV spectators, throughout the first decade of the twenty-first century we were daily confronted with carnage from the aftermath of the invasion of Iraq and the reprisals made on the occupying British and American troops. More recently, the gruesome stories of death squads and sadistic soldiers in Afghanistan have increasingly been brought to light, and have shocked the US and British public, which is still encouraged to believe in the wars which led to the occupation of Iraq and Afghanistan. A single page of the *International Herald Tribune* (p.7) on Tuesday, 5 October 2010 carried two such stories. One depicted the disarray of a woman whose farmhouse was ransacked as a pretext in order to 'justify' a hunt for hidden weapons, after her husband had been ruthlessly and inexplicably shot. The title read, 'Rogue U.S. Soldiers on the Hunt'. Below that article, the trial of Sgt. Calvin Gibbs led to 'grisly reports' which forced Gibbs to declare that he was 'no monster'.

The reports involved violence perpetrated on civilians and on Gibbs' fellow soldiers. 'Several soldiers recalled Sergeant Gibbs and Specialist Morlock [his associate in the US Army in Afghanistan] as tossing severed fingers in front of a soldier who had reported the widespread use of hashish within the unit'.

This is the hidden face of war, which is now increasingly coming to light. Public opinion can now face such truths. But how were the wars themselves justified in the first place? Of course, arguments were used. But rhetoric cannot be simply reduced to the art of presenting arguments. In the build-up to the war in Iraq the very concept of war and the place it holds in our imagination and in the English lexicon was transformed.

Not only were we submerged by news of actual, armed, physical 'war', 'wars' of all sorts, metaphorical 'wars', grabbed our attention. Thus, after fifteen US soldiers lost their lives in an attack on a helicopter on Sunday, 2 November 2003, the BBC World News asserted that: 'The war for hearts and minds is a battle waged not only in Iraq but on home turf'. Bush, it appeared, would have to go to battle once again, this time against a rising popular opinion as he began to prepare for the following year's re-election campaign, fighting the Democrat candidate, the staunchly anti-war war hero, Kerry. The 'war for hearts and minds' makes reference to a familiar metaphorical expression – often used during the Cold War – one that is easily understood by all of us in terms of a more fundamental metaphorical equation: Politics-is-War.

Inevitably, during wartime, 'propaganda' is a word that comes to mind. And in this sense, this case study can be understood as a contribution to the theory of propaganda. But it is also a contribution to ethnolinguistics in the sense that we will be concerned with discerning a crucial moment in the transformation of the 'Anglo worldview', a worldview which would inevitably be exported to other languages via the translation of media representing war.

The diverse media of the Western world presented the war in Iraq in ways that were intended to support their country's or their government's interests, or simply in a way that was intended to reassure the readers and spectators in their preconceived ideas of the conflict. As spectators, we are often struck by the strange (and seemingly clumsy) bias of foreign media in their attempt to 'manipulate' their audience. On the other hand, we are, of course, usually less sensitive to the ways in which the media we are regularly exposed to are manipulating us, by highlighting certain aspects of the conflict while leaving others in the shadows, and by carrying us along with emotive narratives presented on a daily basis.

At first sight, it may seem that critique of propaganda should come from without. In this sense, readers might be interested in the criticism of US policy on war generated in France, which refused to join in the invasion of Iraq. However, the debate in France often showed more about France's own economic and political interests, and protest against the war often degenerated into the joyful condemnation of Bush in another round of anti-Americanism.

Throughout the period, a rising anti-American sentiment had been growing, only to be fuelled by the anti-war movement. A nostalgic *Gaullism* had been on the rise, and President Chirac (who had only managed to get himself elected thanks to an *anti-Front-National* vote) soon found himself with the support of masses of students who saw him as a defender of peace, a courageous contester to the military and economic heavyweight, the USA.

As we saw in our case study on hate, anti-Americanism has a long tradition in France. It adopts diverse forms at different times. To analyse this protest movement in the light of Philippe Roger's eloquent critique *L'Ennemi améric-ain*, we might conclude that this version of anti-American sentiment consisted in believing that little France, a bastion of civil rights blessed with a rich and artistic culture, was being menaced and manipulated by a cruel, crude and ignorant superpower peopled by halfwits, of which George W. Bush was the clown-in-chief. As Roger demonstrated, anti-Americanism revels in clichés and stereotypes. As a result, it shows very little about America and all too much about France; the France that French people want to believe in, the France that defends the *droits de l'homme* rather than the exporter of arms or the ex-colonial power eager to protect or extend its economic influence throughout the world.

Opposition to arguments forms part of rhetoric, but rhetoric fails to explain the emotive power of argument and it fails to prevent us from being swallowed up in the logic of the arguments in which we engage. Throughout the first decade of the twenty-first century, French politicians criticized and rejected American foreign policy measures. But the very fact that they argued that 'This is not the way to fight the war on terrorism', revealed only too well the degree to which they had been swallowed up by the rhetoric of fear and the 'war on terror'. In this sense, even in opposing Bush, they entered into a complicit acceptance of the terms of the world which he was exporting.

French criticism of the United States is situated. It is the discourse of a nation, the discourse of a ruling elite and it is the discourse which confuses freethinking moralism with the strategies designed to protect French business interests. Such a discourse must itself be critiqued from an ethnolinguistic perspective. The French point of view will certainly not suffice to allow us to understand how arguments transformed – in the space of a few months – popular opinion in Britain, and, in turning it around, created the agenda for war that Blair was so eager to establish. In order to elucidate this question, there is no space for anti-Americanism. There is no space for sentiment. Understanding the rhetoric and discourse strategies which transformed our concept of war and which consolidated the neoconservative worldview requires critique in the pure theoretical sense of the term, critique as Marx, Adorno or Williams would understand the term. Only a rigorous critique which strives to maintain an objective stance can allow us to understand the way in which terms are being manipulated and the way this manipulation is used to manipulate the popular conception of why the Second Gulf War took place. In this endeavour a corpus was established which comprized 150 articles from *The Economist* from September 2002 to May 2003. In 2002 something crucial was happening to our concept of war. A complex series of rhetorical strategies was converging to transform it. But to understand this process, we cannot simply denounce or reject the propaganda that came into play, we must first question what we mean by propaganda.

What is propaganda?

The idea of propaganda implies the perversion of 'real' or 'pure' meanings of words and concepts. As Orwell puts it:

Political language – and with variations this is true of all political parties, from Conservatives to Anarchists – is designed to make lies sound truthful and murder respectable, and to give an appearance of solidity to pure wind. (Orwell 1968: 139)

Words are deformed. Meanings are twisted. This is particularly true in periods of war, when enemies are diabolized. During the First and Second World Wars, the British public was bombarded with ridiculous blood thirsty images of the *Bosch* or the *Huns*, as the Germans were called, images which would no doubt have seemed absurd misrepresentations if the hysteria that accompanies war had not made such caricatures palatable to the British public. Only a few decades ago, in 1985, the pop singer Sting was singing 'I hope the Russians love their children too', as though our then Cold War enemies were perhaps too inhuman to be capable of parental attachment. Dehumanising our enemies, depriving them of all that makes them thinking, feeling people acting and breathing in space and time is nothing new, it would seem. Judging from media representations, we seem to feel a deep affection for the production and recycling of ludicrous stereotypes.

Propaganda is nothing new, then. Back in the seventeenth century, Thomas Hobbes, an English philosopher, was well aware of the ways in which different factions twist words. And it was perhaps because of this that he was very suspicious of metaphor, which for him was a perversion of the ordained meaning of the word (1985: 102). Hobbes was no doubt very sensitive to propaganda, given that he lived through the English Civil War. But the fact that he was also the translator of one of the greatest and oldest historians, Thucydides, the author of the chronicles of the Peloponnesian Wars, no doubt made him all the more sensitive. Four centuries before Christ, Thucydides described the ways in which words and concepts were subtly and strategically misused in order to sway public opinion and justify acts which in normal peacetime would seem outrageous. To quote Hobbes' translation:

The received value of names imposed for signification of things, was changed into arbitrary. For inconsiderate boldness was considered truehearted: provident consideration, a handsome fear: modesty, the cloak of cowardice. (Thucydides 1966: 348–9)

In wartime, as Orwell showed in his novel *1984*, propaganda inverts meanings. In his fictional, totalitarian regime, the Ministry of Truth bore three slogans:

> *WAR IS PEACE*
> *FREEDOM IS SLAVERY*
> *IGNORANCE IS STRENGTH*
> (1949: 7)

In Orwell's novel, perpetual war was an important means by which the party maintained order within a society in which the Ministry of Truth, predictably, dealt out the lies of the propaganda machine and the Ministry of Peace concerned itself with war (*ibid.*). As a journalist and a political thinker, Orwell was, like Hobbes and Thucydides, well aware of the workings of propaganda. He was also (once more like Hobbes) suspicious of metaphor; or, to be more precise, metaphors which we are used to seeing in print. Such used, hackneyed metaphors should, he said, be banned from writing by anyone who respected the English language and wished to guard against its decay (1968: 139). Hobbes, Orwell, and in more recent times, Andrew Goatly can be considered thinkers who urge us to guard against propaganda and the strategies it uses, metaphor being one of those strategies.

Hobbes, for his part, joins a long philosophical tradition which condemns metaphor wholesale as part of rhetoric, language play, which, so the argument goes, distracts us from the 'real', 'concrete', 'pure' meaning of words. Orwell, in contrast, was singling out those repeated political expressions that politicians and journalists use; expressions that we ourselves unwittingly adopt and allow to enter into common speech. Such language, he claimed 'consists less and less of "words" chosen for the sake of their meaning, and more of "phrases" tacked together like the sections of a prefabricated hen-house' (1968: 130). Using such hand-me-down, prefabricated, propaganda phrases showed, as far as Orwell was concerned, a kind of 'slovenliness' in our use of language and 'makes it easier for us to have foolish thoughts' (*ibid.*: 128).

It is exactly those prefabricated propaganda phrases that will be examined in the present chapter. But a distinction must be made. As we saw in our comparative study of truth, as soon as we enter into conceptualisation, we find ourselves entangled in metaphors. War is not unique in this respect, no more is truth. Even the most pragmatic discourse on work or money takes us into metaphors. Work is 'hard', money can 'flow' like water, or funds can 'dry up' and present us with a 'cash flow' problem. As soon as we say 'the economy is not taking off' we introduce the conceptual metaphor of the economy as an aeroplane.

Goatly proves more lucid than both Hobbes and Orwell in this respect: he knows that there is no escape from metaphor, if we accept by the term the definition of 'conceptual metaphor' with its 'metaphorical extensions' that Lakoff and Johnson have given us. This chapter is not the place to discuss the merits of metaphor theory (which I discuss in detail in *Creating Worldviews*, 2011). Neither am I concerned here with the question of the efficiency of propaganda and its capacity to condition the way we speak and act. The aim in the following pages is simply to show the underlying logic or rhetorical manipulation and the role metaphoric conceptualisation contributes to this strategy. This will involve showing that as far as the war in Iraq was concerned, metaphors certainly seemed to be inescapable. Metaphors were used again and again in *The Economist* (though not always overtly) to recondition the way we perceive war. The real war was juxtaposed with metaphoric wars such as Business-is-War and Student-Protest-is-War. Moreover, the examples we consider should allow us to establish that the metaphorical and the real intertwined to form part of a hype that represented war in a positive light.

What is war?

First of all, we need a definition of 'war', if we are going to argue that the 'proper' content of war is being perverted. Though we must proceed tentatively in drawing the line between literal and figurative language, we might, I believe, define war in its most literal, core meaning as:

a violent struggle between two or more nations, peoples or large groups of men or women over a sustained period of time, in which the aim of the parties involved is the subjugation or annihilation of the other party or parties or their expulsion from a given territory.

This is, of course, a reductive definition, but it should serve our purposes to allow us to show when some non-violent activity (such as cracking down on tax evasion) is being metaphorically conceived in terms of 'warfare'.

From the early autumn of 2002 the possibility of US intervention in Iraq was called 'war'. Thus far it seems that a spade was being called a spade. How was this war represented, though? In terms of trenches and bombing raids?

In one hundred *Economist* articles covering the build-up to the war and the fighting of the war itself (September 2002 to May 2003), thirteen conceptual metaphors could be identified. These thirteen conceptual metaphors can be divided into ten fairly common or 'traditional' ones, that is to say, metaphorical equations which are found in common usage, and three 'novel' ones, by which I mean metaphorical equations which were newly coined either by *The*

Economist or other media in the period directly preceding the build-up to the second war with Iraq.

Traditional conceptual metaphors for war

War is:

- defence
- acccpting a challenge
- lighting a fire
- a vehicle
- unleashing a wild beast
- a film
- surgery
- execution
- a game
- problem solving.

Ten traditional conceptual metaphors for war

1. War is Defence

30 Nov. 2002, p. 11

(George Bush) 'has rewritten America's **security doctrine around the notion of pre-emption**, so that he can **"confront the worst threats before they emerge"'**.

2. War is Accepting a Challenge

8 Mar. 2003, p. 13

'On most of these issues [Afghanistan, North Korea and Iraq] **America now has little choice but to take up the fight'**.

3. War is Lighting a Fire

30 Nov. 2002, p. 39

'But the full account of its weapons programmes, which Iraq is obliged to give to the weapons instructors and the Security Council on or before December 8th, is likely to be **Mr. Hussein's first big chance to ignite a war'**.

4. War is a Vehicle

5 Apr. 2003, p. 47

(Bush) 'personally took the decision **to kick-start the war with a missile attack** on Saddam's headquarters'.

5. War is Unleashing a Wild Beast

30 Nov. 2003, p. 39

(The advance party of 17 inspectors from Unmovic and IAEA, the two United Nations agencies charged with finding and destroying weapons in Iraq) 'will also be burdened by the knowledge that **their findings could unleash a war'**.

6. War is a Film

30 Nov. 2003, p. 67

'the **no-war scenario** is not necessarily the best for the economy'.

29 Mar. 2003, p. 47

(Donald Rumsfeld) 'A man who has seen only two films in years "Saving Private Ryan" and "Black Hawk Down" – found himself **treated as a matinee idol'**.

7. War is Surgery
29 Mar. 2003, p. 43

'The current combat has limited aims. It seeks to remove Saddam Hussein and his regime without massive damage to Iraq's civilian population and infrastructure. Hence the **surgical strikes against the leadership** and rules of engagement that seek to limit Iraqi civilian casualties, even at the risk of increasing American ones'.

8. War is Execution
29 Mar. 2003, p. 11

'The **"decapitation" strike** with which the war opened failed to kill Saddam Hussein or his lieutenants'.

9. War is a Game
21 Sep. 2003, p. 39

'Given that few expect Iraq's reprieve to last very long, this allows America's strained allies time to prepare for **a less abrupt endgame** than seemed **on the cards** a week ago'.

10. War is Problem Solving
8 Mar 2003, p. 13

'... peace did not break out with the end of the cold war. Even in Europe, there was **bloody tidying up to do** (with American help) in the Balkans throughout the 1990s. And while Europe during the 1990s was **finishing the job of making itself whole and free**, other parts of the world were not so lucky. This was not a decade that established universal peace, which the Bush administration is now needlessly disturbing. It was a decade during which the Clinton administration **neglected too many unresolved problems**'.

Commentary

It is perfectly clear that all of these metaphorical equations enabled *The Economist* to put a positive spin on the war. When the Americans were defending themselves or accepting a challenge, they were presented as reluctantly facing up to an attack. If war became problem solving, how could a down-to-earth, pragmatic, utilitarian nation refuse to get the job done? Action, intervention, declaring war became a moral imperative that only irresponsible nations would refuse to acknowledge. While Bush was presented as a dynamic young biker who 'kick-started' the war, an image geared to endear him to younger readers, the USA was not usually presented as the instigator of the conflict. Saddam Hussein's failure to give a full account to weapons inspectors would be the cause that 'ignited' the war. And if war was represented as unleashing a wild animal, neither the USA nor Britain was responsible. The findings of the weapons inspectors would do the unleashing. Finally, we moved into war as a spectator sport with War-is-a-Film and War-is-a-Game. Both forms of representation allowed real violence to provoke real emotions, but the war was moving more into the realm of Hollywood and ever further from the real carnage of warfare.

Novel conceptual metaphors for war

War is:

- reaching a destination
- a commodity
- crime-fighting.

Novel conceptual metaphors for war

1. War is Reaching a Destination

| 30 Nov. 2002, p. 39 | 'The **paths to war**'. |

2. War is a Commodity

| 30 Nov. 2002, p. 67 | 'Recent studies suggest that even a successful military campaign in Iraq could **carry a hefty price tag**'. |

3. War is Crime-fighting

| 15 Mar. 2003, p. 26 | 'But whereas France, by threatening its veto in the broad way it has, seems to be making the Iraq row a test of wills with America, both America and Britain see it as a test of the Security Council's resolve to enforce its own repeated resolutions against **a serial offender who has shown every determination to resist**'. |

Commentary

To represent victory as an ultimate goal, a destination, would be a conventional representation. But here we have something different: in the build-up to this war, the destination became the actual declaration of the war. War, rather than being represented as a hell that had to be passed through, became the end we were supposed to work towards. War became a solution. This meant, consequently, that those who opposed war were refusing a solution. They were being difficult. War, the ultimate form of destruction, was presented as a constructive option, one that the French, the Germans and the Russians were obstructing.

Elsewhere, war was, in a rather grotesque materialist fashion, presented as a commodity that could be bought off the shelf. The question became, would it be worth it? Was war good value? Perhaps the most frightening novel conceptual metaphor that has imposed itself over the past couple of years, though, is War-is-Crime-fighting. This metaphor was already present (if in a much less elaborate form) in the Vietnam war, but it increasingly came to be a touchstone for the pro-war rhetoric. This metaphor assumes that one country has the right to dictate the laws of a world society, and to enforce them. Indeed, if we accept that a nation can commit 'crimes', as Iraq was portrayed as doing, then 'crime prevention' becomes a moral obligation, an obligation that US soldiers are asked to fulfil. The essential thing about this conceptual metaphor is that Americans are living through this idea. Consequently, they find it difficult to grasp that other nations are unwilling to help them do the job. Bush has been denounced, and Obama's war policy has been shaken by criticism, but the French refusal to engage in the war has never been forgiven, and resentment and a feeling of betrayal continue to animate the bad faith which promoted war as a solution, and presented the USA and Britain as liberators rather than invaders.

It would seem that the attackers remain in denial and continue to see themselves as peace-keepers. There has been much derision in France and elsewhere concerning the peace-keeping role that the USA has attributed itself. Yet, curiously, the conceptual metaphor upon which it is based, War-is-Crime-fighting, has passed directly into the mindsets of people of France, as the phrase 'the war on terrorism' was translated directly into *la guerre contre le terrorisme* in French. Other cultures were similarly influenced by this key moment in the transformation of the 'Anglo worldview'. The war on terror was translated into *válka terorismus* in Czech, for example. And similar terms appear in both Spanish and in German (at least from 2004 onwards, according to my own findings). What ethnolinguistic lessons can be learned from this state of affairs? Certainly, that the 'Anglo worldview' has limits and that those limits are constantly shifting, being redefined and redesigned as that worldview feels the tug of interested parties which seek to refashion the world in their image and according to their interests. But also that critique must move beyond the questioning of arguments and interests, and must delve deeply into the strategies forming questions and defining concepts, deeply into conceptual metaphors and the extensions which support them and which logically branch out from them, once a metaphoric nexus has been established. As much debate and criticism in France, the Czech Republic, Germany and Spain shows, we can oppose something and yet be seduced into using the terms of those we are opposing.

Warfare conceptual metaphors

As we have seen, in the discussion of the Iraq question in *The Economist* from September 2002 to May 2003, war was often not war. A corpus of one hundred articles demonstrates this point, the examples above being only a very brief summary. The total number of articles in the overall corpus was one hundred and fifty, however. The fifty remaining ones had little or absolutely nothing to do with war. Or this, at first glance, appeared to be the case. In point of fact, war was not always absent from these articles, however. But the focus of these articles was on subjects wholly unrelated to the war in Iraq. In these articles, a wide variety of other news items were represented in terms of warfare. In the corpus defined, seventeen conceptual metaphors were found. These seventeen conceptual metaphors can be divided into ten fairly common or traditional ones and seven novel ones.

Traditional warfare conceptual metaphors

- Propaganda
- Trying to alleviate poverty
- Trying to cure disease
- Business
- Party politics
- International diplomacy and politics
- Student protest
- Trying to prevent drug traffic
- Trying to eradicate tax evasion
- Social unrest

is 'war'.

Traditional warfare conceptual metaphors

1. Propaganda is War
29 Mar. 2003, p. 28

'Two factors have emboldened Arab protesters. The first is that Iraq, battered and despised as its regime is, appears to be **winning the propaganda war**'.

2. Trying to Alleviate Poverty is War
26 Oct. 2002, p. 81

'**WEAPONS OF MASS SALVATION**
In this article, Jeffrey Sachs argues that, in the **war against want**, no less than in the war against terror, actions speak louder than words'.

3. Trying to Cure Disease is War
5 Apr. 2003, p. 13

'**Epidemics, like wars, bring out strong emotions**. Fear and anger are chief among them … **Severe Acute Respiratory Syndrome is raging**. The viruses that cause SARS are **formidable foes**. They **are invisible attackers**, spreading with alarming ease across continents and of unknown strength'.

4. Business is War
29 Mar. 2003, p. 66

'FORMERLY **HAWKISH TRADERS** TAKE COVER AS WAR'S REALITY SINKS IN … Stock markets responded by **beating a hasty retreat** from their exuberance in the week before the war began … the **quick about turn** may have caught them (some hedge funds) for a second time … Recent weeks have provided fine evidence of such **violent under- and over-shooting** … Shares will not find it easy **coming home from this war**'.

5. Party Politics is War

21 Sep. 2002, p. 31

(Austria's Jörg Haider) 'Is his **Kampf** really over?'

6. International Politics is War

15 Mar. 2003, p. 39

'More and more, Mr Blair looked like a man caught between growing American impatience with its ally's frenzied but fruitless diplomacy, and the **determination of the French and Russians to shoot down any compromise proposed by the British**'.

7. Student Protest is War

8 Mar. 2003, p. 41

'Students used to see themselves as **intellectual warriors** fighting on behalf of oppressed people everywhere'.

8. Trying to Prevent Drug Traffic is War

5 Apr. 2003, p. 14

'Time to think again about the **rules of engagement in the war on drugs**'.

9. Trying to Eradicate Tax Evasion is War

5 Oct. 2002, p. 64

'IT'S **WAR**

Getting people to pay their taxes [in the Philippines] is the government's biggest challenge … [Gloria Macapegal Arroyo, the president] **ordered all her forces into battle** against the Philippines' pervasive tax evasion. To show how serious she is, she even hauled **a manacled prisoner of the war against tax cheats** in front of the cameras, for a personal dressing-down on television.

The president's **belligerence** is understandable'.

10. Social Unrest is War

19 Oct. 2002, p. 43

'Cruelly oppressive though it may be, the [Iraqi] state does provide security. "The whole **society is a minefield**," said an aid worker who has widely travelled across the country. "Lift the pressure and it could really explode"'.

Commentary

Where the conceptual metaphors had little or nothing to do with the actual war, wars of a metaphorical kind were presented as necessary, beneficial or heroic. Who could pity the gangland drug lord if war was declared upon him? Who would stand up for poverty, suffering and illness, if the government wanted to stamp them out? These metaphors acted as a backdrop to the rhetoric that was used to hype the war and, in a subliminal manner, went some way towards presenting war and warriors in a positive light in the imagination of the readers of *The Economist*.

Where articles touched on the war in Iraq, those nations that advised caution and supported peaceful solutions were represented as declaring war on those advocating invasion. This is exactly the kind of misrepresentation that Thucydides had in mind when he spoke of caution being called cowardice. The conceptual metaphor Politics-is-War allowed pacifists to be portrayed as warriors and war advocates as victims. Similarly, students who resisted the war were somewhat ridiculously portrayed as 'intellectual warriors'. Predictably, rejection and denunciation left little space for enlightened analysis and critical distance. And as the students and protesters were swept away with their chanting, in denunciating Bush they walked straight into his worldview and marched in tune with the very rhetoric they should by rights have been denunciating as pacifists. Students revelled in the idea of themselves as 'warriors', activists who could make a difference. How much difference the millions of demonstrators in France and Britain were to make could be seen months later as the invasion got under way and as the media began to recount the deposing of Saddam Hussein.

Novel warfare conceptual metaphors

- Trying to eradicate terrorism
- Cultural competition
- Pacifism
- Economic planning
- The consolidation of the European Union
- Making peace
- Harming the environment

is 'war'.

Novel warfare conceptual metaphors

1. Trying to Eradicate Terrorism is War
7 Sep. 2002, p. 84

'Rohan Gunaratna's "Inside al-Qaeda: Global Network of Terror", embraces the notion of Mr bin Laden as the godfather of **an army of terror with foot soldiers in every region of the world**'.

2. Cultural Competition is War
7 Dec. 2002, p. 72

'THE **MISS WORLD WAR**
... Given all of the talk of a **clash of civilisations**, might Miss Morely (Miss World's chief executive) deserve praise for fearlessly promoting western "culture"?'

3. Pacifism is War
15 Feb. 2002, p. 40

'**BOMBS AWAY**
Britain's anti-war movement is booming but divided'.

4. Economic Planning is War
15 Mar. 2003, p. 13

'WORLD ECONOMY: BEARING DOWN
The case for **pre-emptive policy action**'.

5. The Consolidation of the EU is War
5 Apr. 2003, p. 35

'The European Union's expansion is roaring
ahead, with destination unknown.
Operation EU enlargement is going well.
The **European Union's advance into central Europe is meeting little opposition**;
the natives are greeting the **invading army
of Eurocrats** with flowers and celebration'.

6. Making Peace is War
31 May 2003, front cover

'Now, the **waging of peace**'.

7. Harming the Environment is War
29 Mar. 2003, p. 71

'A few years ago, the [Iraqi] government
decided to drain the marshes of lower
Mesopotamia, in what amounted to an **act
of environmental warfare**'.

Commentary

Some of these novel metaphors were invented by the creative muse that
inspires the journalists of *The Economist*, which prides itself on the level of
education of its readership and displays a cultivated style of journalism that
often makes use of literary and philosophical references. Others were invented
during the period by politicians and journalists, and recycled or adapted by
the journalists of *The Economist*. Several of the above examples, such as the
consolidation of the EU and economic planning, might be regarded simply as
a form of 'rhetorical overspill'. Indeed public events often tend to condition
the creativity of media discourse. After the French team won the World Cup
in 1996, the French financial press was full of references to soccer, to train-
ing and to goals, applied to the field of business strategies and takeovers. The
celebration of the fall of the Berlin Wall, in turn, spread throughout the press,
almost like a contagion. Soon the sports press in France was talking about 'the
wall' in cycling, and marathon running, a term referring to the period of heavy
fatigue that comes about after two or three hours of intensive activity, when
sugar levels are depleted and the body must begin transforming carbohydrates
into energy.

   Other metaphors are, however, less innocent and cannot be accounted
for as simple 'overspill'. Saddam Hussein was once more represented as a
warmonger when he harmed the environment. Even the apolitical youth of
today are 'green'. Green is good, is a slogan that seems to all intents and purposes unassailable. Such a metaphor was unlikely, therefore, to win Hussein
any allies. More importantly, pacifists were turned into bombers who were
dropping bombs on a soft-spoken Mr Blair, who was advocating a peaceable

European consensus on war. Even making peace was transformed into war, a war that would, it seemed, require the resolute fortitude and courage of soldiers. Once more, Bush was portrayed as a hero fighting for liberty by this conceptual metaphor.

Switching

Both Pacifism-is-War and Making-Peace-is-War constitute full inversions of the kind Orwell described in *1984*. Here, one concept is transformed into its opposite. This is a curious form of metaphor which seems to defy outright the Aristotelian view that metaphor works by virtue of an intuitively perceived similarity between two things. That making peace could be seen in terms of waging a war is indeed curious enough in itself. The justification seems to be that making a lasting peace will take the same unswerving determination as a war campaign. 'Waging the peace', we were invited to believe, is a daunting task that takes guts, resolute courage and skill. This might be accepted, even if the metaphor appears very ill-chosen, but the representation of those forces which resisted immediate engagement in war in Iraq was even more absurd in *The Economist*'s articles. Because politics is conceived of in terms of war, the anti-war movement could 'kill' Blair. The only way Tony Blair could 'defend himself' against their 'attacks' (which were represented as 'bombing raids') was by defusing this threat. That Blair may have viewed anti-war supporters as a threat to his career is perfectly possible, and understandable, but that such metaphorical reasoning leads us to tar pacifists as terrorists is nonetheless bizarre, if not ridiculous.

The conceptual metaphor Pacifism-is-War did, quite naturally, extend to both Schröder and Chirac, whose attempts to calm things down were seen as 'sabotage'. Doubtless this rhetoric was animated by that particularly insidious form of bad faith that shapes our unconscious reasoning and refuses to allow us to see a pretext for what it is. This unconscious reasoning did, however, structure itself along logical lines: because refusing war was 'war' (of a political kind), then a 'peaceful' solution to the political conflict would be the establishment of a consensus-based alliance that would promote the declaration of war. This was the only 'solution' both Blair and Bush seemed inclined to accept, and they themselves seem to have found their arguments for that 'solution' reasonable enough. These are forms of out-and-out 'inversion'.

Although this might be a striking example, it does not allow us to account for the interpenetration of warfare metaphors between source and target domains. My corpus has allowed me to present a considerable amount of evidence to support the claim that while one thing (war) was being transformed into another, other things were being transformed into the concept which was being transformed. Since, to my knowledge, this curious form of metaphorical interpenetration has yet to be given a name, I would like to suggest we call it *the switch*.

As we have seen, when *The Economist* spoke of war, it seemed to transform it into such alternative concepts as problem solving, accepting a challenge, a game or a film. This was my own impression at least. However, is it true then that *The Economist* refused to represent war as war?

The answer to this question is a definite NO. Although in my attempt to demonstrate how *the switch* works, metaphors have been quoted which transform the meaning of war, the term 'war' was very much present in discussion of Iraq. In a one-and-a-half-page article on the subject in the 7 January 2003 edition, for example, *The Economist* used the term war to designate its prototypical meaning no less than twenty-seven times. Similarly, when it came to actually fighting the war, *The Economist* frequently called a tank a tank, a bombing raid a bombing raid and gave ample scope to technical military language in discussions of manoeuvres and military strikes.

It would seem that we should be careful, therefore, not to allow the striking nature of novel metaphors to mislead us by giving a false impression or imbalanced view of the workings of political rhetoric. Although I initially imagined that the switch had utterly evacuated the meaning of the term 'war', it had merely contributed to blurring its definition. Moreover, rather than being a sole or primary rhetorical strategy used to promote war, the switch proved to be one of several devices which came into operation. Other devices included:

- well-tailored rational arguments in favour of the war;
- the use of images to present the 'defenders' of war in a sympathetic light and images used to suggest defenders of peace were aggressive interventionists;
- the use of alliteration (reminiscent of the 'gutter press') such as *the world awaits the battle for Baghdad* (29 Mar. 2003 p.22), *What turned it for Tony* (22 Mar. 2003 p.37) and *A fight to the finish* (22 Mar. 2003 p.22).

This alliteration served to foreground selected phrases that hyped up the apology for war, and gave pro-war rhetoric a sonorous power which, like poetry or advertising jingles, acts on our irrational unconscious. What resounds, somehow seems to us to be apt and right. The alliterative phrases quoted above were often used as headlines to attract the attention of the reader.

Nonetheless, the switch cannot be considered to be the poor cousin of the inversion, and it seems reasonable to expect that its rhetorical power of persuasion is no less forceful. Inversions are striking, they draw attention to themselves. The switch does the very opposite, it allows meanings to glide into new domains, and thereby curtails the dimensions of a reality which propagandists are interested in occulting. Inversions turn white into black. But it is in the shadows that most rhetorical manipulation takes place, and the switch, which excels in disseminating the grey areas of doubt, and in blurring the contours of concepts and the links they form to other concepts, is well equipped for spreading the shadow of the neoconservative worldview.

The neoconservatives paved the way to war and left the Americans to pay for their wars: they have left regions in chaos and left Obama to pick up the pieces. But the success of their war rhetoric both in home and foreign policy lies in their ability to play with polysemy. They have set up war in their domestic discourse, made a home for it in civil society. Meanwhile, they continue to perpetuate the illusion that the war efforts were waged in the name of peace. Escaping from the neoconservative worldview will not be easy, but this is the endeavour facing the citizens of America today, and this is the endeavour we, too, in other countries, in other linguistic communities, must engage in. Redefining war and limiting the tentacles with which it reaches out into other domains of life and experience must count as one of the main steps on the road to escaping from the world-according-to-Bush.

Escaping from the neoconservative worldview

There has been a widespread desire to turn the page on Bush's worldview. Given the catastrophic polls concerning Republican war and home policy, both the Republican candidate John McCain and his running mate, Sarah Palin, were eager to disengage themselves from the worldview which had precipitated the country into conflict and the culture of fear. A contender for the place of Republican candidate, Michael Huckabee, took a much firmer stance than McCain in relation to Bush and his administration when he denounced its 'bunker mentality'. This did not turn out to his advantage, however. Despite widespread mistrust for the administration, the idea of a Republican turning on his party alienated many right-wing voters. This resentment was, predictably, enflamed by the conservative media: authors publishing on the www. freerepublic.com website, for example, made a series of devastating attacks on Huckabee.

For his own part, McCain made more restrained criticisms: he took issue with the 'mismanagement' of the war in Iraq, and he focused, strategically, on individuals, the 'managers' who could be blamed for the whole crisis, without forcing voters to consider whose backing had been needed to put such people into positions of power 'managing' the war. Rumsfeld was thus selected and denounced by McCain as 'one of the worst secretaries of defense in history' (*The North Country Times*, 28 April 2007). Rumsfeld went down in the attempt to keep the Republican administration intact, afloat.

McCain avoided frontal attacks on both his Republican campaign competitors, the existing administration and even, to a certain, degree, on his opponents, Obama and Clinton, who were vying for the candidacy of the Democrats. Politics-is-War is a rhetorical discourse which McCain (a war hero himself) carefully kept clear of. This was clearly part of a strategy designed to send electors to sleep. With his bonhomie, his discreet charisma, his sense of humour and his spontaneity, the ageing McCain was presented as the friendly grandfather, representing continuity, traditional values, authority and serenity. In one sense, he would avoid a brutal break with the Bush administration, and in another, he would trigger a return to the traditional values, which the neoconservative hawks had broken free from. McCain claimed he could reassemble the Republicans, a strategy which explains his tireless use of 'my Friends' in his speeches.

To his credit, to the very end, McCain played this hand to the full, and he graciously congratulated Obama on his election. Throughout the election, McCain made it plain that the competition for election was a natural and 'American' ritual, almost a sports competition: let the best man win, and let each man (and woman) strive to do his or her best thanks to the inherently healthy ritual of setting people against one another in competition. That appeared, at least, to be McCain's view. And it was largely successful as a media strategy: none the less so because it contrasted so greatly with the more brutal confrontations between Clinton and Obama, which the *New York Times* described as a 'slugfest'.[5]

But if war rhetoric was on the decline, the wars in Iraq and Afghanistan were still fully aflame, and McCain could not avoid commenting on them. He spoke not of hope and invasion but of 'bringing security to Iraq' and of 'cautious optimism', in his major speech on the subject on 26 March 2008. Like a true soldier, McCain refused to accept defeat: 'We're no longer staring into the abyss of defeat', he affirmed. 'Abyss' is a patently biblical word, one which thereby situates us well within the scope of Bush's sacred war on terror and against the Evil of the world. McCain embraced, therefore, not only the project of the Bush administration's expansionist policy, but its rhetoric and the driving forces of its underlying postulates. Together, the Americans could succeed. And what did success entail for McCain? His answer merely reiterated the ambition of the Bush administration:

Success: the establishment of a peaceful democratic state that poses no threats to its neighbors and contributes to the defeat of terrors.

The words, the concepts, the fears and the resolute optimism, that unshakable faith in America's capacity as a nation to do good in the world, are the very convictions of George W. Bush and Rumsfeld. The success those two had reached out for was 'within reach'; McCain stressed optimism, rejecting both a rising sense of defeatism and the revelling in the horrors of war to which the media had succumbed towards the end of the decade. To pessimists, McCain sent out a challenge: 'Don't tell me what we can't do. Don't tell me we can't make our country stronger and the world safe'.

In this short phrase, we find the three cardinal desires of the Bush administration expressed: to protect the USA militarily in the post-Cold-War period, to protect its economic interests and to play the role of world sheriff. In this worldview, the security of the USA conflates with and subsumes the security of the world. At this stage, we enter the totalitarian worldview: the USA represents the centre and the essence of the world as a whole, and all that rises up against that centre rises up against the world as a whole. At this point, it becomes logical that a discourse of war should increasingly disappear, since warfare paradigms posit the existence of binary forces, opposing armies. In a world in which the USA protects the interests of the whole, on the other hand, the whole world is embraced within the goodwill of the States. Good stamps out Evil in the world. Evil can return, Evil will always rise up again, but the Good, the whole, the USA will always remain, vigilant, ready to serve the interests of us all.

McCain in 2008 adhered fully to the worldview which Fukuyama had proclaimed fifteen years before. According to Fukuyama, the American Hegelian sociologist, the lesson we must draw from the failure of socialist republics to sustain themselves, and from the end of the Cold War, was that one system alone was fit to rule the world, the regime adopted by the USA, liberal democracy. Social and economic well-being was safeguarded best by this system, Fukuyama believed, and it was for this reason that the free peoples of the West had chosen to adopt it. Liberal democracy represented the 'end of history' for Fukuyama. This was what made Fukuyama a Hegelian: history had a destiny and it was following its logical and unalterable course. History could know only one outcome, and that outcome was the American form of liberal democracy.

This spirit inhabits the neoconservative worldview. The Bush administration does not have any philosophers, but it does have a philosophy of sorts, and McCain had inhaled its zeitgeist. And all that he said would demonstrate that fact. It is, therefore, in Fukuyama's terms that we must understand McCain's pronouncements when he spoke of destiny and war. McCain believed that the Americans were 'on the right side of History' (NBC News). Even after losing the elections, McCain did not abandon this rhetoric, and on 21 June 2009 he was claiming once more, in relation to the Iran crisis, that the USA must be on 'the right side of history'.[6]

In other words, if McCain avoids violent rhetoric, it is not because of his timid nature (his personal courage is beyond question). Neither is it because he denounced the violence of the Bush administration; it is because, in all strategic matters, he was not a catalyst for rupture: he incarnated the continuity of the Bush administration and its worldview. Most of all, he incarnated the Republicans' incapacity to hear the criticisms which were being levelled at them and their administration. Calmness was not simply a cover: it was a symptom of a deeper complacency, an intellectual and moral lethargy which passed itself off as conviction. When it came down to strategy, McCain, when pushed, would rehash the righteous biblical rhetoric of the

Bush administration. And it was on this very point that Obama was able to score points by mocking his style and pointing out that McCain had no policy of his own. As he put it:

John McCain may like to say he likes to follow Osama bin Laden to the gates of hell, but so far all he's done is follow George Bush into a misguided war in Iraq. (*Caucus New York Times*, 27 February 2008)

Throughout the campaign against Clinton and, later, against McCain, Obama won praise for his calmness and his respect for his adversaries. In the 'war of words', the 'slugfest', curiously, it was the woman who, because of the violence of her attacks, came off looking worse. Was it because Hillary Clinton belongs to a generation of women who were forced to 'outdo' men in affirming their strength in order to make their way in a man's world, that she allowed her discourse to become vitriolic at times? That remains to be seen. At any rate, the aggressiveness of her posturing seemed, in the face of the calmness of both Obama and McCain, to belong to another period, to bygone days. Her claim that the USA would 'annihilate Iran', if attacked (a fairly obvious reaction to a highly improbable hypothesis), was widely publicized and invariably misquoted on internet sites, a fact that did much to harm her campaign.

What both McCain and Obama had understood about the discourse of the Bush administration was that 'warring with words' had outrun its term in office. This was part of a deeper change in sentiment regarding the administration and its objectives. On 23 March 2007, Dr Zbigniew Brzezinski, President Carter's adviser, weighed up the Bush administration in a way that reflected the public opinion's disappointment:

- The 'war on terror' has created a culture of fear in America. The Bush administration's elevation of these three words into a national mantra since the horrific events of 9/11 has had a pernicious impact on American democracy, on America's psyche and on US standing in the world.
- The phrase itself is meaningless. It defines neither a geographic context nor our presumed enemies.
- A recent BBC poll of 28,000 people in 27 countries that sought respondents' assessments of the role of states in international affairs resulted in Israel, Iran and the United States being rated (in that order) as the states with 'the most negative influence on the world'. Alas, for some that is the new axis of evil!
- Only a confidently determined and reasonable America can promote genuine international security which then leaves no political space for terrorism. (*Washington Post*, 23 March 2007)

In this light, Obama's administration has distanced itself from war rhetoric. Clinton was appointed Foreign Secretary in 2008 on Obama's victory, but when she told reporters as she travelled to a United Nations-led conference on Afghanistan: 'The administration has stopped using the phrase [war on terror], and I think that speaks for itself', she was merely reaffirming a stance that had long since come to be established.

Corpus linguistic research testifies to the eradication of war-on-terror rhetoric. The COCA corpus found only nine references linking Obama to the word 'terror', only one from 2010: and of those, most were commentaries upon his policies rather than the pronouncements of the President himself. However, the discourse of war-on-terror has not been buried. That rhetoric has migrated from the field of political discourse to nest in the American imagination. The war-on-terror is no longer a restricted concept. It continues, unsurprisingly, to be used in relation to the fate of prisoners in Guantanamo and their trial by civilian courts. But it has taken on a much greater scope and significance. In 2010, war-on-terror was still animating the discourse of *Fox News*, *NBC*, *CSM*, *Newsweek*, and *The Washington Post*.

In fact the real test of a term's anchorage within the lexicon is its ability to be creatively used and placed in new contexts. From this perspective, claims that 'Kashmir as new frontier of global war on terror' are interesting. This proves the point: the war on terror exists, and it can move from one territory to another. This rhetoric taps into the American spatial imagination. The USA is engaged in a 'global' war, but the very conception of 'global' turns out to be very 'national'. The American nation created itself by 'pushing back frontiers'. Now it continues to push frontiers back as it redoubles its efforts to 'civilize' and 'secure' the world and rid it of terrorism. Ironically, the words spoken by Condoleezza Rice on 8 April 2004, testifying at the 9th Public Hearing of the 9/11 Commission, seem very apt, when it comes to considering the way the American imagination and its linguistically coded world-perceiving and world-conceiving have been transformed: 'The world has changed so much that it is difficult to remember what our lives were like before that day'.

The Bush administration may have been ousted from power by the elections, but their worldview has taken root even in academia, where we might have hoped for a critical distance when it comes to their rhetoric. Carl J. Ohlson used 'war on terror' as if it was an unproblematic term, in the *Journal of Psychology* (September 2009, volume 36:3). And the *Anthropological Quarterly* in the same year (Summer 2009, vol. 82:3) was declaring that 'India has joined the ranks of nations engaged in a global "war on terror"'.

In other words, all we can hope for from academia as it adopts this rhetoric is inverted commas. Criticism of Bush has been rampant, and, in the beginning at least, it took the form of a joyful retaliation. But if we are to understand the way in which war rhetoric has been effaced, we should try to see what has replaced it, and how the alternatives have maintained some of the central tenets of American foreign policy. On one point, Clinton and Obama join with Brzezinski's reappraisal of Bush's foreign policy, and, ironically, in doing so, they join with McCain. All four advocate the promotion of a 'real international security' and leaving no space for terrorism. And indeed, in 150 articles taken from the *International Herald Tribune*, which I considered during the build-up to the 2008 elections, war had largely been replaced by the discourse of 'security'. In this discourse, the world exists as a space to be managed, a series of opposing forces to be mastered, a series of interests to be preserved and promoted. It goes without saying that for Obama and Clinton, the USA is best suited and best qualified to be appointed as 'manager' in this newly conceived 'secured' space.

A rhetorical shift has taken place. Opposition has won out in its struggle with Bush and his rhetoric, but in entering into combat with that rhetoric, the opponents have, predictably, been conditioned by the fight. They have encountered Bush and his worldview, to a large extent, on the terms forged by the Bush administration. And those terms involve not only words themselves, but, at a very fundamental level, the concepts which invent reality and political space. Metaphors for conflict, invasion and suppression and oppression, and, above all, a certain tone and rhythm of rhetoric, belong to the style of Bush's discourse. Reagan may have ended his speeches by asserting with a Hollywoodesque conviction 'God bless America!', but the tone and rhythm of his speeches was measured. George W. Bush introduced a very different tone and rhythm to the presidential speech, the language of the convert. The events of 9/11 shocked and shook the American people so greatly that the incantatory rhetoric of the Evangelicals came to seem apt and reassuring on the centre stage of American politics. The language and the worldview of a minority of American citizens came to resonate more and more with the shellshocked majority looking for reassurance in public debate.

This explains not only Bush's own personal success, the charismatic charm he undoubtedly held for many electors in his first term of office, but also the kinds of rhetoric which would replace him once he fell from grace. Obama's oratory skills have often been praised. But what are they? An ability to articulate a rational argument, but to do so with a rounded, undulating rhythm which, without overdoing it, reminds us of the Baptist-style speeches of Martin Luther King. With the tone, goes the sentiment: hope, brotherhood, sharing and, increasingly, 'reaching out'. Obama in 2009 and 2010 was 'reaching out to Muslim nations'. But what exactly does 'reaching out' involve, if not inviting other nations 'to come back within the fold'? And if those nations do not accept the hand that reaches out to them? Will they be considered spiteful and resentful dogs that 'bite the hand that feeds them'? Obama's hope is a religious hope. Obama's religion is a religion of love, not of hatred. He does not share the weakness for hell and brimstone which animated the rhetoric of Bush and McCain. He does not speak of the 'abyss' or the 'menace of evil'. Nevertheless, in his *Audacity of Hope*, he made it plain that America had the right to protect its own economic interests by making use of its military power, and he asserted that the diplomacy he would advocate would not be made of empty words: it would be enforced, if necessary, by firepower.

Democrats allowed themselves to be submerged by the war-on-terror rhetoric of the Bush administration. Ironically, now that Obama is preaching a New Testament love, the love of reaching out, the Republicans seem to have chosen to dance in tune to this new rhetoric. Sarah Palin is a very authentic exponent of the Evangelical community. Well versed in scripture, she makes use of it in her speeches. And in November and December 2010, she was promoting her book entitled *American by Heart*, subtitled *Reflections on Family, Faith, and Flag*. There is a certain logic in this: the Evangelicals have often been staunch allies of the Republican Party. For this reason, the pro-Democrat media pounces upon her biblical references and turns them against her. This makes it often difficult to ascertain the true nature of her remarks. When Palin intelligently expresses her faith and stresses that we must all ask ourselves if we are fighting on the side of God, media sites caricature her position, affirming that she has asserted that God is on her side. This is unfortunate, because the caricature makes it difficult to understand the true charm that Palin's positions have for her electorate and for her supporters. As a mother who sends her son to war to fight for his country and for liberty, as a patriot, as a Christian, Palin incarnates a symbol. She is reaching out, offering herself, and bowing down to something greater than her own personal interests. This discourse resonates with the American people. It is, after all, the same rhetoric that Obama employs. It is the rhetoric of love, the rhetoric of the New Testament.

Bush appealed to fear and fury. Obama and Palin appeal to the heart. They want the heart to hear them. Palin's book tour was a tour of the homeland, but she replaced that loaded political term (which has become irreparably harnessed to 'security') with 'heartland'. In 2002, the American academic David K. Naugle celebrated 'the heart' in similar terms when he made an oblique attack on the concept of 'worldview' in his *Worldview: The History of a Concept*. As a Christian, Naugle believes the term 'worldview' belongs to a relativistic, amoral tradition, and he quoted Karl Jaspers as a main exponent of the term (though Naugle himself made a detailed and erudite study of the usage of the word since Kant). In contrast to the existentially subjective usage of the term, Naugle was concerned with defending the worldview of 'the heart': 'the subjective sphere of consciousness which is decisive for shaping a vision of life and fulfilling the function typically ascribed to the notion of *Weltanschauung*' (Naugle 2002: 267). What Naugle was analysing in the history of ideas, Palin is preaching at political gatherings at a grassroots level.

Refusing to accept that different worldviews exist, that culture and language and political interests separate us and divide us, Palin (and Obama) are preaching the discourse of unity. Deep down, both believe that God has made us equal and in the same mould. It then follows that we must reach out to others and gather them in. In warfare, such rhetoric clearly defines Obama and Palin as generals waging what Clausewitz would call an 'ideological war', a 'religious war', a war between Good and Evil. The problem with such wars is that their conception makes pulling out impossible. Nelson, or Bismarck could capitulate or negotiate for strategic military reasons. We can negotiate with antagonists, and we can respect our enemies and their right to defend themselves against our attacks. But we can't do deals with evil-doers.

If we refuse to relinquish the illusion that we incarnate Good's struggle over Evil in this world, we find our hands tied. It therefore remains questionable whether such arguments of love, backed with firepower, will make the world more secure. Such questions belong to geopolitical analysis not to ethnolinguistics. But the language of geopolitics will always involve struggles to define words. This is what ethnolinguistics has to teach politics.

The lessons to be learned for ethnolinguistics from political discourse, on the other hand, are four in number. Firstly, all language is political, and in comparing cultures we cannot hide from this fact. Secondly, worldviews exist within worldviews, and they are often at war with one another. Thirdly, opposing a worldview does not necessarily allow us to escape it. Bush's religious rhetoric paved the way for Palin's and Obama's calls for love. Fourthly, worldviews spread from dominant languages, and we cannot simply oppose their influence. We must question the very modes by which language is fusing metaphorical and literal frames of thinking, and we must try to disentangle ambiguity, obscurity and semantic blurring in order to re-establish a truth that 'war' proves, but which is the case of countless words: that they mean many things. Accepting polysemy as a linguistic fact, we should, nevertheless, be alert as to the ways in which polysemy is being tugged in new directions by new policies. The switch, the strategy of rehabilitating war in metaphoric scenarios while denying its existence in reality, is only one of the strategies which is threatening us and our vision of the world. If we have managed to unmask this insidious rhetorical trope, then we will have taken one step towards 'washing the mind' as Goatly would put it, rendering ourselves a little more lucid in our world-perceiving.

7   A final word

This is not a book about ethics, but about ethnolinguistics. It is not a book about politics, but about the poetics of language, about worldviews and how humans live through an adventure in language, conceiving their own personal world within the world of politics and in relation to one another. Ethics and politics obviously overlap, but no more so than language and ideology. This was the crucial fact that Aristotle understood, and which has been forgotten by the rhetorical tradition. For Aristotle, rhetoric formed part of politics and politics formed part of ethics. To persuade will not suffice, Aristotle taught. To lead others where we wish is pointless unless we know where we want to lead them. And in order to understand the nature of the good, we must first understand politics, which in itself entails understanding our own natures and the destinies to which we should by nature tend. Only philosophy can teach us the goals towards which we should strive, and in striving, guide others towards them. In this sense, this book is intended as one small step towards a philosophy of language.

What Aristotle did not take in to account, however, was the nature of language, since, for him, language was Greek. Though he was anything but complacent about language, and though he went some way towards reinventing Greek with the introduction of words such as 'science', a concept which has become irreplaceable throughout the majority of the world's languages today, Aristotle had little time for other languages and had no real theory of language difference. Somewhat naively, Aristotle believed that nouns referred to things and adjectives referred to their observable qualities. Languages other than Greek did not, he believed, introduce different forms of conceptualising the universe and all that is in it.

In this respect, Aristotle stands no further behind those among the contemporary cognitive linguists and neuroscientists who investigate the relationship between language and the mind without taking into account different languages. The absence of a theory of worldview and the incapacity to take on board the activity of translation forms part of the same wilful ethnocentric blindness. For those who do not master other languages, it appears more convenient to ignore them.

The Humboldtian project was of a much wider scope. Believing that knowledge, its refinement and its exchange among people all derive from language use, speech, Humboldt set out the guidelines of a great adventure of the mind. His quest became the investigation of the various courses which linguistic communities had taken in reaching out into the world and in drawing it back into consciousness. His ethnolinguistic approach was soon to be overshadowed by the exciting findings of those of his fellow countrymen who were investigating the Indo-European family of languages. Humboldt, for his part, had sought to reach beyond the scope of the Indo-European languages, to the Amerindian languages. But the 'American project' was to gather less support as the Indo-European project waxed strong, and anthropologists soon moved in to take over the study of Amerindian languages as a part of the societies to which they belonged. Since those anthropologists often lacked the necessary knowledge to understand speech, they were invariably reduced to discussing 'words' and considering archetypes, cultural models and myths in translation.

But can we understand a language in translation? To some extent, we can move into the world of Balzac and Tolstoy in reading their works in translation. But at another level, most French speakers or Russians find themselves bewildered, disorientated and irritated on reading the works of their writers in translation. They perceive a mutation as the words and concepts, the feelings and the phrases, are coloured by translation. Concepts seem to couple together differently. The translated words set off different networks of associations. At this stage, it is clear that the translator has made the jump between worldviews at the level of the language system. Is this betrayal? It is fairer to say that the translator has done his or her job: the translation 'trans-forms' the original, in order to transplant it into the soil of a foreign culture. If the work begins to breathe within that culture, if the words stretch out to activate (different but coherent) meanings and associations, then the translation 'works'. And if it 'works' as a 'work of art' it will take its place in the literary tradition. That Tolstoy and Balzac continue to be read in English proves the possibility of moving between worlds. And that our central text, the one which has never ceased to shape and organize our culture, *The King James Bible*, is itself a translation asserts the truth that the foreign can be assimilated and appropriated. Not only do we make foreign texts our own, but they themselves make us a little more 'their own'. We grow to be like what we appropriate, just as, in proverbial wisdom, we are what we eat.

Humboldt believed, and ethnolinguistics teaches us, that the further we reach into foreign worldviews, the more we perceive their strangeness, and the more we realize our own conceptual limits; we understand more and more that we are engaged in attempting the impossible: assimilating the foreign concept into the frameworks of our language system. This is not simply a question of words, but much more manifestly a question of the relationship between words. This is a question of patterning. The frameworks of thinking differ from language to language. In this respect, the contemporary quest to establish whether emotions are universal is doomed to come up with spurious and insubstantiated conclusions. Unless we first accept that the concepts of emotions are conceived of in the mind and in language, then we will set off to find the same concept with a different label in another language.

Whorf and Sapir, translators, lexicographers and etymologists, all of those who have reached deeply into language, know this to be a false quest. Contrary to what Aristotle believed, words do not refer to entities outside of the mind whose contours are traced by them and whose essence is encapsulated within them. Even simple nouns such as 'crows' and 'tangerines' prove difficult to translate directly from one language and back again, because they demonstrate that languages define, arrange and harness concepts in different categories. Words allow us to create 'objects of understanding' and to take them into the mind in order to order, arrange and use them.

This implies no existentialism or lack of faith in reality. Neither does it involve a critique of language. The linguistic nihilists will always see a weakness or lack of efficiency in language. Those who wish to 'use' language and hold it up as a 'mirror' to reality will always feel that language 'betrays' the philosophical project to 'grasp' things. The ethnolinguist is dogged by no such cynicism. To the ethnolinguist, language, each language, seems to embody a bold new creative adventure into reality.

The ethnolinguist is not primarily concerned with the true nature of things, but about the generation of meaning. The analysis of the way language allows us to make meaning of the world and communicate with one another meaningfully: this is the central core of ethnolinguistic study. Far from espousing a nihilistic existentialism, ethnolinguists see language as enabling linguistic communities to live together meaningfully.

Entering into the worldviews of foreign languages involves learning the ways words take their place within that worldview. This presupposes that we acknowledge that what we are trying to comprehend is something 'strange', something which will inevitably escape comprehension to some extent. We might gain an insight into the way key terms organize thoughts and take root in the mindset of a culture, but in tracing their outlines, the full definition of those words will remain dim and obscure to us to a great degree. Even after decades of speaking a foreign language, a person will betray their foreign origins, if not by their accent, then by the way they link ideas and concepts together in phrases which appear curious and inappropriate to native speakers. At this level, it becomes clear that worldviews are conflicting, and that the worldview of the foreigner is still asserting itself as the 'natural' and 'normal' patterning of conceptual organisation. This difficulty of mastering the patterning of a foreign language is partly explained by the polysemy of language which enables us to branch off into a whole array of complex metaphorical meanings by abstraction and association. As we saw with the word 'truth', even this noun takes flight within the language systems of English, French, German and Czech, to take on forms which are difficult to follow and to master for the non-native speaker.

Ethnolinguistics is more an attitude to thought than a clearly defined approach. In this respect, there is no codified methodology. Wierzbicka will approach languages differently than Sapir. Humboldt employed a number of angles of attack, taking on board the analysis of syntax, wordlists, texts and by engaging in the activity of translation himself. In our studies of truth, love, hate and war, we have likewise adopted a number of approaches. No one approach can be considered more appropriate than another. The efficiency of each one will be proven only in as much as it allows us to enter into the foreign, and thereby ascertain a more lucid insight into the limits and shapes of the patterning of our own language-dependent worldview.

At one level, it will be appropriate to study the etymology of hate or the conceptual metaphors organising our concept of truth. But this only reveals to us facets of the problem of how languages make meaning. In order to understand how languages work, we need to leave behind the naive subject–object model in which language guides thought, and look at things from the other end: we must investigate what we do with language. How do people make sense? How do arguments hold together? How do individuals adopt the patternings of the language in order to appropriate arguments, and to transform them, as they invent and defend their own discursive strategies?

At this level, we found that the ethical impulse of condemning hate and war was absurd and naive. Far from annihilating love, hate (as a concept at least) appears to be essential to love. Hate can define love. But hate can also hide behind love. And, indeed, how many wars are declared out of love? Alliances serve as pretexts for the declaration of war. In this sense, one of our first paradigms for war, the seduction of Helen of Troy, becomes a meaningful narrative: one which allows lovers on both sides to defend both invasion and defence.

War exists and has always existed. There seems little evidence to indicate that we will ever see an end to war. And language therefore has a vested interest in the term. Because of the economy of speech, we preserve only what is useful for us in language, and we have great need of a clear-cut concept of what exactly we mean by war. But over and above the concept of war itself, the term shatters into a kaleidoscopic constellation of meanings at a non-literal level. Wars against want and wars against disease do make sense. And to denounce such expressions would be to misunderstand the very nature of language in which a great many terms are used more as metaphors than as non-figurative expressions. 'Shallow', for example, is used less to describe rivers and lakes than to describe people's personalities.

What Orwell was denouncing in metaphor was the unwitting adoption of 'loaded' metaphorical phrases: 'the war on terror', 'securing an area' and 'reaching out' are all phrases which invite us to think within ideologically constructed frameworks of thought. They belong to the neoconservative worldview which posits that the vocation of the USA is to bring democracy and freedom to the world. That discourse was one which Obama denounced to some extent, but in opposing the neoconservatives' positions and policies, he took his stance within the overarching concepts which constructed them, and in adopting their wars he perpetuates their policies. To this extent, 'reaching out to Muslim cultures' entails defending occupation and setting up pro-American regimes which will strengthen US influence throughout the region. How far is that from the 'nation building' of which Bush spoke? How far is Obama's discourse of love and his condemnation of hate from Reagan's crusading capitalism and his evangelical discourse of love and his fight against evil empires?

Obama is engaged in war, but he dreams of peace, or more precisely 'security'. Withdrawal of troops might be on the agenda, but withdrawing from the world is not. He made this clear in 2006 in his *Audacity of Hope*, when he affirmed:

To begin with, we should understand that any return to isolationism – or to a foreign policy that denies the occasional need to deploy U.S. troops – will not work ... Frustration with the war in Iraq and the questionable tactics the Administration used to make its case for the war has even led many on the left to downplay the threat posed by terrorists and nuclear proliferators. (303–4)

Obama does put 'evil-doers' in inverted commas when he adopts ideas taken from the neoconservatives, and he disparages their promotion of hate. But to what degree does he dissent from their promotion of war as a means of securing economic gain for the States?

Globalization [Obama affirmed] makes our economy, our health, and our security all captive to events on the other side of the world. And no other nation on earth has a greater capacity to shape that global system, or to build consensus around a new set of international rules that expand the zones of freedom, personal safety, and economic well-being. Like it or not, if we want to make America more secure, we are going to have to help make the world more secure. (304)

Obama has remained true to the convictions he announced in *The Audacity of Hope*. He is engaged in a fight against 'the growing threat ... of weak, of failing states ... hostile to our worldview' (305). Obama has sought to improve the conditions of detainees suspected of terrorist activities and to ensure them fair trials. But he is careful to avoid being perceived as being 'soft on terrorism', as he put it (203), a criticism that he knew the right would pounce upon once he gained office.

He described being 'disturbed' by Ronald Reagan's re-election in 1980, and by his 'John Wayne, *Father Knows Best* pose' (Obama 2006: 31). But he shared Reagan's faith in the American worldview and in the American people. Despite misgivings about the reasons for and the execution of the invasion of Iraq, Obama wrote in 2006:

[T]he entire enterprise in Iraq bespoke American ingenuity, wealth, and technical know-how; standing inside the Green Zone or any of the large operating bases in Iraq and Kuwait, one could only marvel at the ability of our government to essentially reerect entire cities within hostile territory, self-contained communities with their own power and sewage systems, computer lines and wireless networks, basketball courts and ice cream stands. More than that, one was reminded of that unique quality of American optimism that everywhere was on display – the absence of cynicism despite the danger, sacrifice, and seemingly interminable setbacks, the insistence that at the end of the day our actions would result in a better life for a nation of people we barely knew. (297)

Obama's 'end of the day' is drawing out into what Eugene O'Neill described as 'The Long Day's Journey into Night' in the title of one of his plays. Obama is celebrating hope. He is celebrating the Americans' desire and their capacity to make a difference for the better. This is the song of the settlers, a speech fit for Thanksgiving. After two years in office, the American people appear more sceptical, and the army is uncertain of the degree to which their Commander-in-Chief is capable of leading them, or whether he even believes in the operation. Caught in the rhetoric of the 'total war', the war of Good against Evil, as Clausewitz defined and analysed it, and as Reagan unthinkingly adopted and promoted it, Obama cannot withdraw, however little headway the occupying forces seem to be making in imposing 'security' in Iraq or Afghanistan. Obama cannot do deals with 'evil' forces, terrorists. Nor can he admit the incapacity of hope. To do either would be to betray the neoconservative worldview to which he clearly subscribes.

To some extent, Obama is the victim of his times. He would never have been able to win the elections unless he had learned to speak the 'language of Bush'. The 2004 election had revolved around the war in Iraq, but by the time Obama's chance came around, US policy had become established. As Chomsky remarked:

Not long before the presidential campaign of 2008, it was taken for granted that the Iraq war would be the central issue, as it was in the mid-term election of 2006. But it virtually disappeared, eliciting some puzzlement. There should have been none. (2010: 121)

The Americans were concerned with the war in Iraq, but the political elite and the forces driving the media were not in favour of a debate. Asked by colleagues at my university in Grenoble to analyse the media representation of the 'war on terror' during the build-up to the 2008 elections, I considered refusing after observing an almost total absence of real content or analysis concerning debate on the occupation of Iraq and Afghanistan while reading the American press over a period of three months. Chomsky may have shared my perplexity but not my puzzlement. As he pointed out in his chapter 'Good News, Iraq and Beyond' in *Hopes and Prospects* (2010: 121–42), events were following the same scenario as the one the media had acted out during the Vietnam War. The reason was simple: no real question of policy change was on the agenda. A real debate would have exposed the unforgiveable: the complicity of adversaries.

In entering into the neoconservative narratives and in adopting their concepts and their objectives, Obama now finds his hands tied. And it is love and hope that ties them. His love of the American people, and his belief in them, his acceptance of the narrative of the good people on the brink of Armageddon makes Obama speak and act as a neoconservative. His interpretation of the 9/11 attacks and the response of the Government coincide perfectly with the language of Bush: 'Now chaos had come to our doorstep. As a consequence, we would have to act differently, understand the world differently. We would have to answer the call of a nation' (Obama 2006: 292).

Condemned to hope, Obama strides on, and however lucid and eloquent he proves, that stride has something of the swagger of John Wayne when he announces: 'With justice at our backs and the world by our side, we drove the Taliban government out of Kabul in just over a month' (*ibid.*).

No one can blame Obama for his patriotism. He remains a statesman worthy of the term. He is capable of moving and directing a nation, as his vocation requires him to do. But for we who do not belong to his nation, the question of the American ideology, and the worldview that Americans share, be they Reagan or Obama, be they the shopkeeper in Detroit or the trade unionist in Illinois, two questions remain. If Obama has, to a large extent, failed to escape the neoconservative transformation of the American worldview, how are we as English speakers to critically appraise that world view and to resist its expansion as the universal paradigm for understanding world affairs that neoconservatives would obviously like to see it become? And how are we to translate the neoconservative worldview into other languages?

Ethnolinguistics will provide no easy answers to these two questions. Ethics inevitably transcends language study. But ethnolinguistics teaches us that worldviews are ingrained in words and phrases, in patterns of thought, and in conceptual metaphors. Synonyms replace and efface one another in discourse, until 'peace' has been displaced by 'security'. Conceptual links are forged, and 'security' begins to rhyme with 'anti-terrorist measures'. 'Homeland' begins to take on an aggressive connotation, where it used to evoke peace or defence. 'Terrorists' are replaced by 'terrorism', and 'terrorism' is replaced by 'terror'. Soon we find ourselves fighting the fear within, not the enemies without. Obama may have taken some steps to set this process in reverse, by abandoning the discourse of the 'war on terror', but 'reaching out' has replaced 'nation building' without any significant change in fundamental economic or military policy.

The coupling of words, the use of metaphor and the use of euphemism all form part of rhetoric. And at one level we prove we are lucid about our own capacity to use language to express our ideas and to justify our actions. At another level, however, language, the collective use of speech as it shapes the worldview we share with other speakers, induces us into courses of thought which are politically and philosophically positioned. We are capable of standing back from political positions and philosophical beliefs. But we do not step outside of language any more than we step outside of history when we reflect upon language. And the lesson that ethnolinguistics has to teach us is that the freedom which speech opens up for the mind is found within language: within that specific language to which we belong. It is in language that we affirm our identity, as subjects living within a linguistic community. But the worldview of our language provides the clay with which we mould our personalities and forge our destinies.

To what degree those destinies will be personal or political depends upon us. To what degree they will be carved by love and will oppose hate or will use hate to define more clearly what we love will nevertheless be made possible by our understanding of what we mean as a community by love and hate. And politics is no stranger to the private sphere. As we saw in our study of love, study of the English and French worldviews reveals an increasingly market-oriented conception of love as a product to be consumed. Meanwhile, the end of Czech communism has coincided with a mutation in the concept of love which takes Czech speakers some way in the same direction. Resisting this trend is possible, but only if we realize to what extent it is reorganising one dimension of personal space within the worldview of the cultural mindset of our times and within our own personal worlds.

Likewise, though we might critique discourse, we cannot escape from worldviews or from language. We can only take up a position towards ideas within our language. Whether we support or denounce a declaration of war will depend on what we understand by 'war' and to what degree we believe in the 'truth' of the arguments used to defend it. Truth, love, hate and war are only fragments of our worldview. If they have served to show how concepts entail linguistic patterning, and if they prove to what extent those patterns of speaking and thinking are only partially translatable, then the ethnolinguistic project Humboldt dreamed of will have taken a small step further.

Notes

1 HOPE, OBAMA AND THE NEOCONSERVATIVE WORLDVIEW

1. www.economist.com/node/14961345.
2. It would, of course, be interesting to compare the degree to which both Indo-European languages and non-Indo-European languages objectify experience and privilege the use of the noun-form. A. H. Bloom, working in the psycholinguistic field, attempts to draw conclusions about hypothetical thinking in the Western mindset by looking at the way nouns are formed from adjectives ('sincerity' from 'sincere'), allowing more abstract levels of thought in English than in Chinese, in which no lexical distinction is made between adjectives and nouns (see Bloom quoted in Lucy 1992: 232–342). It remains unclear, though, whether the Chinese do not make a conceptual distinction between concepts which are divided up in French and English into 'parts of speech'. At any rate, it does seem highly unlikely that abstractions and hypothetical thinking are unavailable to the Chinese understanding.

2 ETHNOLINGUISTICS

1. In explicating this example of the repetition of the word 'war' (*guerre*), Tullio de Mauro posits that von Clausewitz, the great German philosopher of war would not have in mind the same concept as the good soldier Schweik (Švejk in Czech). This would no doubt be true, provided both von Clausewitz and Švejk, the absurd and buffoon-like anti-hero of Hašek's novel on the First World War, were speaking French. But de Mauro's reasoning is flawed: he reveals that he is working with a model which might by termed a 'languageless linguistics' in making this point. Von Clausewitz, as a German, would be speaking of *Krieg*, and Švejk (if fictitious characters could conceive and communicate), as a Czech, would be speaking of *válka*. From the ethnolinguistic perspective, this is an unforgiveable oversight. It is a great mistake to translate such terms, thereby giving the impression that they fit snugly into the conceptual constellations composed by our own linguistic universe. Such an error would certainly not have been made by a Swiss, like Saussure, whose very nation is made up of speakers of French, German and Italian. The point de Mauro and Saussure wish to make, however, is perfectly legitimate: concepts do have meanings within a linguistic community, but those meanings change from person to person and from context to context, as concepts combine with and enter into opposition with different concepts.
2. My own research into this question leads me to conclude that Kochanowski's interpretation is a free or inspired one, because neither *The King James Bible*, nor

Meschonnic's translation of the Psalms in *Gloires* (from the Hebrew, 2001), provide anything to support this translation as an 'authentic' one.

4   LOVE

1. Kövecses' research is intriguing in that he is one of the few cognitive researchers to master a non-Indo-European language, Hungarian. This makes his findings of great interest. Kövecses compares whether conceptual metaphors such as 'anger is hot liquid' can be found in Hungarian as in English (see Goatly 2007: 247). Whorf and Humboldt reached out beyond the pale of the Indo-European thought-world, intuiting that the Amerindian languages would confront us with modes of conception and cognition which would force us to revise our own 'givens', but Kövecses, as a bilingual, is far better equipped in that he 'inhabits two worlds'. Like many of his colleagues in the fields of cognitive linguistics and psycholinguistics, Kövecses reaches beyond the languages he masters when he contrasts conceptual metaphor frames in Japanese and Chinese (in Goatly 2007: 247). It is certainly interesting that he finds conceptual metaphors such as 'loss of control is an explosion' in Japanese, Hungarian and Chinese, as we find it in English: but can we consider his finding that 'anger is the production of pressure' exists in Japanese and Hungarian but not in Chinese to be conclusive? Presumably, Kövecses masters neither Japanese nor Chinese (certainly to the level of corpus-based research or discourse analysis). And if he believes, like many of his colleagues, that hard and fast conclusions about worldviews can be established based upon second-hand knowledge, he would appear to be undermining the force of his findings by overreaching himself.

5   HATE

1. The Cathars were in fact far more widespread than is usually depicted in traditional accounts, which focus upon persecution in precise regions. At one time the Cathars were found from Catalonia to Burgundy. In contrast to the views on free sexuality espoused in certain regions, the Cathars were, like the Franciscans of later centuries, known for their extreme austerity in contrast to the opulence of the Catholic Church. This, of course, constituted one more reason for them being seen as a threat to the Church's power and influence.
2. The Cathars denounced the institution of marriage as a symbol of worldy satisfaction and joy. In the most austere expression of their cult, all terrestrial life was condemned as belonging to evil. Eating meat was banned and sexual abstinence was advocated. But with the celebration of marriage being the main focus of their denunciation, over time, sexual freedom began to impose itself as an alternative system governing relations.
3. As Robert A. Pois shows in his *National Socialism and the Religion of Nature* (1986), Himmler's reflection upon lice and parasites was not a simple turn of phrase. The Nazi *Weltanschauung* involved a 'religion of nature' and a religion of the world order in which an abstract principle of life was celebrated. According to the Nazis, this life principle was constantly gnawed away at by weak, impure destructive elements. The role of the party was, consequently, to preserve it from such pernicious influences. Thus the extermination of the Jews was promoted as protecting life itself. And qualms about the Final Solution were presented as giving in to an insipid weakness which would ultimately have catastrophic cosmic consequences.

4. 'Obama to gay group: "Still laws to change, hearts to open"', *CNN Politics*, 11 October 2009, http://edition.cnn.com/2009/POLITICS/10/10/obama.gay.rights, last accessed 15 November 2011.

5. 'Holder pushes for hate-crimes law; GOP unpersuaded', *CNN Politics*, 25 June 2009, http://edition.cnn.com/2009/POLITICS/06/25/holder.hate.crimes, last accessed 15 November 2011.

6. 'Obama signs hate crimes bill into law', *CNN Politics*, 28 October 2009, http://edition.cnn.com/2009/POLITICS/10/28/hate.crimes, last accessed 15 November 2011.

7. 'Federal hate crime cases at highest level since '01', *New York Times*, 17 December 2009, www.nytimes.com/2009/12/18/us/18hate.html, last accessed 15 November 2011.

8. 'Blair "prayed to God" over Iraq', BBC News, 3 March 2006, http://news.bbc.co.uk/1/hi/uk_politics/4772142.stm, last accessed 15 November 2011.

9. 'Blair: "God will be my judge on Iraq"', *The Independent*, 4 March 2006, www.independent.co.uk/news/uk/politics/blair-god-will-be-my-judge-on-iraq-468512.html, last accessed 15 November 2011.

10. 'George Bush: "God told me to end the tyranny in Iraq"', *The Guardian*, 7 October 2005, http://www.guardian.co.uk/world/2005/oct/07/iraq.usa., last accessed 15 November 2011.

11. The translation becomes obscure at this point in the *King James Version* with the phrase 'in their selfwill they digged down a wall', where Meschonnic translates the meaning as 'in their fit of rage they maimed the bulls' (*dans leur fureur ils ont estropié des taureux* (233)). The *Scofield Reference Bible* (1917) follows the *King James Version* word for word, but the *New International Version* (1973/2000 (NIV)) and *The English Standard Version* (2001 (ESV)) both support Meschonnic's direct interpretation from the ancient Hebrew text. The former translates it as 'for they have killed men in their anger / and hamstrung oxen as they pleased' (NIV: 58). The latter opts for 'in their anger they killed men, and in their willfulness they hamstrung oxen' (ESV: 42).

12. Curiously, this is a relatively modern tradition, which dates back to the post-revolutionary period. Republicans and Napoléon III were anxious to unearth a Gallic origin to celebrate French culture, while accepting the inevitability of Gaul being conquered along with its hero, Vercingetorix. Rome and Caesar were accepted as legitimate conquerors. Conquest was considered an inevitable part of the process of civilisation from the point of view of exponents of the Gallo-Roman roots of France. This is very much an ideological interpretation, however. Napoléon and Napoléon III were trying to efface the long-standing aristocratic tradition which had celebrated the Kings of France and the Frankish tradition, the tradition of the Germanic chevaliers who had conquered Rome.

13. Napoléon was a Romantic in other ways. Before invading Germany, he read the great literary success of the time, Goethe's *The Sufferings of Young Werther*. The novel seems rather insipid and self-indulgent now, and it certainly belongs to another age, the age of the Old Order. It is the story of excessive and hopeless love which ends in suicide. Napoléon considered it one of the great classics of literature.

14. Competition is the modern equivalent of that chivalry that sent knights hurtling towards one another in jousting, trying to unsaddle one another. This spirit of

rivalry is as fundamental to the conception of man in the Middle Ages as the stirrup was to the development of medieval warfare.

15. 'Les raisons de la colère: paroles d'émeutiers', *Socialisme International*, No. 17/18, January 2007. http://revuesocialisme.pagesperso-orange.fr/s17mucci.html, last accessed 15 November 2011.

16. The native speakers who I consulted on this question all affirmed that it was impossible to say 'I have hate' in German and that *Ich habe haß* was not idiomatic.

17. 'Hillary Clinton scrubs Ronald Reagan from history', *The Telegraph*, 10 November 2009. http://blogs.telegraph.co.uk/news/nilegardiner/100016373/hillary-clinton-scrubs-ronald-reagan-from-history, last accessed 15 November 2011.

18. 'Remarks at the Annual Convention of the National Association of Evangelicals in Orlando, Florida', 8 March 1983. www.reagansheritage.org/html/reagan03_08_83.shtml, last accessed 15 November 2011.

19. In opposition to the cult of power, Nietzsche set up the resentment of the weak, the pitiful and perverted perspective of those who cannot face up to the reality of greatness and power, but who deride and misrepresent it. Nietzsche attributes 'slave morality' (the opposite of this 'master morality') to the Jews. Is this fair, though? Our study of Old Testament discourse makes this affiliation problematic. The spontaneous, self-affirming celebration of life and power is very much the force that animates the Psalms of David, after all, and it is only in exile that the Hebrews will disparage the cult of power. Nietzsche's opposition appears more illuminating if we remember that he is critically reappraising the Christian heritage which seeks its inspiration in the Judaic tradition: the Jews who preoccupied Nietzsche were the vanquished Jews, those who were excluded from this celebration of force and will. Nietzsche believed that in the periods in which they were dominated, the Jews inverted master morality and perverted it. In its place, they celebrated all that was wretched and alone. The poor, the weak, the wretched, the despised and the ugly were alone to be considered good (1989: 34). The celebration of piety formed an excessive and perverted form of *agapē*. Nietzsche, a curious and complex character, was himself often commended in his personal life for this very form of fraternal love, but, admittedly, it played no real part in his philosophy and his idealism. The essential point concerning this 'slave morality' for our discussion of hatred was that Nietzsche rightly believed that weakness is invariably transformed into resentment. Nietzsche associated a specific form of small-minded, spiteful resentment with the French term *ressentiment*. There is little justification for this, philologically speaking, but this has not prevented his use of the term in German from developing into a crucial philosophical concept, and the term is invariably preserved in French and English translations from the German.

20. Hegel's contempt for America is ironic, given Fukuyama's claim to be Hegelian. What Fukuyama sees as the End of History, its culmination in US democratic capitalism, Hegel saw as a 'dead end'.

21. The word *jingoïsme* enters the French language during this period.

22. Ironically, this contrasts greatly with the fashionable trend at the beginning of the twentieth century for impoverished aristocrats in Britain to search for profitable marriages for their offspring with new money in the States. The aristocratic interdiction to speak of money at home did not prevent them from reaching out for it in America, while discreetly despising the mercantile Americans for their grasping

pursuit of profit. Such an ambivalence is hardly surprising, and, ultimately, predictable; the courting of the nouveau-riche oligarchs of Russia's new capitalist economy has followed the same pattern in London and Paris, on the French Riviera and on the slopes of the most prestigious Alpine ski resorts (such as Courchevel and Méribel). Rather than opposites, hate and love appear to be inextricable. We resent what we depend upon. And British financial circles and French tourism find it difficult to resist the attraction of this new moneyed class.

6 WAR

1. A fair reading of Sun Tzu would stress the simple pragmatic sense of many of his teachings. Sun Tzu teaches, for example, that by far the most efficient means of vanquishing an adversary is to transform him into an ally.
2. http://outsports.com/olympics2008/2008/08/06/gender-testing-as-art-of-war/, last accessed 16 November 2011.
3. Access to Arabic media would obviously allow us to tell an entirely different story about the invasion of Iraq and the occupation of Afghanistan. It is possible to trace in English the 'muzzling' of the media by national governments eager to side with the US perspective or afraid of being included in the 'axis of evil', given the Bush administration's 'either you stand with us or against us' stance. But the everyday details of the war and the narratives they open up would serve to expose the strategies of the Bush administration far more fully. Not personally having any knowledge of Arabic, I am indebted to Abdulkrim Ziani's study of Al-Jazeera's reporting on events in his PhD thesis (2007).
4. The following quotations are my translation from the French at www.islamophile. org/spip/Le-Jihad-sa-vraie-signification-et.html, last accessed 28 November 2011.
5. 'Big Sky Slugfest', *New York Times*, 5 April 2008, www.nytimes.com/2008/04/05/ opinion/05egan.html, last accessed 17 November 2011.
6. The US must be on 'the right side of history' (www.cbsnews.com/38016-503544_ 162-5101183-503544.html, last accessed 26 February 2010).

Glossary

Analogical negation Term designating the introduction and negation of the comparison of two terms. While many of the adherents of the Lakoff–Johnson approach to metaphor are concerned with the way we understand things and experiences in terms of metaphors, corpus study, discourse analysis and ethnolinguistic studies make it clear that many analogies are invoked only to be debunked. That is to say, a metaphor is used as a starting point to allow the speaker or writer to refuse a given or accepted conception, often in order to modify it or supply an alternative conception. Love-as-Fire can be debunked by analogical negation. We were told that passion 'dies down'. Analogical negation can be a creative process: the Love-as-Unity metaphor was, for example, debunked in a curiously imaginative manner in our love corpus. A man was no longer to be considered a 'bolt-on' – an attached part – one writer argued. Elaborating frames of analogical negation provides us with meaningful oppositions in contrast to which we can further refine our definitions of concepts such as love. If love is 'heat', then, consequently, lack of love is 'coldness'. Frigidity and cooling off belong to a whole network of concepts used to define the lack of love or desire in various languages. Similarly, if love implies the metaphor of tastiness, as in 'honey', in English, or *belle à croquer* ('beautiful enough to bite into') in French, then we might suppose this commonplace analogy would give rise to converse analogical networks in both languages. This turns out to be the case: both French and English speak of lack of love in terms of disgust, i.e. a physical desire not to taste someone. Vomiting forms the basis of many slang expressions for sexual aversion. Analogical negation is therefore a basic feature of conceptual and lexical organisation. It structures the way we understand things and express them. We reactivate analogical and negative analogical patterns when we speak: we improvize upon them as we give expression to our thoughts and feelings in conventional, imaginative and original ways.

Ascription In Eubanks' work, this term is used to define the discursive strategy by which we attribute (ascribe) a conceptual metaphor to another party. We accuse others of acting as if 'trade is war', for example. In this example, the metaphoric frame is invoked only to be debunked or disparaged. As Eubanks points out, a great deal of bad faith is found in the use of ascription. We accuse others of doing what we ourselves do.

Attributed world conception The idea, commonly held among linguists, language students and translators, that each language engenders its own specific world conception (usually referred to as 'worldview').

Blend In second-generation cognitive theory, the 'blend' was widely disseminated by the work of Fauconnier and Turner. Opposing the binary model of metaphor constituting a target and source, Fauconnier and Turner argued, often a third concept emerges from the fusion of two concepts. They gave examples such as dog-man, and 'chunnel' (from tunnel and channel). For these scholars, it was important to understand that metaphor transforms the two terms into a third, where Lakoff and Johnson, following more traditional theories of metaphor, tended to work with a model of interaction. Blends can fuse conceptual metaphoric frames. We might, for example, speak of the taste of love, calling it bittersweet. But a counter conceptual metaphor posits love as a journey. One woman in our English corpus of texts from women's magazines fused the two frames in order to enable her to speak of difficulties, break downs and the act of resuming loving in terms of stopping off and moving on. In such a model, infidelity was conceived of in terms of 'straying' from the path. This was the bitter part. Transforming love itself from a journey into a quest, the object of a journey, she spoke of her experience of love as 'a bittersweet journey'.

Cognitive unconscious Term used by cognitive linguists (see Lakoff, Johnson, Turner, Fauconnier and Sweetser) to designate the organized network of 'folk theories' which pattern understanding and which enable us to interpret the world and act within it. The contention of cognitive linguists is that language is fundamental to folk theories and behaviour. Conceptual metaphors offer us models for understanding the world and the way people behave in society, in both personal and public life. The cognitive unconscious is used to invoke all that 'goes without saying' in language: up is good, down is bad, love is hot, frigidity is cold, going beyond frontiers is exciting, turning inwards and closing off to others is pitiful and depressing.

Conceptual frames Relying on Fillmore (1982), Lakoff and Johnson (1999: 116–17) described conceptual frames as semantic frames which 'provide an overall conceptual structure defining the semantic relationships among whole "fields" of related concepts and the words that express them' (116).

Conceptual metaphor (originally referred to by Lakoff and Johnson as 'protometaphor' (1980) and referred to before them by other scholars as 'root metaphor') Term denoting an underlying metaphorical equation. If a man describes a woman as 'spicy', the expression can only be understood fully by virtue of the underlying conceptual metaphor which invites us to understand sexual congress as eating, and partners as food. Describing men as 'hunks' or 'beefcakes' in English, or describing them in French as *alléchants*, a term which translates as 'lickable' or 'tasty', testifies to the fact that such expressions are not gender restricted and that the cognitive unconscious at work in both men and women operates with largely the same conceptual resources.

Counter metaphor Term used in this work to designate a modification to, or refusal of, one metaphor as another metaphor is proposed in its place. Many examples of counter metaphors were found in the English, French and Czech corpora of women's magazines in which love was defined and discussed. For example, one French author argued that love is not about collecting love stories (*histoires d'amour*) but about a woman offering herself as a 'precious gift', aware of her own 'value'. Counter metaphors can be original proposals intended to open up new modes of conception. Frequently, however, they take the form of reminders. Since metaphors (as Lakoff and Johnson insist) highlight and hide aspects of a concept, counter metaphors can serve to highlight exactly what another metaphor hides by providing an alternative form of representation. The counter metaphor does not necessarily debunk the existing metaphor: it simply awakens us to other aspects of experience.

Cultural mindset Term used in this work to designate that relatively rigid and fixed way of seeing the world which frames our perception and conception of politics, society, history, behaviour, the individual's place in the world and the organising conceptual frameworks of social relations. When groups and generations who speak the same language fail to understand each other, it is because their cultural mindsets have grown into very different expressions of the world, though those differing expressions are derived from the same world-perceiving and world-conceiving which organizes the language shared by all groups within their linguistic community.

Discourse Form or style of language which can be attributed to an individual, a group, an institution or a period of a culture's history. It is, however, important to distinguish between the way in which the individual discourse contrasts with and resists reigning ideologies and cultural mindsets.

Discursive strategy Term used by Eubanks to denote the arguments and positions we formulate by harnessing conceptual metaphors and directing them in ways which serve our purposes and consolidate our positions. Conceptual metaphors are often harnessed in ways which bolster our strategies. Bush presented the destructive force of war as a project to 'build democracy' and to 'bring freedom'. Obama tends to present the continued US presence in the Middle East as 'reaching out' to Muslim cultures. Those on the receiving end of such policies no doubt find such conceptual metaphors absurdly inappropriate.

Diversification When a single target is referred to by a range of sources. Goatly (2007:12) cites the example of Milton referring to 'Satan's legions' as locusts and autumn leaves. Our corpus of war metaphors generated a diverse range of sources (war as crime-fighting, building democracy, picking up a challenge, lighting a fire and so on).

Essentialisation Process, common to many European languages, in which the various members of a group are reduced to the category in which they are enclosed. The most fundamental example would be 'Man', whose use often bears little relation to many of the 'men' it is believed to refer to and to enfold. That the term also applies to women is obviously problematic. In ethnolinguistics, anthropology and ethnology, essentialisation proves especially problematic, because investigators seek out and present individuals as incarnating their culture. Men and women are reduced to one essential model, supposed to disclose for us (outsiders) the worldview of a community. History and social conflict, both internal and external, tend to be downplayed by essentialisation. Personality in language study disappears totally from view as soon as we reduce a culture to one single essence.

Ethnolinguistics In English-speaking linguistics this term is often considered as a synonym for *linguistic anthropology*. Although it has gained little or no recognition in English-speaking countries, the Lublin School of Poland has been developing a forceful analysis of language and culture in its school of ethnolinguistics since the 1980s. See Bartmiński in Polish, and, in English, Wierzbicka, who has managed to introduce a philological approach which preserves a concern for the interaction between literature and the language system. Humboldt's linguistic project involved an 'ethnology of language': the study of the world's variety of worldviews, as expressed by the linguistic communities of mankind. In this way, Bartmiński and Wierzbicka can be seen as contributing to Humboldt's ethnolinguistic project to uncover the character of languages.

Ethnology of speaking The study of linguistic competence in the way individuals and groups use language pragmatically in specific social and cultural contexts. In contradistinction to Chomsky's generative linguistics, the reigning paradigm in post-war linguistics in English-speaking cultures, Dell Hymes (1974) advocated that linguists should aim to develop a descriptive theory in which the ethnographer should record settings, participants, ends, act sequences, keys, instrumentalities, norms and genres. The ethnology of speaking takes us closer to present-day discourse analysis. The similarity of the aims of Hymes to those of Goatly and Eubanks is striking: all three are interested in the rhetorical strategies driving discourse and the means which allow individual speakers to situate themselves in the powerplay of negotiations.

Ethnosemantics Forming part of the American branch of linguistic anthropology, and more specifically of cognitive anthropology, ethnosemantics was a mode of study which emerged in the 1960s and which took on the task of studying the ways in which different cultures organize and categorize different domains of knowledge, such as plants, animals and kinship systems. Taylor, one of the main exponents of ethnosemantics, set out to explain the underlying principles organising behaviour.

Folk theory A model or framework of understanding shared by a linguistic community. Folk theories are often unconscious or subconscious paradigms used to interpret and understand the world around us. In capitalist democracies, relationships are invariably understood in terms of the folk theory of exchange: relations are about giving and receiving. Giving and receiving are obviously universal experiences, as any ethnologist or anthropologist will affirm. To this extent, the exchange model proves to be useful in that it allows us to order our understanding of the world. Nevertheless, other cultures often perceive and experience relationships by conceiving them in the framework of different folk theories. Jewish, Christian and Islamic perceptions of relationships differ to some degree, but all three worldviews conceive of relationships more in terms of sharing than of exchange. In competing against, and in prevailing over these religious worldviews, market economics, with its model of individualism and isolated atoms, individuals engaging in the exchange of products and services, has thus shaded our understanding of relationships and intimacy. Our study of love offered ample examples to support this: individuals spoke about what they 'put into' and what they 'got out of' relationships. The idea of an 'emotional investment' underlines the extent to which this model of understanding has become 'naturalized' in our worldview.

The identity function of language Joseph (2004) and Riley (2007) both argue that the function of language cannot be restricted to the dual functions of representation and communication. Language enables us to construct our identity and to attribute identity to others. The construction of identity depends upon models (stereotypes in Bartmiński's theory), but these models are sustained and reconstructed by individual speakers and by groups defining themselves in relation to others, and defining other groups in relation to their own and society's conceptions of norms and habitus. The identity function of language entails two converse but inextricable activities. We define ourselves in terms of others within language and within our worldview. At the same time, our language and our worldview make up a great part of our identity, our mode of interpreting the world and expressing our place within it.

Latent ideology Language is political and the reigning ideology reaches out and structures the way we organize concepts in the language system. Speaking of the 'upper class' is not innocent, since it activates the conceptual metaphor that up is good and down is bad. Speaking of 'urban regeneration' activates a commonly accepted conceptual metaphor which invites us to see towns and cities as organisms which develop in and of themselves. As Henri Lefebvre pointed out, though, this tends to obscure the social and economic struggles involved in urban development. Is 'the Second Harlem Renaissance' which is taking place at this very moment, to be considered a 'revival' of 'the spirit of the neighbourhood', as property developers portray it, or as a process of gentrification which will eventually exclude the black poor from Upper Manhattan? Ideology is evidently present in discourse strategies, but it is contained within the very concepts with which we think and it patterns the way we harness concepts together. Marx, Adorno, Williams, Bourdieu and metaphor theoreticians, such as Goatly (2007: 25–7), see their task as uncovering the ideologically configured concepts and associations which are latent in language, and continually reactivated in discourse.

Linguistic worldview conception An adaptation of Humboldt's concept of *Weltansicht* within the context of the Polish Ethnolinguistics School of Lublin and its exchange with Czech scholars (see Vaňková 2001) and their concept of 'world picture' (*obraz světa*). Jerzy Bartmiński (2009: 213) gives the following definition: 'The linguistic worldview conception is semantic, anthropological and cultural in nature. It is based on the assumption that language codes a certain socially established knowledge of the world and that this knowledge can be reconstructed and verbalized as a set of judgements about people, objects and events. The knowledge results from the subjective perception and conceptualization of reality by the human mind; it is anthropocentric and relativized to languages and cultures.'

Mirror metaphors Metaphors which work by setting in motion the logic of existing metaphoric frameworks, but by setting them in reverse. This is a fundamental process in language. Heat and coldness are set up as opposites and we can exploit the explorative and innovative frameworks of the one by setting up a contrasting network of frameworks in the other. Desire can 'heat up' and 'cool down'. Similarly, representing desirable partners in terms of delicious foods enables us to activate equally rich frames of disgust and repugnance for other types of food in order to represent the absence of desire or physical repulsion. There is nothing intrinsically perverse about the logic of mirror metaphors. However, perversion is particularly well served by mirror metaphors, because they allow us to twist and invert traditional forms of representation. In our study of love we quoted Valérie Tasso, the French author of an autobiographical book about her own 'sexual marathon': Tasso inverted traditional representations of relationships when she claimed she experienced life in a socially accepted relationship as 'rape', while, for her, prostitution was a 'liberation'. Here the enslavement of the sexual object in prostitution is projected onto the powerplay of the contemporary couple. Fauconnier and Turner (2002/3) discuss related forms of converse definition using the concept of 'disanalogy'.

Multivalency The use of the same source applied to various targets in metaphor theory (Goatly 2007: 13). Our corpus of war metaphors generated examples of multivalency: war was used to represent fighting tax evasion, finding cures for diseases and even for cultural competition.

Patterning The routes along which we think. Patterning involves harnessing concepts together. Language provides us with conventional paths for thinking. Since speech is by nature creative, it goes without saying that we can resist or break out of patterning. Nevertheless, critical discourse analysis seeks to uncover the strategies and interests which lie behind much linguistic pattern-ing. The theory of patterning was best explained in English by Sapir and Whorf (see Lee 1996 on Whorf's unpublished works). In German, Humboldt used the expression *Wechselwirkung* to describe a largely similar concept of linguistic configuration, but he did not stress the political dimension, being primarily interested in the nature of culture as a whole and the way it was engendered by the worldview of the linguistic community (or what he called *Nation*).

Personal world Term used in this work to designate the mode of perception and conception of the world which is specific to each individual. This 'personal world' constitutes the individual's own version of the 'cultural mindset' he or she adheres to both consciously and unconsciously. This world constitutes a stance, and as such it may change over time: nevertheless, the personal world remains coherent and is to a large extent a permanent aspect of the life and personality of the individual. Though malleable, it cannot be abandoned or supplanted. In contrast to this, a person's 'perspective' changes with circum-stances and as he or she interacts with others. Our views and our ideas may change, but our way of seeing the world and our way of conceiving it belongs to a deeper level of feeling and consciousness.

Personified reification A complex and paradoxical rhetorical process. Once people or relationships have been sufficiently reified by the imagination and reclassified as inhuman objects of experience (for example, when men are con-sidered experiences to 'try out'), then discourse can personify its own objecti-fications. This complex and paradoxical process is surprisingly widespread in everyday language. In our French corpus of women's magazines, one young woman reduced her lover to a 'love story', but when the relationship broke down, instead of being forced to consider the man in question, she continued to conceive of him as an object, and when the man was dismissed from her life, it was, curiously, the object which became personified: the love story (rather than the man himself) was 'kicked out of the door'. Communist discourse tended to represent the people prior to socialism as 'the masses', a group of inanimate, unmotivated, latent forces. The role of the party was to 'awaken' those 'sleeping' masses. This conception of revolution attributes to the party the divine role of transforming matter into living souls. A 'spiritual dynamics' frames much of the communist system of ideas, and that system's charm can be attributed largely to the fusion of the metaphysical and the mechanical.

Perspective Term used in this work to designate the changing nature of the way each person perceives and conceives of the world. An individual's 'perspective' changes as he or she moves through the world, interacting with others and discovering new and different experiences. In this, it contrasts with the individual's 'personal world' (see above) which can be said to be a more or less stable form of consciousness which frames the individual's experience, worldview and identity. Perspective is active, or rather interactive, and for that reason it is constantly changing. Just as the changing nature of the world to some extent fashions the perspective we have of it, so we ourselves are constantly changing.

Sociology of knowledge What passes for 'knowledge' in society? This is the domain of the sociology of knowledge. What are the social factors which give rise to that knowledge and sustain it, and what is the relationship between social structures and thought? How is social reality constructed and maintained? And what interest groups condition the social knowledge system? Riley (2007) attributes this series of interrelated questions to Mannheim (1936), who gave this framework its name and its first synthetic and systematic expression. Riley does, however, find precursors in Bacon, Vico, Marx, Durkheim and Simmel. The sociology of knowledge is concerned with everyday knowledge (what 'everybody knows') and the way that knowledge is socially conditioned. To frame this in linguistic terms, the sociology of knowledge is concerned more with meaning than with truth. The sociology of knowledge does not entail the quest for truth, the perennial quest of the philosopher. Instead the sociologist of knowledge asks: why was this true for those people then and there, in a particular socio-historical context? Riley's ethnolinguistics will inevitably open up the dimension of language-specific social spheres to the scrutiny of sociologists of knowledge.

Stereotypes An important element in Bartmiński's ethnolinguistics: stereotypes refer to those archetypes which animate and shape the conceptualisation of the world for each member of a given linguistic community. For Bartmiński, the task of the ethnolinguist is to construct an 'ideal' member of a linguistic community in whose discourse the overarching stereotypes of the linguistic community are expressed. This is inevitably a schematising exercise which will produce a 'model': the actual existence of such an 'ideal member' is, of course, inconceivable. But the attempt is meaningful to the extent that it allows us to see to what extent particular individuals adhere to, grate against, and depart from received ideas and conventionally established conceptions. The search for stereotypes is paralleled in cognitive linguistics by the attempt to establish prototypical meanings. What will surprise cognitive scholars is Bartmiński's attempt to construct the worldview of an ideal rural resident of Poland. This essentialist bent in Bartmiński's work will disturb academics who tend to live and work in cities. The size of the rural population of Poland and the proportion of agricultural workers goes some way to explaining this choice. But Bartmiński's choice entails an implicit critique of our own centralist mindset, which tends to relegate provincials to the outskirts by treating them as the outsiders of culture while focusing upon the centre as the essential part, the essence of our culture. In this way, Bartmiński's methodology reminds us that what we tend to consider as 'marginal' pertains, in fact, to the majority, while our own models generated by cultural capitals such as London, New York, Paris and Tokyo represent little of the cultural experience of most of the individuals of their linguistic communities. Bartmiński's work on 'folk culture' links him to work of Jakobson and Mukařovský, who, as part of the Prague Linguistic Circle in the 1930s, were involved in uncovering the common sources and individual élans of related Slavic languages and their poetic traditions.

Stranger The stranger represents the hidden side of the identity question. No concept of belonging and of identity can dispense with it, but little sociological investigation has gone into the theorisation of 'strangeness'. As Riley (2007) points out, the concept is language specific and problematic. *Étranger*, in French translates into both 'stranger' and 'foreigner'. The Czech word *cizinec* follows the same pattern. German, like English, distinguishes between someone of another nation (*Ausländer*) and 'stranger' (*Fremde*), and the latter term is related to 'strange', 'foreign to us' (*fremde*). According to Riley, the Finnish term *vieras* translates into English as 'foreigner', 'stranger' and 'guest'. The ancient Greeks reserved *barbaros* for 'non-Greeks' and distinguished between citizens and *xenos*, Greeks from other city states. *Metoikos* was used to designate those who had 'changed house', a category of Greeks who came to live in a city state but did not enjoy the rights of citizenship. Such 'immigrants' were often artisans and merchants. Foreigners living within communities are often lucid concerning the definition of cultural models and stereotypes. They perceive all the more clearly the norms which exclude them, while those who observe cultural models often consider them as 'natural' or 'normal'. Simmel (quoted in Riley 2007) defines the stranger in spatial terms. He has a position in space: he is both wandering and fixed. He has a position in time: he comes today and stays tomorrow. He has a social position: he is an element of a group without being part of it. He has a relational position: he imports elements into a society which cannot originate within it. The foreigner represents, in many ways, the complementary antithesis of Bartmiński's stereotype. Both are models which correspond to no individual person but which are active in constructing and maintaining conceptions of identity and difference.

Synecdochical objectification Process of objectification whereby a living thing or person is first reduced to a part and then objectified. Vulgarity makes great use of this process. The other is reduced to the 'essential part' that interests the speaker (often the sexual parts) then that essential part is objectified: e.g. a man is reduced to his penis, and the penis is in turn represented as a functional object, a 'tool'. With a similar degree of vulgarity, a man who feels sexually aroused might say, 'I need a hole' or 'I'm looking for a piece of ass'. Each of these terms objectifies the person in that it considers the body in terms of meat, i.e. dead flesh fit for consumption or use. Since so many speakers of all languages seem to be engaged in 'shooting the shit about ass', how to get 'it' and what to do with 'it', a great deal of linguistic effort goes into innovating new expressions for talking about this cherished subject. In this sense, vulgarity is very similar to literature in that it strives to find fresh and colourful ways of describing the object in question, a process known in literary theory as 'defamiliarisation'. It is clear, however, that the intention of vulgarity is to shock and not to embellish the object of interest. Some literary scholars and poets therefore still contend that poetry and vulgarity remain opposed. Few people, for example, would argue that the comparison of the penis to a 'kidney wiper' is 'poetic'. Indeed there seems something essentially anti-poetic in the comparison between the action of a windscreen wiper and a graphic internal description of the sexual act of penetration. Such a metaphor is intended to shock us into seeing the sexual act from an objectified, dehumanized mechanistic perspective. Nonetheless, though many writers might see it is as their job to 'rehumanize' language and to denounce such metaphors, certain writers of the 1990s, such as the Frenchman Houllebecq increasingly make use of such shock tactics in their writing. Whether this can be read as a denunciation of contemporary decadence, a revolt against romantic conceptions of love, or simply gratuitous sensationalism remains open to question.

Weltansicht Term introduced to German by Humboldt to designate the worldview into which we enter when we learn a foreign language, or the worldview engendered by our own language and of which we are largely unconscious. *Weltanschauung* refers to the system of beliefs or the ideology of a group of people. For this reason, any given language can contain various opposing or incompatible worldviews (*Weltanschauungen*). Ideologies can migrate between languages. *Weltansicht*, on the other hand, refers to the system of concepts and the patterning which holds them together in our mother tongue. We might discuss the 'fate of man' or the 'state of the world', and various groups may disagree about definitions and objectives, but we can only enter into such discussion once we have the concepts of 'fate', 'man', 'state' and 'world'. These concepts are provided for us by the language system. At this level we can speak of languages as having different worldviews.

World-conceiving Term used in this work to designate one aspect of Humboldt's concept of *Weltansicht*, namely the changing and developing manner in which we draw that world into the realm of thought to form concepts and frameworks to represent things and our experience of the world.

World-perceiving Term used in this work to denote one aspect of Humboldt's concept of *Weltansicht*, namely the changing and developing perception we have of the world.

Bibliography

Abdulmoneim, Mohamed Shokr, 2006, 'The Metaphoric Concept "Life is a Journey" in the Qur'an: A Cognitive-semantic Analysis', metphorik.de, October 2006, 94–132.

Adorno, Theodor, W., 1991a, *Minima Moralia* (1951), trans. E. F. N. Jephcott, London: Verso.

1991b, *Notes to Literature*, ed. Rolf Tiedemann, trans. Shierry Weber Nicholsen, New York: Columbia University Press.

Aitchison, Jean, 2003, *Glossary of Language and Mind*, Edinburgh University Press.

St Thomas Aquinas, 1990, *A Summa of the Summa: The Essential Philosophical Passages of St Thomas Aquinas' Summa Theologica, Edited and Explained for Beginners*, edited by Peter Kreeft, San Francisco: Ignatius Press.

Aristotle, 1954, *The Rhetoric and the Poetics*, trans. Ingram Bywater, New York: Random House.

1964, 'Metaphysics', eds., Albert Hofstadter and Richard Kuhns, *Philosophies of Art and Beauty: Selected Readings in Aesthetics from Plato to Heidegger*, Chicago University Press.

1986, *The Politics*, trans. William Ellis, New York: Prometheus Books.

1990, *Poetics*, trans. Hippocrates G. Apostle, Elizabeth A. Dobbs and Morris A. Parslow, Grinell, Iowa: The Peripatetic Press.

Armstrong, Karen, 1993, *A History of God*, London: Mandarin.

Atkins, Beryl T., Duval, Alain, and Milne, Rosemary C., eds., 1993 *Collins Robert French-English, English-French Dictionary*, 3rd edition, Paris: Collins.

Augustine, Saint, 1964, *Les Confessions*, Paris: Garnier Frères Flammarion.

Auroux, Sylvain, 1996, *La philosophie du langage*, Paris: Presses Universitaires de France.

Aquinas, Saint, 1990, *The Summa of the Summa*, ed., Peter Kreef, San Fransisco: Ignatius Press.

Bacon, Francis, undated, *The Essays: Or Councels Civil and Moral*, New York: Dolphin Books. Available at Project Gutenberg: www.gutenberg.org/ebooks/575.

Bartmiński, Jerzy, 2009, *Aspects of Cognitive Ethnolinguistics*, London: Equinox.

Baudelaire, Charles, 1997, *Œuvres Complètes I*, Pléiade edition (1975), Ligugé: Gallimard.

BBC, 2005, *The Shakespeare Collection: All 37 Productions from the BBC Television Shakespeare Series* (DVDs), BBC Worldwide Ltd., www.bbcshop.com/drama+arts/shakespeare-collection-dvd/invt/bbcdvd1767/, last accessed 4 November 2011.

Beauchamp, Paul, 2000, *Cinquante portraits bibliques*, Paris: Seuil.
Beauvoir, de, Simone, 1988, *The Second Sex* (1949), trans. H. M. Parshley, London: Picador.
Benveniste, Émile, 1966, *Problèmes de linguistiques générales I*, Paris: Gallimard.
    1974, *Problèmes de linguistiques générales II*, Paris: Gallimard.
Berlin, Isaiah, 2000, *Three Critics of the Enlightenment: Vico, Hamann, Herder*, Princeton University Press.
The Holy Bible: Containing the Old and New Testaments, King James, Authorized Version, London: Eyre and Spottiswoode Ltd.
La Bible: L'ancien Testament I, 1956, trans. Édouard Dhorme, Paris: Gallimard.
La Bible: L'ancien Testament II, 1959, trans. Édouard Dhorme, Paris: Gallimard.
La Bible de Jérusalem, 2001, reference edition with notes, Rome: Fleurus/Cerf.
Die Bibel nach der übersetzung Martin Luthers, 1999 (re-edited text of 1984 edition), Stuttgart: Deutsche Bibelgesellschaft.
Blay, Michel, 2006, *Dictionnaire des concepts philosophiques*, Paris: Larousse.
Boas, Franz, 1973, *Introduction to Handbook of American Indian Languages* (1911), Lincoln: Nebraska University Press.
Bonte, Pierre, and Izard, Michel, eds., 1991, *Dictionnaire d'ethnologie et d'anthropologie*, Paris: Presses Universitaires de France.
Bouffartigue, Jean, and Delrieu, Anne-Marie, 2008, *Trésors des racines grecques*, Paris: Belin.
Brooke-Rose, Christine, 1965, *A Grammar of Metaphor* (1958), London: D.R. Hilman and Sons.
Buber, Martin, 1923, *Ich und Du*, Stuttgart: Reclam.
    1958, *I and Thou*, 1937, trans. Ronald Gregor Smith (1937), Edinburgh: T&T Clark.
    1969, *Je et Tu*, trans. G. Bianquis, Paris: Aubier.
Cassin, Barbara, ed., 2004, *Vocabulaire européen des philosophes, Dictionnaires des intraduisibles* (1531), Paris: Robert.
Cassirer, Ernst, 1953, *Language and Myth* (1946), trans. Susanne K. Langer, New York: Dover.
    1968, *The Philosophy of Symbolic Forms, Volume One: Language*, trans. Ralph Manheim, New Haven and London: Yale University Press.
Catena, Angels, and Lamprou, Effi, 2009, 'Les prédicats d'affect dans des dictionnaires monolingues coordonnés espagnol/grec/français', in Iva Novakova, and Agnès Tutin, *Le lexique des émotions*, Grenoble: Ellug.
Certeau, de, Michel, Julia, Dominique, and Revel, Jacques, 1975, *Une politique de la langue: La révolution française et les patois – l'enquête de Grégoire*, Paris: Gallimard.
Chabrolle-Cerretini, Anne-Marie, 2007, *La vision du monde de Wilhelm von Humboldt: Histoire d'un concept linguistique*, Lyon: ENS Éditions.
Chomsky, Noam, 1972, *Language and the Mind* (1968), 2nd edition, New York: Harcourt Brace.
    2010, *Hopes and Prospects*, Chicago: Haymarket Books.
Clausewitz, Carl von, 1997, *War, Politics, and Power*, trans. Edward M. Collins, Washington: Regnery.
Čmejrková, Světla, 2000, *Reklama v Čestině* (Publicity in Czech), Prague: Leda.
Colin, Jean-Paul, 1990, *Dictionnaire de l'argot français et de ses origines*, Paris: Larrousse.

Copleston, Frederick S. J., 1962, *A History of Western Philosophy*, in nine volumes, New York: Image Books.

Crystal, David, 1997, *The Cambridge Encyclopaedia of Language*, 2nd edition, Cambridge University Press.

2000, *Language Death*, Cambridge University Press.

Cuddon, J. A., 1991, *Dictionary of Literary Terms and Literary Theory* (1976), 3rd edition, London: Penguin.

Dalby, Andrew, 2003, *Language in Danger*, London: Penguin.

Dalrymple, Theodore, 2001, *Life at the Bottom: The Worldview That Makes the Underclass*, Chicago: Ivan R. Dee.

Dalzell, Tom, and Victor, Terry, 2008, *Sex Slang*, New York: Routledge.

Damasio, Antonio, 2003, *Looking for Spinoza: Joy, Sorrow, and the Feeling Brain*, Orlando, FL: Harcourt.

Danesi, Marcel, 2004, *A Basic Course in Anthropological Linguistics*, Toronto: Canadian Scholar's Press.

Dictionnaire d'ethnologie et de l'anthropologie, 1991, ed. Pierre Bonte and Michel Izard, Paris: Presses Universitaires de France.

Dictionnaire des ethnologues et des anthropologues, 1997, ed. Gérard Gaillard, Paris: Armand Colin.

Dubois, Jean, Giacomo, Mathée, Guespin, Louis, Marcellesi, Christiane, Marcellesi, Jean-Baptiste, and Mével, Jean Pierre, 1994, *Dictionnaire de linguistique et des sciences du langage*, Paris: Larrousse.

Ducrot, Oswald, and Schaeffer, Jean-Marie, 1995, *Nouveau dictionnaire encyclopéique des sciences du langage*, Paris: Seuil.

Dupriez, Bernard, 1984, *Gradus, Les Procédés Littéraires (Dictionnaire)*, Paris: Union générale d'Éditions.

Duranti, Alessandro, 1997, *Linguistic Anthropology*, Cambridge University Press.

Emanatian, Michele, 1995, 'Metaphor and the Expression of Emotion: The Value of Cross-cultural Perspectives', *Metaphor and Symbolic Activity*, 10(3), *info-metaphore.com*: Lawrence Erlbaum Associates.

1999, 'Congruence by Degree: On the Relation between Metaphor and Cultural Models', *Metaphor in Cognitive Linguistics*, Current Issues in Linguistic Theory series, New York: Cambridge University Press.

Encrevé, Pierre, 2007, 'Politiques et Enjeux', *Politiques & Usages de la Langue en Europe*, ed. Michael Werner, Collection du Ciera, *Dialogiques*, Ciondeé sur Noireu: Éditions de la Maison des sciences de l'homme.

Eubanks, Philip, 2000, *A War of Words in the Discourse of Trade: The Rhetorical Constitution of Metaphor*, Carbondale and Edwardsville: Southern Illinois University Press.

Fauconnier, Gilles, 1985, *Mental Spaces: Aspects of Meaning Construction in Natural Language*, Cambridge, MA.: MIT Press.

Fauconnier, Gilles, and Turner, Mark, 2002/3, *The Way We Think: Conceptual Blending and the Mind's Hidden Complexities*, New York: Basic Books.

Fergusson, Rosalind, 1983, *The Penguin Dictionary of Proverbs*, London: Penguin Books.

Fidelius, Petr, 1986, *L'esprit post-totalitaire*, Paris: Bernard Grasset.

1998, *Řeč komunistické*, Prague: Triada.

Fillmore, C., 1982, 'Frame Semantics', in Linguistic Society of Korea, *Linguistics in the Morning Calm*, Seoul: Hanshin, 111–38.

Fingl, J., et al., 1962, *Stručný Slovník Politický* (A Short Dictionary of Political Terms), Prague: Nakladatelství Politické Literatury.

Fishman, Joshua A., 1999, *Handbook of Language & Ethnic Identity*, Oxford University Press.

Foley, William A., 1997, *Anthropological Linguistics: An Introduction*, Malden, MA.: Blackwell.

Fontanier, Pierre, 1977, *Les Figures du discours* (1830), Paris: Flammarion.

Foucault, Michel, 2004, *Philosophie, Anthologie*, Paris: Gallimard.

Fought, Carmen, 2006, *Language and Ethnicity*, Cambridge University Press.

Geddie, William, ed., 1964, *Chambers's Twentieth Century Dictionary*, Edinburgh: W & R; Chambers Ltd.

Géraid, Marie Odile, 2000, *Notions clés de l'ethnologie*, Paris: Armand Colin.

Goatly, Andrew, 2007, *Washing the Brain: Metaphor and Hidden Ideology*, Amsterdam / Philadelphia: John Benjamins.

Gobineau, de, Arthur, 1983, *Oeuvres*, Pléiade edition, Dijon: Gallimard.

Grady, J., 1997, *Foundations of Meaning: Primary Metaphors and Primary Scenes*, PhD thesis, Berkeley: University of California.

La Grande Encyclopédie, Inventaire raisonnée des sciences, des lettres, et des arts, 1885–1902, in 31 volumes, under the direction of M. Berthelot, Paris: H. Lamirault et Cie.

Hagège, Claude, 1985, *L'homme de paroles: Contribution linguistique aux sciences humaines*, Paris: Fayard.

  1996, *Le Français: Histoire d'un combat*, Paris: Editions Michel Hagège.

  2000, *Le souffle de la langue*, Paris: Odile Jacob.

  2002, *Halte à la mort des langues*, Paris: Odile Jacob.

  2006, *Combat pour le français: Au nom de la diversité des langues et des cultures*, Paris: Odile Jacob.

Harvey, David, 2005, *The New Imperialism*, Oxford University Press.

Hersant, Yves, 2001, *La métaphore baroque: D'Aristote à Tesauro, extraits du Cannocchiale aristotelico*, Paris: Seuil.

Hobbes, Thomas, 1985, *Leviathan* (1651), London: Penguin.

Hodgson, Terrence, 2006, *Eyes Like Butterflies: A Treasury Of Similes And Metaphors*, Edinburgh: Chambers.

Hofstadter, Albert, and Kuhns, Richard, eds., 1964, *Plato to Heidegger*, Chicago University Press.

Holub, Josef, and Lyer, Stanislav, 1978, *Stručný Etymologický Slovník Jazyka Českého* (A Short Dictionary of Etymology for the Czech Language), Prague: Statní Pedagogické Nakladatelství.

Humboldt, Wilhelm von, 1971, *Linguistic Variability and Intellectual Development* (1836), trans. George C. Buck and Frithjof A. Raven, Philadelphia: Pennsylvania University Press.

  1995, *Schriften zur Sprache*, Stuttgart: Reklam, Universal-Bibliothek.

  1999, *On Language: On the Diversity of Human Language Construction and its Influence on the Mental Development of the Human Species* (1836), trans. Peter Heath, ed. Michael Losonsky, Cambridge University Press.

  2000, *Sur le caractère national des langues et autres écrits sur le langage*, trans. Denis Thouard, Paris: Seuil.

2003, *Über die Verschiedenheit des menschlichen Sprachbaues/Über die Sprache*, Berlin: Fourier Verlag.

Hymes, D., 1974, *Foundations in Sociolinguistics: An Ethnographic Approach*. Philadelphia: University of Pennsylvania Press.

'Ibn Arabï, 1986, *Traité de l'amour*, trans. Maurice Gloton, Paris: Albin Michel.

Jaspers, Karl, 1962, *Plato and Augustine*, trans. Ralph Manheim, ed. Hannah Arendt, New York: Harcourt Brace Jovanovich.

Johnson, M., 1987, *The Body in the Mind: The Bodily Basis of Meaning, Imagination and Reason*, University of Chicago Press.

Joseph, John E., 2004, *Language and Identity: National, Ethnic, Religious*, New York: Palgrave Macmillan.

2006, *Language and Politics*, Edinburgh University Press.

Kant, Immanuel, 1993, *Critique of Pure Reason*, a revised and expanded translation based on Meiklejohn, ed. Vasilis Politis, London: Everyman.

The Kingdom Interlinear Translation of the Greek Scriptures, 1985, New York: Watchtower Bible and Tract Society of New York.

Klemperer, Victor, 1975, *LTI: Notizbuch eines Philogen*, Leipzig: Reklam.

2000, *The Language of the Third Reich, LTI Lingua Tertii Imperii*, trans. Martin Brady, London/NewYork: Continuum.

The Koran, 1956/1999, transl. N.J. Dawood, London: Penguin.

Kövecses, Zoltán, 1986, *Metaphors of Anger, Pride, and Love: A Lexical Approach to the Structure of Concepts*, Amsterdam/Philadelphia: John Benjamins.

2000/2003, *Metaphor and Emotion: Language, Culture and Body in Human Feeling*, Cambridge University Press.

Lakoff, George, 1987, *Women, Fire and Dangerous Things: What Categories Reveal about the Mind*, University of Chicago Press.

1991, 'Metaphor and War: The Metaphor System Used to Justify War in the Gulf' (Parts 1 and 2), Viet Nam Generation Journal & Newsletter, Vol. 3, No. 3. http://www2.iath.virginia.edu/sixties/HTML_docs/Texts/Scholarly/Lakoff_Gulf_Metaphor_1.html, last accessed 4 November 2011.

1996, *Moral Politics*, University of Chicago Press.

2003, 'Metaphor and War, Again', *AlterNet*, internet journal www.alternet.org/story/15414, last accessed 4 November 2011.

Lakoff, George, and Johnson, Mark, 1980, *Metaphors We Live By*, University of Chicago Press.

1999, *Philosophy in the Flesh: the embodied mind and its challenge to Western thought,* New York: Basic Books.

Lakoff, George, and Turner, Mark, 1989, *More Than Cool Reason: A Field Guide to Poetic Metaphor*, University of Chicago Press.

Langham Brown, Roger, 1967, *Wilhelm von Humboldt's Conception of Linguistic Relativity*, The Hague/Paris: Mouton & Co.

Lee, Penny, 1996, *The Whorf Theory Complex: A Critical Reconstruction*, Amsterdam/New York: John Benjamins.

Levi-Strauss, Claude, 1961, *Race et histoire*, Paris: Gonthier.

Littré, Emile, 1962, *Dictionniare de la langue française*, France: Gallimard, Hachette.

Locke, John, 1964, *An Essay Concerning Human Understanding* (1689), Glasgow: Fontana, Collins.

Lucy, John A., 1992, *Language, Diversity and Thought: A Reformulation of the Linguistic Relativity Hypothesis*, Cambridge University Press.

Malmkjaer, Kirsten, 1991, *The Linguistics Encyclopedia*, London: Routledge.

Malotki, Ekkehart, 1983, *Hopi Time: A Linguistic Analysis of the Temporal Concepts in the Hopi Language*, Berlin: Mouton.

Manchester, L. Martin, 1985, *The Philosophical Foundations of Humboldt's Linguistic Doctrines*, Amsterdam/Philadelphia: John Benjamins.

Mannheim, K., 1936, *Ideology and Utopia*, London: Routledge.

Matoré, Georges, 1962, *L'espace Humain*, Paris: La Colombe.

Meschonnic, Henri, 1982, *Critique du rythme: anthropologie historique du langage*, Paris: Verdier.

1985, *Les états de la poétique*, Paris: Presses Universitaires de Vincennes.

1995, *Politique du rythme: politique du sujet*, Paris: Verdier.

1997, *De la langue française: Essai sur une clarté obscure*, Paris: Hachette.

2001, *Gloires: Traduction des psaumes*, Paris: Desclée de Brouwer.

2002, *Au commencement: Traduction de la Genèse*, Paris: Desclée de Brouwer.

2003, *Les Noms: Traduction de l'Exode*, Paris: Desclée de Brouwer.

Meschonnic, Henri, ed., 1995, *La Pensée dans la langue, Humboldt et après*, Paris: Presses Universitaires de Vincennes.

Messling, Markus, 2010, 'L'homme? Destruktion des Menschen in der Humboldt-Rezeption bei Gobineau', *Wilhelm von Humboldt: Universalität und Individualität*, Munich: Fink.

de Mijolla, Alain, ed., 2002, *Dictionnaire international de la psychanalyse*, Paris: Calmann-Lévy.

Mitterand, Henri, 1981, *Les mots français*, 3rd edition, Paris: Presses Universitaires de France.

Mleziva, Emil, 1996, 'Vliv spolecenských změn na vznik nových významu a vzrazu v ceském jazyce' (The Influence of Social Developments on the Creation of New Meanings and New Expressions in the Czech Language), *Slovo a slovesnost*, 57, Prague: Karlova Univerzita.

Morier, Henri, 1989, *Dictionnaire de poétique et de rhétorique* (1961), Paris: Presses Universitaires de France.

Mukařovský, Jan, 1948, *Kapitoly české poetiky*, Volumes I and II, Prague: Statní Pedagogické Nakladatelství.

Mukarovský Jan, 1964, 'Standard Language and Poetic Language', *A Prague School Reader*, ed. Joseph Vachek, University of Indiana Press.

Müller, Ralph, 2005, 'Creative Metaphors in Political Discourse: Theoretical Considerations on the Basis of Swiss Speeches', metaphorik.de, 53–73.

Naugle, David K., 2002, *Worldview: The History of a Concept*, Michigan/Cambridge: Grand Rapids, W.B. Eerdmans.

Nerlich, Brigitte, Hamilton, Craig A., and Rowe, Victoria, 2002, 'The Socio-Cultural Role of Metaphors, Frames and Narratives', metaphorik.de, 90–108.

Nettle, Daniel, and Romaine, Suzanne, 2000, *Vanishing Voices: The Extinction of the World's Languages*, Oxford University Press.

Nietzsche, Freidrich, 1989, *On the Genealogy of Morals and Ecce Human*, ed. Walter Kaufmann, New York: Random House.

Novakova, Iva, and Tutin, Agnès, 2009, *Le lexique des émotions*, Grenoble: Ellug.

Nussbaum, Martha, C., 1994, *The Therapy of Desire: Theory and Practice of Hellenistic Ethics*, Princeton University Press.

Obama, Barack, 2006, *The Audacity of Hope: Thoughts on Reclaiming the American Dream*, Crown/Three Rivers Press.

Orwell, George, 1949, *1984*, London: Secker and Warburg.

    1968, *Collected Essays, Journalism and Letters, 1940–1943*, vol. III, London: Camelot.

Oster, Pierre, 1990, *Dictionnaire de citations françaises I, de Villon à Beaumarchais*, Paris: Robert.

    1993, *Dictionnaire de citations françaises II, de Chateaubriand à J. M. G. Le Cézio*, Paris: Robert.

Ottenheimer, Harriet Joseph, 2006, *An Introduction to Linguistic Anthropology*, Belmont, A: Thomson.

The Oxford Concise Dictionary of English Etymology, 1986, edited by T. F. Hoad, Oxford University Press.

The Oxford Dictionary of Quotations , 1992, Oxford University Press.

Palmer, Gary B., 1996, *Toward a Theory of Cultural Linguistics*, Texas University Press.

Paprotté, E. Wolf, and Dirven, René, eds., 1985, *The Ubiquity of Metaphor: Amsterdam Studies in the Theory and History of Linguistic Science*, Amsterdam/Philadelphia: John Benjamins.

Peckham, Aaron, ed., 2005, *Urban Dictionary*, Kansas City: Andrews Publishing, LLC.

    2007, *Mo' Urban Dictionary*, Kansas City: Andrews Publishing, LLC.

Picoche, Jacqueline, 1994, *Le Robert dictionnaire étymologique du français*, Paris: Robert.

Pinker, Steven, 1994, *The Language Instinct*, London: Penguin.

    2007, *The Stuff of Thought: Language as a Window into Human Nature*, New York: Penguin.

Plato, 1961, *The Collected Dialogues*, ed. Edith Hamilton and Huntington Cairns, Princeton University Press.

    1968, *The Republic*, trans. Allan Bloom, New York: Basic Books.

Pois, Robert A., 1986, *National Socialism and the Religion of Nature*, Kent: Croom Helm.

Poldauf, Ivan, 1986, *Česko–anglický slovník*, 2nd edition, Prague: Státní Pedagogické Nakladatelství.

Preminger, Alex, and Brogan, N. T. V. F., 1993, *The Princeton Encyclopedia of Poetry and Poetics*, Princeton University Press.

Rey, Alain, 1998, *Dictionnaire historique de la langue française* (1992), Paris: Robert.

Rey-Debove, Josette, 2004, *Le Robert Brio, Analyse des mots et régularités du lexique*, Paris: Robert.

Rey-Debove, Josette, and Rey, Allain, 1993, *Le Nouveau Petit Robert*, Paris: Robert.

Ricoeur, Paul, 1975, *La métaphore vive*, Paris: Seuil.

Riley, Philip, 2007, *Language, Culture and Identity: An Ethnolinguistic Perspective*, London: Continuum.

Ripert, Pierre, 1993, *Dictionnaire des citations de la langue française*, Paris: Booking Internationale.

Roger, Philippe, 2002, *L'Ennemi américain: Généalogie de l'antiaméricanisme français*, Paris: Seuil.

Salzmann, Zdenek, 1999, *Language, Culture, and Society; An Introduction to Linguistic Anthropology*, 2nd edition, Boulder, CO: Westview Press.

Sapir, Edward, 1949, *Language: An Introduction to the Study of Speech* (1921), New York: Harcourt, Brace & World.

1985, *Selected Writings in Language, Culture, and Personality* (1949), ed. David G. Mandelbaum, Berkeley: University of California Press.

Saussure, Ferdinand de, 1994 *Cours de linguistique générale*, critical edition prepared by Tullio de Mauro, Paris: Payot.

Scholze-Stubenrecht, W., and Sykes, J. B., 1999, *The Oxford-Duden German Dictionary*, Oxford: Clarendon Press.

Schulte, Joachim, 1992, *Wittgenstein: An Introduction*, trans. William H. Brenner and John F. Holley, Albany: State University of New York Press.

Scruton, Roger, 1996, *Kant* (1982), Oxford University Press.

Šefčík, Vladimir, *Ekonomická válka– Staronový fenomén mezinárodní bezpečností* (Economic war – Ancient-New Phenomena of International Security), www.army.cz, last accessed 27 September 2010.

Shakespeare, William, 1976, *The Sonnets*, ed. M. R. Ridley, London: Everyman's Library.

1987/1990, *The Complete Oxford Shakespeare*, in three volumes, ed. Stanley Weks and Gary Taylor, London: Oxford University Press.

Sire, James W., 2004, *Naming the Elephant: Worldview as a Concept*, Illinois: InterVarsity Press.

Smith, Adam, 2009, *The Theory of Moral Sentiments* (1759), New York: Penguin.

Spinoza, Benedict de, 1989, *Ethics: Including The Improvement of the Understanding* (1677), trans. R. H. M. Elwes, New York: Prometheus.

Steiner, George, 1992, *After Babel, Aspects of Language and Translation* (1975), 2nd edition, Oxford University Press.

Sun Tzu, 1993, *The Art of War*, trans. Yuan Shibing, Ware: Wordsworth.

Swaan, de, Abraham, 2007, 'Le sentimentalisme des langues (Les langues menacées et la sociolinguistique)', *Politiques & Usages de la Langue en Europe*, ed. Michael Werner, Collection du Ciera, *Dialogiques*, Condé sur-Noireau: Éditions de la Maison des sciences de l'homme.

Sweetser, Eve, 1990, *From Etymology to Pragmatics: Metaphorical and Cultural Aspects of Semantic Structure*, Cambridge University Press.

2006, 'Negative Spaces: Levels of Negation and Kinds of Spaces', *La negation: formes, figures, conceptualisation*, ed. Stéphanie Bonnefille and Sébastien Salbayre, Tours: Presses Universitaires François Rabelais.

Sweetser, Eve, and Fauconnier, Gilles, 1996, *Spaces, Words, and Grammar*, Chicago University Press.

Taylor, John, R., 2002, *Cognitive Grammar*, Oxford University Press.

2003, *Linguistic Categorization* (1989), 3rd edition, Oxford University Press.

Thomas, Linda, Wareing, Shân, Singh, Ishthla, Peccei, Jean Stilwell, Thornborrow, Joanna, and Jones, Jason, 2004, *Language, Society and Power: An Introduction* (1999), 2nd edition, London: Routledge.

Thucydides, 1966 [1651], *The English Works of Thomas Hobbes of Malmebury*, edited by Sir William Molesworth, Volume VIII, London: reprinted by John Bohn, III.

Trabant, Jürgen, 1992, *Humboldt ou le sens du langage*, Liège: Madarga.

1999, *Traditions de Humboldt* (German edition 1990), French edition, Paris: Maison des sciences de l'homme.

2003, *Mithridates im Paradies: Kleine Geschichte des Sprachdenkens*, Munich: Beck.

2007, 'L'antinomie linguistique: quelques enjeux politiques', *Politiques & Usages de la Langue en Europe*, ed. Michael Werner, Condé-sur-Noireau: Collection du Ciera, *Dialogiques*, Éditions de la Maison des sciences de l'homme.

2008, *Was ist Sprache?*, Munich: Beck.

Trask, R. L., 1999, *Key Concepts in Language and Linguistics*, London: Routledge.

Turner, Mark, 1987, *Death is the Mother of Beauty: Mind, Metaphor, Criticism*, University of Chicago Press.

1996, *The Literary Mind: The Origins of Thought and Language*, Oxford University Press.

Underhill, James W., 2003, 'The Switch: Metaphorical Representation of the War in Iraq from September 2002–May 2003', metaphorik.de, December 2003.

2004, 'Métaphores dans le marché, ou le marché en métaphores', *Les Cahiers de l'ILCEA*, Numéro 6, *Traduction/adaptation des littératures et textes spécialisés*, Grenoble : ILCEA, ELLUG Presses Universitaires de Grenoble.

2007, '"Making" Love and "Having" Sex: An Analysis of Metaphoric Paradigms in English, French and Czech', *Slovo a smysl: Word and Sense*, Karlova univerzita, Akademie.

2008, 'War and Peace: A Story of International Trade: A Critical Appraisal of Philip Eubanks' *A War of Words'*, Lille: Presses Universitaires de Lille.

2009a, 'Dérive et déformation de la pensée: Vision du monde et métaphore', *Dérives de la métaphore'*, ed. Denis Jamet, Paris: Harmattan.

2009b, *Humboldt, Worldview and Language*, Edinburgh University Press.

2011, *Creating Worldviews: Metaphor, Ideology and Language*, Edinburgh University Press.

Vaňková, Irena, 2007, *Nádoba plná řeči* (Dishes Full of Speech), Prague: Karolinum.

Vaňková, Irena, ed., 2001, *Obraz světa v jazyce* (The Picture of the World in Language), Prague: Desktop Publishing.

Vaňková, Irena, Nebeská, Iva, Římalová, Lucie Saicová, and Šlédrová, Jasňa, 2005, *Co na srdci, to na jazyku* (What's on Your Heart Is on the Tip of Your Tongue), Prague: Karolinum.

Vlasák, Vaclav, and Lyer, Stanislav, 1987, *Česko-Francouský Slovník*, Státní Pedagogické Nakladatelství.

Watkins, Calvert, 2000, *The American Heritage Dictionary of Indo-European Roots*, Boston: Houghton Mifflin.

Whorf, Benjamin Lee, 1984, *Language, Thought and Reality: Selected Writings* (1956), ed. John B. Caroll, Cambridge, MA.: MIT Press.

Wierzbicka, Anna, 1992, *Semantics, Culture and Cognition: Universal Human Concepts in Culture-specific Configurations*, New York, Oxford University Press.

1996/2004, *Semantics: Primes and Universals*, Oxford University Press.

1997, *Understanding Cultures through their Key Words*, Oxford University Press.

1999, *Emotions across Languages and Cultures*, Cambridge University Press

2010, *Experience, Evidence & Sense: The Hidden Cultural Legacy of English*, Oxford University Press.

Williams, Raymond, 1983, *Keywords: A Vocabulary of Culture and Society* (1976), revised edition, Oxford University Press.

Wittgenstein, Ludwig, 1969, *The Blue and Brown Books*, 2nd edition, New York: Harper and Row.

1993, *Tractatus logico-philosophicus* (1922), trans. Gilles-Gaston Granger, Paris: Gallimard.

2001, *The Philosophical Investigations, The German Text with a Revised English Translation* (1953), 3rd edition, trans. G. E. M. Anscombe, Oxford: Blackwell.

2002, *Remarques mêlées*, trans. Gérard Granel, Paris: Flammarion.

Ziani, Abdulkrim, 2007, *La chaîne Al-Jazira et la guerrre contre l'Irak: Couverture médiatique et traitement de l'information*, unpublished PhD thesis directed by Bernard Miège, and defended at Stendhal University, Grenoble, France.

Index